THE ORIGINS OF CRITICAL RACE THEORY

The Origins of Critical Race Theory

The People and Ideas That Created a Movement

Aja Y. Martinez *and* Robert O. Smith

NEW YORK UNIVERSITY PRESS

New York

NEW YORK UNIVERSITY PRESS
New York
www.nyupress.org

Library of Congress Cataloging-in-Publication data.
Names: Martinez, Aja Y., 1982- author. | Smith, Robert O. (Robert Owen), 1974- author.
Title: The origins of critical race theory : the people and ideas that created a movement / Aja Y. Martinez and Robert O. Smith.
Description: New York : New York University Press, [2025] | Includes bibliographical references and index.
Identifiers: LCCN 2024019104 (print) | LCCN 2024019105 (ebook) | ISBN 9781479832675 (hardback) | ISBN 9781479832682 (paperback) | ISBN 9781479832699 (ebook) | ISBN 9781479832729 (ebook other)
Subjects: LCSH: Critical race theory--United States. | Racism--United States. | Racism in education--United States. | Race discrimination--Law and legislation--United States.
Classification: LCC E185.61 .M3637 2025 (print) | LCC E185.61 (ebook) | DDC 305.800973--dc23/eng/20250122
LC record available at https://lccn.loc.gov/2024019104
LC ebook record available at https://lccn.loc.gov/2024019105

This book is printed on acid-free paper, and its binding materials are chosen for strength and durability. We strive to use environmentally responsible suppliers and materials to the greatest extent possible in publishing our books.

The manufacturer's authorized representative in the EU for product safety is Mare Nostrum Group B.V., Mauritskade 21D, 1091 GC Amsterdam, The Netherlands.
Email: gpsr@mare-nostrum.co.uk.

Manufactured in the United States of America

10 9 8 7 6 5 4 3 2

Also available as an ebook

For Derrick

CONTENTS

LIST OF FIGURES

ACRONYMS

AALS Association of American Law Schools
BLSA Black Law Students Association
CLS critical legal studies
COINTELPRO Counterintelligence Program of the FBI,
    1956–1971
CORE Congress of Racial Equality
CRT critical race theory
FBI Federal Bureau of Investigation
HEW United States Department of Health, Education, and
    Welfare (1953–1979)
HLR *Harvard Law Review*
HLS Harvard Law School
HUAC House Un-American Activities Committee (1938–1969)
KKK Ku Klux Klan
LDF The NAACP Legal Defense and Educational Fund, Inc., also
    known as the Legal Defense Fund, the Fund, or NAACP LDF
LLM Master of Laws (degree)
NAACP National Association for the Advancement of Colored
    People
NOI Nation of Islam
SAG Screen Actors Guild
SCLC Southern Christian Leadership Conference
SNCC Student Nonviolent Coordinating Committee
TWC Third World Coalition
YLS Yale Law School

TIMELINE OF THE BOOK

1787 September 17: Signing of US Constitution

1863 Emancipation Proclamation

1866 Civil Rights Act of 1866

1868 Fourteenth Amendment to the US Constitution is adopted.

1896 *Plessy v. Ferguson*, 163 US 537, upholding racial segregation laws

1909 February 12: NAACP is founded on centennial of Lincoln's birth.

1934 W. E. B. Du Bois resigns from NAACP board.

1940 Thurgood Marshall founds NAACP Legal Defense and Educational Fund (LDF).

1946 Constance Baker Motley graduates from Columbia Law School, hired as LDF assistant counsel.

1950 Ralph Bunche is awarded Nobel Peace Prize.

1954 *Brown v. Board of Education of Topeka*, 347 US 483, outlawing racial segregation in public schools

Derrick Bell returns from US Air Force deployment in Korea, enters law school at the University of Pittsburgh.

1957 Derrick Bell receives JD from University of Pittsburgh School of Law and enters US government service.

1960 Derrick Bell begins work with the LDF.

1961 Thurgood Marshall assigns James H. Meredith case to Constance Baker Motley.

President John F. Kennedy appoints Thurgood Marshall to US Court of Appeals, Second Circuit.

Jack Greenberg is appointed LDF director-counsel.

1962 January: Meredith case for admission to University of Mississippi is elevated to federal court.

October: Meredith registers for classes at University of Mississippi.

1963 June 12: Medgar Evers is assassinated.

August 28: March on Washington for Jobs and Freedom

1964 July 2: President Lyndon B. Johnson signs into law Civil Rights Act of 1964.

June–August: Freedom Summer (Mississippi Summer Project for Voter Registration)

August 4: Bodies of James Chaney, Andrew Goodman, amd Michael Schwerner are discovered.

September 1: Carthage School in Leake County, Mississippi, is desegregated by first grader Debra Lewis, escorted by Derrick Bell and Jean Fairfax.

1965 President Lyndon B. Johnson increases US involvement in Vietnam.

Jean Fairfax joins the LDF staff.

August 6: President Lyndon B. Johnson signs into law Voting Rights Act of 1965.

October/November: Richard Delgado participates in Run for Peace against US involvement in Vietnam.

1966 Derrick Bell departs LDF to work as deputy director, Office for Civil Rights, Department of Health, Education and Welfare.

President Lyndon B. Johnson appoints Constance Baker Motley as first Black female federal judge.

1968 April 4: Martin Luther King Jr. is assassinated.

1969 Derrick Bell is hired by Harvard Law School.

Paulo and Elza Freire, exiled from Brazil, arrive at Harvard.

1971 Derrick Bell is awarded tenure at Harvard Law School

Richard Delgado commences studies at University of California, Berkeley, School of Law.

1972 Patricia Williams commences studies at Harvard Law School.

1976 Derrick Bell publishes "Serving Two Masters: Integration Ideals and Client Interests in School Desegregation Litigation."

Bell writes against Jack Greenberg in ACLU *Civil Rights Review*, describing LDF as a "penthouse plantation."

1977 Supreme Court decides *Regents of the University of California v. Bakke*, 438 US 265, limiting racial quotas.

1980 Bell publishes *"Brown v. Board of Education* and the Interest Convergence Dilemma."

President Jimmy Carter appoints U. W. Clemon as Alabama's first Black federal judge.

1981 Bell departs Harvard Law School to become dean of University of Oregon Law School.

Kimberlé Crenshaw commences studies at Harvard Law School.

1982 James Vorenberg becomes dean of Harvard Law School.

Harvard Law School student protest over lack of civil rights course.

Stephanie Y. Moore commences studies at Harvard Law School.

1983 January: Third World Coalition boycotts Greenberg/Chambers course.

Alternative Course is announced.

1984 March: Richard Delgado publishes "The Imperial Scholar: Reflections on a Review of Civil Rights Legislation."

Jack Greenberg resigns from LDF director-counsel position, goes to Columbia Law School.

Julius Chambers named LDF director-counsel.

Harvard Law School invites Linda S. Greene to become first African American woman to teach at the Law School.

October: Jean Stefancic begins work at the University of San Francisco Law Library.

1985 June: Critical Legal Studies Feminist Conference

Bell publishes "The Civil Rights Chronicles" as the Foreword to *Harvard Law Review*'s Supreme Court issue.

1986 Derrick Bell suffers infamous Stanford Incident.

Richard Delgado and Charles Lawrence travel to Oregon to support Bell, initiating "Bell-Delgado Survey" on minority law professors' lives.

1987 January: CLS Conference "Sounds of Silence" focused on race criticism

January: Charles Lawrence publishes "The Id, the Ego, and Equal Protection: Reckoning with Unconscious Racism."

Spring: *Harvard Civil Rights-Civil Liberties Law Review* publishes CLS panel papers from Richard Delgado ("The Ethereal Scholar"), Mari Matsuda ("Looking to the Bottom"), and Patricia Williams ("Alchemical Notes").

David Trubek is denied tenure at Harvard Law School; Bell goes on protest leave.

September 17: Derrick Bell publishes *And We Are Not Saved.*

1988 Richard Delgado and Patricia Williams seek Law Review support for legal storytelling special issue.

Kimberlé Crenshaw returns to Wisconsin for research fellowship.

Kimberlé Crenshaw publishes "Race, Reform, and Retrenchment: Transformation and Legitimation in Antidiscrimination Law."

1989 Kimberlé Crenshaw publishes "Demarginalizing the Intersection of Race and Sex: A Black Feminist Critique of Antidiscrimination Doctrine, Feminist Theory and Antiracist Policies."

April: Legal storytelling conference organized by *Michigan Law Review.*

June: Randall Kennedy publishes "Racial Critiques of Legal Academia."

July: First meeting of Critical Race Theory Workshop (Wisconsin); movement is named.

September/August: Bell issues memos encouraging storytelling (counterstory).

August: Special issue on legal storytelling, containing first theorizations of counterstory method, is published in the *Michigan Law Review.*

November: Richard Delgado and Jean Stefancic publish "Why Do We Tell the Same Stories? Law Reform, Critical Librarianship, and the Triple Helix Dilemma," their first cowritten study,

1991 Patricia Williams publishes *Alchemy of Race and Rights: Diary of a Law Professor.*

1992 Derrick Bell publishes *Faces at the Bottom of the Well: The Permanence of Racism.*

2001 Richard Delgado and Jean Stefancic publish *Critical Race Theory: An Introduction.*

Introduction

Humanizing Critical Race Theory

Virtually every state enacted what were called Racial Tolera-
tion Laws. These Measures severely restricted—and, in some
states, banned outright—public teaching that promoted racial
hatred by focusing on the past strife between blacks and
whites. . . . State officials enforced these laws with vigor, severely hampering the ability of blacks to carry out their healing campaign. Whites whose fears were not allayed by the
government's actions organized volunteer citizens groups to
help rid their communities of those whose teachings would
destroy the moral fabric of American society.
—Derrick Bell, "The Chronicle of the Slave Scrolls" (1985)

In 2021, we received an email from a local news channel in upstate
New York. The reporter, who covered local school board meetings, had noticed that critical race theory (CRT) was becoming
an increasingly prevalent and contentious topic. She shared a
video containing impassioned pleas from mothers on behalf of
their school-aged children—mothers who were women of color,
speaking English with foreign accents, identifying themselves as
immigrants and asylees from communist countries with totalitar-
ian governments. These mothers, speaking one after the other,
were in tears as they described fears that their children were being
brainwashed by Marxist propaganda they had been trained to call
"critical race theory."

Everything had changed the previous year. Aja had published
her award-winning book *Counterstory: The Rhetoric and Writing of Critical Race Theory*, in May 2020.[1] In September, then

President Trump issued his "Executive Order on Combating Race and Sex Stereotyping."[2] This ban shined a national spotlight on CRT and in many ways placed targets on those of us who are identifiable culprits charged with pushing CRT's "different vision of America."[3] As a result of this recent controversy, CRT has been misunderstood (often intentionally) as a catchall for everything associated with the political left by pundits promoting ethnonationalist responses to demographic shifts in the US electorate.

In March 2021, media strategist Christopher Rufo, the primary inspiration for President Trump's executive order, tweeted, "We have successfully frozen their brand—'critical race theory'— into the public conversation and are steadily driving up negative perceptions. We will eventually turn it toxic, as we put all of the various cultural insanities under that brand category."[4] By that point, Rufo's tried-and-true market branding exercise had largely succeeded in framing CRT as a monster, a villain, the boogeyman waiting for your children at school. It was a manufactured sociopolitical crisis intended to stir up the masses, create havoc and confusion, and promote intentionally deceptive definitions, terms, and concepts. Rufo and his ilk were crafting lies and telling tall tales about CRT. *The Origins of Critical Race Theory* tells the movement's story.

As even longtime CRT critic Randall Kennedy, a colleague of Derrick Bell's at Harvard Law School, has admitted, any student of Bell's will not be "thrown off-kilter" by right-wing political discourse.[5] Recent attacks on CRT represent little more than repeated and intensifying cycles in an ongoing culture war. Bell's words from "The Chronicle of the Slave Scrolls" that open this introduction are from 1985, confirming that we are indeed fighting a battle that has been waged before. Michelle Alexander, acclaimed author of *The New Jim Crow*, described Bell's writings as "eerily prophetic, almost haunting."[6] But could Bell tell the future? Or, as he wrote, does "the gift of prophecy, when practiced by earthly oracles, [entail] a risky willingness to predict future events based on an examination of the present using the insight provided by an evaluation of the past"?[7] *The Origins of Critical*

Race Theory revisits the past, telling the story—the many inter-woven stories—of CRT's founding and development through the people and interpersonal relationships that breathed life into this movement.

While this is a history of the CRT movement within con-temporary US legal studies, it is also a chronicle of the human experiences, relationships, and interconnections that give the movement its spirit and resolve. Through this history, we see how CRT's founders came together, what they created, and why they created it. Much of what is already known about CRT from the movement's own perspective is couched in academic discourse that boils CRT down to key figures, key dates, and theorized tenets. The tenets are articulated as follows (see appendix 3 for expanded definitions):

The permanence of race and racism
Challenge to dominant ideologies
Interest convergence
Race as social construct
Intersectionality and anti-essentialism
Interdisciplinarity
Centrality of experiential knowledge and/or unique voices of
    people of color
Commitment to social justice
Accessibility

While this approach has provided important insights for scholar-ship, the academic style of much CRT writing has often presented more of a barrier than an invitation for other audiences who might benefit from accessing the rich insights of CRT. In this cur-rent moment, academic concepts have often been weaponized to instill fear and disinformation.

The intentional storytelling approach in this book humanizes CRT, a movement flattened and demonized by opponents at every turn. We have visited the archives. We have read deeply in sources not often referenced. We have engaged in conversation with CRT founders. Through this effort, we have gathered the strands of people's stories to weave the tapestry of CRT's founding history.

The idea that eventually became CRT was always about people and their relationships. We share the stories of how the people who informed CRT's founding period cared for one another as they navigated the intersecting injustices of US institutions, all while encountering the same broken record of resistance to CRT work and ideas. Through these stories, we trace timelines and characters unknown or previously unassociated with CRT, lifting up hidden figures foundational to the movement. What readers will find within this book is how immensely human CRT is, with a beating heart dependent on story and a storytelling tradition.

The story of CRT is one of collective courage. Throughout the history of the movement, people have taken risks to define and defend the tenets of CRT, values that existed long before the movement was given a name. In the 1960s, Mississippi was nothing less than a war zone. In the 1970s, people of color at Harvard Law School experienced its culture as nothing less than a psychic assault. In the 1980s, those who went on to become CRT's founding core learned the painful lesson that liberal institutions and ideologies will, in the end, *never* defend the interests of minoritized people. In the 1990s, under regular attack from both liberal intellectuals and conservative politicians, it became clear that sustaining the movement would require the cultivation of courage. "At a time of crisis, critics serve as reminders that we are being heard, if not always appreciated," Bell wrote in 1995. "For those of us for whom history provides the best guide to contemporary understanding, criticism is a reassurance."[8]

But conflict isn't the only narrative thread. The stories within this crucible of conflict also illustrate how the people at the heart of CRT came together to support each other, care for each other, and navigate systems and structures of inequity together. CRT is built by people who have welcomed each other into their homes, fed each other spaghetti dinners, people who have nourished each other at every level. The story of CRT is a quintessentially American story; the movement's deep roots are intertwined with key figures and flashpoints of US history at every twist and turn of its development. The history of CRT *is* US history. We look forward to sharing these stories with you.

Navigating the Book

Aja's previous book *Counterstory* made the case for critical race counterstory as a methodology by reviewing counterstory through its CRT origins and influences. She focused especially on CRT storytelling exemplars Richard Delgado, Derrick Bell, and Patricia Williams. The list of founders who are counter-story writers can be expanded to include Mari Matsuda, Charles R. Lawrence III, Margaret Montoya, Robert Chang, Robert A. Williams Jr., and Jean Stefancic. Each has written in various counterstory methods (styles), including narrated dialogue, fantasy/allegory, and autobiographic reflection, influencing many other scholars, such as Gloria Ladson-Billings, Daniel Solórzano, David Gillborn, Adrienne Dixson, Dolores Delgado Bernal, Tara J. Yosso, Lindsay Pérez Huber, Daniella Ann Cook, Carmen Kynard, and Frankie Condon.

We consider this current book, categorized as creative historical nonfiction, a work of counterstory. We seek to bring readers into scenes of high drama and create imagined dialogue between historical figures based on meticulously researched sources in order to explore race-critical themes. The form of the founding CRT counterstory exemplars inspires; we see this project as a work of counterstory in practice.[9]

The Origins of Critical Race Theory is a book of stories— many counterstories—strands woven together, producing a new tapestry of the history of CRT. One of the major tenets of CRT, also the anchor-point of counterstory, concerns the centrality of the experiential knowledge and/or unique voices of people of color. Experiential knowledge and the resulting unique voice are best communicated through story. Reflecting on what counterstory is and what is it not, education scholar Gloria Ladson-Billings cautions would-be counterstorytellers, saying, "The point is not to vent or rant or be an exhibitionist regarding one's own racial struggle."[10] Narratives like that often fall short of principled argument based on verifiable sources. Our aim, along with the aims of other race crits—the shorthand term many critical race theorists use to refer to themselves—is to construct counterstory with a deep commitment to social justice and the elimination of racial oppression as part of the broader goal of ending all forms of oppression.[11]

That said, we did not set out to write this book. And we certainly did not intend, at first, to write a book together. The process hasn't always been easy! At first, we thought this would be a single-authored book for Aja's academic field of rhetoric and writing studies, one focused on a much narrower question concerning Derrick Bell's writing process. Because of the controversy around CRT, Aja had many opportunities to speak to groups of academics and other learners about how Bell transformed academic arguments and insights from his law review articles into bestselling collections of science fiction short stories. Robert, as an historian, discovered that Bell had an archive at New York University that might help answer those questions about Bell's writing process.

That question—How did Bell revise academic work to become more accessible to the public?—is what first drove Aja into the NYU archive that Robert had located. Because we are a married couple, Robert went along to help document whatever might be found. Although Aja was lucky enough to secure some funds—a University of North Texas Scholarly and Creative Activity Award—visiting New York City is expensive, so our first visit was short. Too short, as we were to soon discover; we encountered an archive that is meticulous, massive, and close to comprehensive, covering Bell's writings—especially his correspondence—from the mid-1950s through the end of his life in 2011. In the archive, we entered a world of names, dates, and stories. We expected to encounter one person; we instead entered an entire world of relationships. At times, it felt as if Derrick Bell himself, with a broad smile, invited us into his home office for story hour with a CRT founder.

It was overwhelming in the best of ways. Before this project, neither of us had engaged in archival research. We made many mistakes, especially when it came to accurately documenting the myriad historical details we encountered. We resolved to go back. During our second visit, equipped with a better strategy for cataloguing and with a clearer sense of what we were looking for, we were able to focus our search. Still, we encountered many more people than we expected to find, many of whom are still alive and reachable by social media or email. For example, we found several rounds of correspondence between Bell and Richard Delgado—one document even featured a cute little doodle of the Loch Ness monster from Richard's own pen. As a result, we reached out to Delgado and his spouse and writing partner, Jean Stefancic.[12] They appreciated how the story of CRT was coming together and decided to help us. We were overjoyed to receive the support of these powerhouse mentors and models for what partnered research and cowriting can be. We pressed further into the journey.

What also became clear was that just about every door we knocked on—virtual and, in some cases, real—would open to us. Whether it was CRT founders, former Harvard Law School students, *Harvard Law Review* editors, academic collaborators, or community leaders—just about anyone who had known and worked with Derrick Bell was open to speaking with us. What's more, many of them responded with great love and affection for the positive impact Bell had on their lives. Yes, Bell clashed with many people. As two of his book titles assert, he had no problem confronting authority with ethical ambition. But he also inspired meaningful connections and sustained relationships around shared values.

One thing that struck us, particularly in the archive's many boxes of correspondence, was the tireless support Bell offered to anyone who asked for it, from community leaders in Mississippi, to hourly workers facing racial discrimination, to former students seeking clerkships and teaching positions, to judges on the highest benches seeking advice and counsel. In an archive—at least in a near comprehensive one—you cannot hide who you are. Very few secrets can be kept. We saw again and again the genuine efforts Bell put forth on behalf of individuals, organizations, and society. Derrick Bell, we came to learn, was a good person.

Through all these connections and doors that opened, we realized we were holding many strands of data from archival research. Conversations turned into interviews and oral histories. Each encounter led us to additional key figures and documents we may not have thought to read. Sometimes, it was a matter of mining the excellent (and sometimes juicy) footnotes that legal scholars compose; often, this is where the most humanizing details were and where the best storytelling takes place. In some cases, people shared unpublished manuscripts that provided key historical details. Some email inquiries were answered with hyperlinks to recorded presentations, events, and panel discussions we needed to view. Some queries resulted in people sharing their own work in progress that enhanced our own. We were like detectives following leads in an investigation, the map of CRT's origins taking shape before our eyes.

All these encounters helped us humanize the origin story of CRT. These conversations helped us fill in blank spots, the interstices between previously published histories. Moreover, the very human details allow us to share a story with texture and nuance. This book is the result of our research journey. This research has taken us to many places, from the law library at the University of San Francisco to the Bobst Library of NYU and back again to the West coast, eating Aja's famous chicken tacos dorados at Richard and Jean's dining table. We have spent countless hours in the Bell archive, finding personal details like grocery lists, coffee-ring stains, and bits of his hair pressed between the pages of letters from Supreme Court justices and a Harvard Law School student who would someday become the first Black president of the United States.[13] We were surprised to find Anthony Scaramucci in the footnotes of a Derrick Bell publication and even more surprised to find ourselves in Scaramucci's Midtown Manhattan office after he enthusiastically agreed to an interview to discuss how Bell, a teacher he loved, still informs his own political philosophy.[14]

We have also benefitted from conversations with people in chance encounters throughout the United States who cheered us on as we field-tested components of these stories in community spaces. The response has been heartening. In Manhattan, bartenders offered us free drinks with a toast once they learned what we were in town to research. In one heartfelt conversation with a chef, he lamented the loss of a relationship with his mother over alt-right news media and hoped she might one day read this book. In Nashville, Robert, seated upstairs in a Broadway Street honky-tonk, had an in-depth conversation with a famous pedal steel player who expressed deep concern about rising fascism and the political heritage of country music. We have learned a great deal from our students at the University of North Texas and in classroom visits throughout the country. We have deeply enjoyed the thrill every librarian has expressed upon learning that Jean Stefancic, a giant in CRT, is one of their own. This project has taken us to many places, humble and grand; each encounter has been precious to this process.

The result is a series of chapters intended to introduce readers to the tenets of CRT, the main framework of the discipline. Through story, the chapters show how the founders of CRT arrived at those concepts and commitments. Rather than starting at the end, with the concepts fully formed, we made the choice to start at the beginning, showing how CRT came to be.

How did we get to the idea of interest convergence? From what lived experience did the concept of racial realism arise? Why is it distinctive for CRT to challenge dominant ideologies? Which dominant ideologies does CRT challenge? What lived experiences led the founders of CRT to arrive at these tenets, making up what would eventually be labeled CRT? We hope *The Origins of Critical Race Theory* contributes to answering those questions.

In each chapter, we highlight and draw attention to these tenets in the context of their development. Our storytelling approach emphasizes dimension and texture; it results from a refusal to be extractive or flat. Recent opponents of CRT want the movement reduced to a few statements and commitments, a collection of dry bones or simple equations that can be picked apart or rearranged.

The chapters that follow will introduce people whom you may know but may now understand from a different point of view. You will also meet people whose names you likely have never heard and learn of their centrality to the story of what becomes CRT. While at some points, the stories can read like fiction, they are not. As Patricia Williams says of her own writing, we often intend our writing to be "playfully fictive, not fiction but fictive."[15] This is an important distinction, since although we are charting history in a storytelling mode, the stories are not about fictional characters; we are describing the experiences of real people. At the same time, we are not aiming to write comprehensive biographies, even of main characters like Derrick Bell. When one of Bell's mentors, Rev. Jefferson Rogers, whom we'll discuss later in more detail, encouraged Bell to write a proper autobiography, Bell recalled that one of Rogers's own influences at Howard University, philosophy professor Alain LeRoy Locke, once "said he would never write autobiography because he believed in telling the truth." Laughing, Bell continued, "There's some aspects of my life I'm not sure I want out there!"[16] While *The Origins of Critical Race Theory* contains many names—some of which you may not have realized had anything to do with this movement and its history—our aim has been to make CRT itself the star of the show.

Looking at the lives of people who shaped the story of CRT offers new insights into the movement itself. We have benefited from Mari Matsuda's recent reflections on the method of prosopography, understood as investigation into the common characteristics of a group of people whose biographies, when considered in parallel, give collective insight into social and historical realities.[17] The central trunk of *The Origins of Critical Race Theory* is the founding story of CRT; that story's many roots and branches are the people—some prominent, some relatively unknown—whose constellated stories contributed to its making.

The Chapters

Our story begins with Derrick Bell and a particularly thrilling find in his archive: his law school application essay. In 1954, he was on a ship headed home from his year-long tour of US Air Force duty in Korea. In the same year that Bell decided to apply to the University of Pittsburgh School of Law, the US Supreme Court announced its decision in *Brown v. Board of Education*. This launch point for chapter 1 immediately challenges bad-faith accusations that CRT is or ever has been communist, Marxist, or anti-American. Through the witness of Bell's life as a service member, a devout Christian, and eventually a dedicated civil rights litigator in service to communities in the US South, we demonstrate how the tenets of permanence of race and racism, race as social construct, and commitment to social justice came to be.

In the second chapter, we introduce readers to the storied lives of critical thinkers and cowriters Richard Delgado and Jean Stefancic. They each had full lives before meeting one another and deciding to research, write, and publish together. We explore how their unique combination of backgrounds, interests, and personal experiences produce an indelible, humanities-based, and storytelling-infused mark on CRT. Once teamed up, they have been an unstoppable force in the world of legal studies. Delgado, often cowriting with Stefancic, is the top-cited critical race legal scholar of all time.[18] Their most successful contribution, *Critical Race Theory: An Introduction*, now in its fourth edition, is still the best entry point for learners at all levels. As such, both Delgado's and Stefancic's life stories and their decision to write for popular audiences exemplify the tenets of accessibility, challenging dominant ideologies, interdisciplinarity, and commitment to social justice.

During the spring of 1985, the student-led staff of the *Harvard Law Review* extended a major accolade to Derrick Bell, inviting him to write the Foreword to the journal's annual Supreme Court issue. The invitation provided Bell an opportunity, along with a featured platform, to do something different, something *big*. Through this venue, the world was introduced to Geneva Crenshaw. In the third chapter—through interviews, archival documents, and published accounts—we trace the various sources of the composite character of Geneva Crenshaw. We explore key moments in Bell's life and trace influences and relationships, particularly with Black women, that propelled Bell toward developing the tenets of the permanence of race and racism, interest convergence, intersectionality and anti-essentialism, and interdisciplinarity.

The fourth chapter considers a variety of historical accounts of what led to the development of CRT, informed by frameworks like Kimberlé Crenshaw's concept that became the CRT tenet intersectionality. We trace several strands of CRT's history to flashpoint moments such as the 1983 Harvard Law School student protest and boycott resulting in the Alternative Course, the 1985 and 1987 critical legal studies (CLS) conferences, and Bell's infamous 1986 incident at Stanford Law School, illustrating the CRT tenet centrality of experiential knowledge and/or the unique voices of color. The chapter identifies several lesser-known contributions to the seedbed from which CRT grew, specifically tracing influences from other liberation movements, including the struggle for ethnic studies, informing the CRT tenet of interdisciplinarity. In this chapter, conflict between longtime LDF director-counsel Jack Greenberg and Derrick Bell takes center stage. Helping explain the source of CRT's tenet challenging dominant ideologies, we detail tensions between liberalism and Black liberation throughout the United States in the twentieth century, particularly in the NAACP, the Legal Defense Fund, and the legal studies field.

After a long process of coming into being, CRT finally gained a name in July 1989. Once the discipline, also a social movement, took shape, different groups approached it in very different ways. Scholars in various academic fields, especially in education, almost immediately began applying CRT's insights. Not everyone was so positive. Critics of various sorts began lodging their assessments of CRT and its core commitments. This fifth chapter highlights some of these critiques, distinguishing good-faith, reasonable criticism from scholars like Randall Kennedy from more recent political attacks from media manipulators, including the likes of Christopher Rufo. Throughout this chapter, we address the CRT tenets of the permanence of race and racism, interest convergence, challenge to dominant ideologies, and the centrality of the unique voices of people of color.

This book's conclusion gestures toward new CRT directions in incorporating class analysis alongside racial critique, contemporary turns within legal studies toward storytelling and transdisciplinarity, and the promise found in greater engagement with the humanities. Despite current challenges to CRT's credibility, the movement's deep rootedness in relationships of human concern is not easily overcome. The superficial word games of the current critiques can do their best; CRT is an idea that cannot be killed. Let's get to it.

1

Deeply Rooted

Derrick Bell and the Foundations of
Critical Race Theory

CRT TENETS COVERED: Permanence of Race and Racism;
Race as Social Construct; Commitment to Social Justice

Derrick Bell is a towering figure, a giant in civil rights and critical race theory. Bell was also a social and cultural critic, writing
and speaking, often through story, to audiences ranging from
community members in rural Mississippi, to fourth graders in
Washington, DC, to patrons at Black-owned bookstores in Dallas,
Oakland, and other cities. In other words, this first tenured Black
professor at Harvard Law School—an ivory tower bastion if there
ever was one—was deeply rooted in his life-long commitment to
the lives, welfare, and rights of communities of color throughout
the United States.

Bell tells a story about his time as an NAACP Legal Defense
Fund (LDF) lawyer litigating desegregation cases in Leake
County, Mississippi. It was 1964, and he was driving the dusty
rural roads with American Friends Service Committee field
director Jean Fairfax (whom we discuss further in chapter 3),
trying to locate Black first-graders who would be the first to desegregate the county's public schools. But Black parents, acutely
aware of the risks of white violence, resisted the LDF efforts. In
the mid-1970s, Bell first considered writing a memoir; he tentatively titled it *Still Looking for the Pony*.[1] This memoir would explain his changing perspectives on civil rights law, as he recalled
how parents responded "with long, agonizing silences and then
with tears. We knew all too well why they were so upset. We did

not have the power to end their tears, and out of frustration and sympathy, we cried too."

Bell's work in Leake County supplemented the efforts of two sisters, Winson and Dovie Hudson, who had long worked for civil rights in Mississippi. Along with their family and friends, the Hudsons faced severe consequences for their efforts. As Bell recalled, "They had lost jobs and loans, their homes had been shot into. And yet they persevered, grew stronger with the dangerous proof that whites at least were taking them seriously." He recalled walking down a Leake County dirt road beside Mrs. Behonor McDonald—a first cousin and coworker of the Hudsons.

"Why do you do it?" Bell asked.

She thought for just a moment before her answer came strong and certain.

"I am getting old now," she said, "and I think sometimes I lives to harass the white folk."[2]

Harass? And harass white folk? "But I thought civil rights was all about getting along and finding ways to coexist," the reader might object. "You know—the MLK photo where he's marching, arms linked with folks of all hues!"

Before anyone gets too worked up, pause for a moment. Focus on the word—*harass*. What does harass mean? To readers versed in white parlance, it might connote gratuitous irritation. But in the way Bell and Mrs. McDonald meant it, harassment has everything to do with keeping people focused, vigilant, and non-complacent. Harassment is about shaking people into consciousness, awareness, and an educated literacy about inequality, oppression, racism, and injustice. Mrs. McDonald was well aware of where power resided in her world, that of an elderly Black woman fighting for civil rights in 1964 Mississippi. She knew who had most of the guns—and who had the law on their side to use them. She knew who had the vote. And she knew who had full rights as citizens in the United States of America.

In the face of all this inequity, however, she also had hope, an enduring hope that sustained her community-organizing and

Figure 1.1. Mrs. Behonor McDonald (1908–78). Photo courtesy of Dotson/McDonald/Jackson family.

resistance efforts—in short, effectual harassment of the white folk in Leake County who would rather she stayed silent and satisfied with her lot in life. Mrs. McDonald's bold statement took root within Derrick Bell and grew to become a centerpiece of the foundation for his overall creed of racial realism—a comprehension of how race, racism, and law works in the United States. This racial realism provides the foundation for a major tenet of critical race theory: the permanence of race and racism.

The Law School Application

A landmark year—1954. The NAACP Legal Defense and Educational Fund, Inc. (LDF), founded by Thurgood Marshall in 1940, won a decisive victory in *Brown*. The sole woman on Marshall's team, a young lawyer named Constance Baker Motley, had written the original complaint. Also in 1954, two young Black US military veterans submitted applications to law school. One of them, Medgar W. Evers, applied to the University of Mississippi Law School in Oxford and received a prompt rejection. The other, Derrick A. Bell Jr., applied to the University of Pittsburgh School of Law, which admitted him as the only Black student in a class of 140. Although Motley, Evers, and Bell were on very different paths in 1954, their worlds would collide in 1961, talents assembling behind James Meredith's quest to become the first officially enrolled Black student at the University of Mississippi.

A draft of Bell's typewritten law school application essay, written during his year-long tour of duty in the US Air Force in Korea, rests in his archive at NYU.[3] When the US Supreme Court announced its decision in *Brown* on May 17, 1954, Bell was on a ship headed home.[4] This first essay draft, written when Bell was twenty-two, is filled with typed corrections, handwritten notes (in Bell's recognizable hand and that of an anonymous collaborator), and strikethroughs, denoting likely edits in a final version. In other words, it illustrates his writing process—a true first draft. We discuss it in later sections of this chapter.

Raised in Pittsburgh on a prospering edge of the culturally vibrant, predominantly Black neighborhood known as The Hill, Bell's childhood involved few instances where his worth was called into question. His father, Derrick Bell Sr., who had been raised in Dothan, Alabama, and through whom Bell received family lore of Choctaw and Blackfoot lineage, was concerned when the younger Bell received military orders to travel deep into the South of the United States.[5]

During his undergraduate studies in political science and journalism at Duquesne University, the unreservedly patriotic

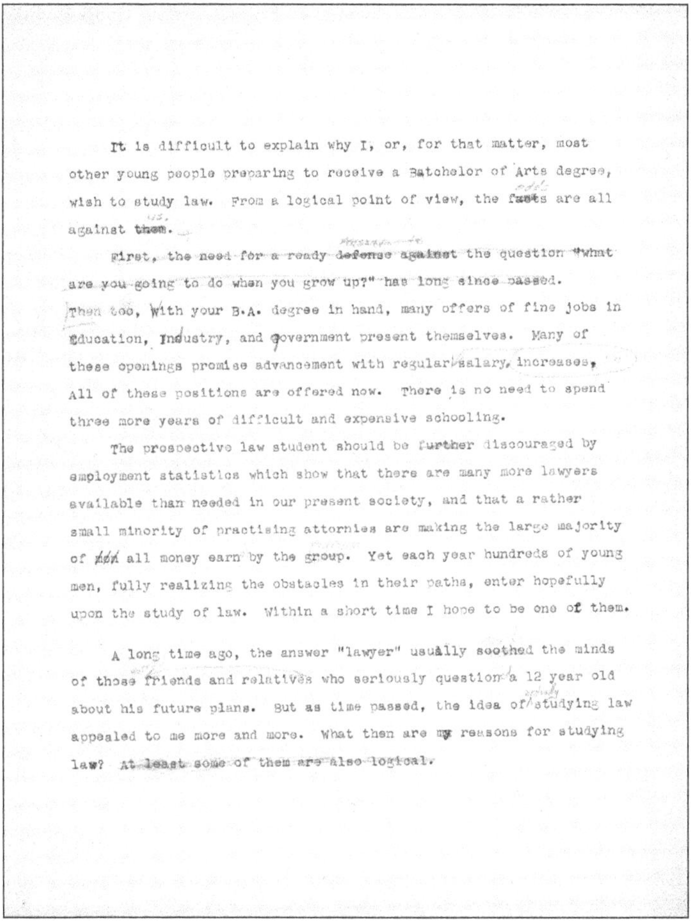

It is difficult to explain why I, or, for that matter, most other young people preparing to receive a Batchelor of Arts degree, wish to study law. From a logical point of view, the facts are all against them.

First, the need for a ready defense against the question "what are you going to do when you grow up?" has long since passed. Then too, with your B.A. degree in hand, many offers of fine jobs in Education, Industry, and government present themselves. Many of these openings promise advancement with regular salary increases, All of these positions are offered now. There is no need to spend three more years of difficult and expensive schooling.

The prospective law student should be further discouraged by employment statistics which show that there are many more lawyers available than needed in our present society, and that a rather small minority of practising attornies are making the large majority of all money earn by the group. Yet each year hundreds of young men, fully realizing the obstacles in their paths, enter hopefully upon the study of law. Within a short time I hope to be one of them.

A long time ago, the answer "lawyer" usually soothed the minds of those friends and relatives who seriously question a 12 year old about his future plans. But as time passed, the idea of studying law appealed to me more and more. What then are my reasons for studying law? At least some of them are also logical.

Figure 1.2. Fourth page of Derrick Bell's Law School application essay, written in 1954, showing his commitment to Negro causes. NYU Archive.

younger Bell had joined the Air Force Reserve Officer Training Corps. Upon graduation, he received orders to report to an Air Force base in South Carolina. Derrick Bell Sr. wasn't at all eager for his son to experience the realities of Jim Crow. "I remember my father . . . was very concerned about me having to ride segregated trains and all that, and he'd just bought a new Plymouth and he said why don't you take the Plymouth," Bell recalled in an oral history interview. And Bell's father wasn't pleased when his son decided to bring along a white classmate heading to the same base. The pair's first taste of southern reality came, Bell said, when "we stopped in Richmond [Virginia] and I had this name of this Black rooming house and we both went up and . . . the landlady had a fit. 'Get this white boy out of here, what you trying to do? You take him down to that hotel and you come back.' She kind of laid me out." Soon after the pair reported to their base, Bell noticed that his white companion, Ed Trainer, was no longer speaking to him. "As northerners often do, he got to the South and he had to, you know, fit in with the group."[6]

Bell's father had good reason to be concerned for his son's experiences in the South, far beyond being shunned by erstwhile white friends. Derrick Sr. had left Alabama under duress, driven out by racist violence and its aftermath. "My father left Alabama, I learned later, hurriedly," Bell recounted in a story he learned from his sister. As a young man, Derrick Sr. "had gone to a county fair with . . . this beautiful white shirt on, . . . and a couple of white boys . . . had a real whip and proceeded to beat him with it, so that the white shirt was all tattered and covered with blood." Afterward, local police took Derrick Sr.'s father, Albert, a minister with prestige in the community, to see if they could find the attackers. Soon afterwards, Bell's father "ran into these two guys without their whip and beat both of them down to the ground."[7] This experience propelled the elder Derrick Bell to Pittsburgh, one of the many thousands of experiences that made up the Great Migration.[8] No less than the landlady at the Black safehouse in Virginia, Bell's father knew in his bones, in the whip marks he carried on his skin, that the officers' bars on his son's Air Force uniform would not protect him from white supremacist violence.

From there, Derrick Bell Jr. went to Korea, but not before starting what Rep. John Lewis would later call "good trouble" by complaining about the racial segregation of buses once they left his second base in Alexandria, Louisiana. Bell had visited a local Black church but found it to have "a lot of spirit but very little substance." Since "there was no Black Presbyterian church" like the one he had attended in Pittsburgh, Bell recalls, "I went to the white church." Eventually, he inquired about whether he might be allowed to sing in the choir. He never received an answer from the choir director and contented himself with sitting in the church balcony until he was deployed overseas.[9]

When Bell wrote his law school application essay, his core principles were already highly formed. The values we see there—commitment to hard work, devotion to Christian faith, and a commitment to pursuing social justice within the legal frameworks of the United States—would remain consistent throughout his life. These values run counter to accusations hurled against CRT in recent years, especially from the alt-right and echoed among activists from the religious right, that assume CRT's roots are in European Marxist critical theory. The implication of those accusations is that CRT is irredeemably anti-American and anti-Christian. If Derrick Bell is central to understanding CRT, if only in a background sense, the witness of his own life—as a veteran, a lifelong Christian, and a committed family man—refutes those accusations.[10]

Plainclothes Minister

In a portion of the application essay about his personal character, Bell shares that other people had "noticed certain 'religious' characteristics about my nature" and had inquired if he had "ever thought about ministry." He believed, however, that society needed "men willing to lead really Christian lives not only in the Church, but also in business [and] government. What is needed are more 'plainclothes ministers.'"[11] Baptized in a Pittsburgh African-Methodist-Episcopal congregation, Bell later "joined a black Presbyterian church where [he sang] in the choir during [his] high school [and] college years."[12] His mother hoped he would become a preacher like his paternal grandfather, Albert Bell. Derrick Bell would remain devoted to his Christian identity throughout his life, attending Black and liberal Protestant churches. In fact, his love story with Jewel Hairston Bell, his first wife of thirty years, can be credited to their shared faith.

Derrick first met Jewel in their Pittsburgh neighborhood, The Hill. This historically Black and working-class neighborhood was the cultural center of Black life and a major center for jazz and literature. Jewel and Derrick had been friends since they were children. Both came from working-class families and attended the mostly white Schenley High School, where they were two of the three Black students tracked into a special program for gifted and talented learners. "On math and science, Jewel helped me a lot," Derrick said of their high school years. "We were . . . really close friends, but it wasn't a romance."[13] Derrick graduated in 1948, a year ahead of Jewel.

After high school, they wouldn't meet again until the late 1950s when they were both—unbeknown to each other—living in Washington, DC. With a bachelor of science degree (with honors) from Margaret Morrison Carnegie College, the women's college of Carnegie Mellon University, and a graduate degree in psychiatric social work from Case Western Reserve University in hand, Jewel launched into careers in psychology and community-based social work. According to Derrick, however, Jewel had always wanted to be an actor. She was very active in high school theater and, while in Cleveland for studies at Case, was heavily involved with Karamu House, a Black theater company that developed and premiered many Langston Hughes plays.[14] After relocating from Cleveland to Washington, DC, she became an active participant in the Church of the Redeemer Presbyterian, a startup church community led by Rev. Jefferson P. Rogers and his wife, Mary Grace.

Derrick Bell relocated to DC in 1957 to work for the US Department of Justice. He would eventually work in the Civil Rights Division, established in the same year. Jewel Hairston, already an NAACP organizer, was someone Rev. Rogers described as "preordained [with a] powerful spiritual force." She helped Jeff and Mary Grace Rogers structure their new church (founded that same year) "as a fellowship without barriers as to race or class" so as to "put a new face on a community plagued with centuries of racism and burdened with needless social pain."¹⁵ Upon realizing Derrick now also lived in DC, Jewel invited her former school friend to church.

The home of Jeff and Mary Grace Rogers became a lifelong model for Derrick and Jewel. Their living room was a space of warm familial hospitality and community-based vocational clarity that served as an intellectual parlor. Originally from Quincy, Florida, Jeff had been aggressively recruited to graduate school by Benjamin Mays, founding dean of Howard University's School of Religion. Mays even went so far as to appeal to Jeff's grandmother, Hattie Paramore, a fierce educator and activist in her own right.¹⁶ At Howard, Jeff came to know and study under prominent Black theologian Howard Thurman.

When Mays and Thurman encouraged Jeff to further his theological studies, the two Rogerses headed to Yale, where Jeff completed a graduate degree in social ethics from the Divinity School while Mary Grace earned a masters in sociology. Through Mays and Thurman, Jeff became an early confidant of Martin Luther King Jr., heading the DC chapter of the Southern Christian Leadership Conference (SCLC), founded in 1957. The Rogers's living room would often host SCLC strategy meetings with King, Andrew Young, Wyatt T. Walker, Jesse Jackson, and others.¹⁷

In that same living room, as Derrick recalls, "I watched Jeff Rogers, one of the best-read persons I know, and Jewel argue for hours over any of a variety of subjects."¹⁸ Seeing how Jeff and Mary Grace operated, Derrick began to understand that with the right person, marriage could be a support rather than a burden. Later, Jeff would recall how the young couple worked together with "effortless grace and the spiritual magnetism that we all know as Jewel and Derrick. All of us in that young fellowship knew that [they] were destined for permanent togetherness even if Derrick didn't know it then."¹⁹ The next summer, while Jewel was serving as program director for the Urban League–supported James Weldon Johnson Summer Camp in a state park west of Pittsburgh, Derrick proposed to her under the stars.²⁰

Derrick and Jewel are both the product of and the shapers of Black uplift and self-determination, the beneficiaries of cultural movements like the Harlem Renaissance. They participated directly in the civil rights movement of the 1960s, and they went on to build the critical race consciousness of the post–civil rights era. For them, Black Christian hope was never separate from the struggle for equality. The social and theological insights of Reinhold Niebuhr, which Jeff Rogers studied at Yale while Reinhold's brother, H. Richard Niebuhr, was on the faculty, contributed to the basis of what would become Bell's racial realism, later a central premise informing CRT.[21] The Bells carried their Christian convictions to Harvard during fall 1969, when Bell began his term as a lecturer at Harvard Law School. They rapidly connected with Harvard Divinity School and the Memorial Church. It's an interesting coincidence that another couple with deep commitments to Christian social action, Paulo and Elza Freire, arrived at Harvard during that same period. Indeed, this convergence with Paulo Freire would provide a significant thread through the rest of Bell's teaching career.

Throughout the 1970s, Bell offered several sermons during morning prayer at Harvard's Memorial Church.[22] The Bell home gained a reputation as a safe haven for lonely artists, scholars, and Harvard Law students who were seeking human connection. It was a place of kindness and psychological comfort.

Jewel and Derrick opened their home to students, making them feel like family; this was especially important for marginalized and oppressed students at Harvard Law School for whom activism some days was, in the words of Patricia J. Williams, "simply surviving, . . . simply getting up every day and coming to class." Williams, who would become a central figure in the CRT movement, described Jewel as providing what "in today's world we'd call a certain kind of group therapy." However, as civil rights stalwarts in their own right, with mentors like Jefferson and Mary Grace Rogers in DC just over a decade before, the Bells represented and provided much more than simply friendship to this Harvard Law School community. Students found the Bells and

Figure 1.3. Derrick Bell and Jewel Hairston Bell. Steve Liss, Getty Images.

their home to be a space of refuge similar to safe houses in the Jim Crow Deep South. As Williams put it, "I think [they] provided . . . part of a history of the civil rights movement, a little bit like the houses that put you up in the Deep South when you couldn't go into a hotel. Or the homes that would greet you with a full meal when there was no supper to be found on the road."[23]

Bell's reflections on law and religion find their central note in Gospel hymns and in his lifelong love of music. It is no coincidence that Derrick and Jewel initiated their union at Camp James Weldon Johnson. That community's message of hope rang out in the Gospel choirs of Pittsburgh, Pennsylvania, and Alexandria, Louisiana, and echoed again in his 1996 book, *Gospel Choirs: Psalms of Survival in an Alien Land Called Home*. Bell's calling to be a "plainclothes minister"—a thought already present in his 1954 Law School application essay and nurtured in the living room of Jeff and Mary Grace Rogers—comes full circle in the course Bell later co-taught with George Taylor in 2006 on race, religion, and law at the University of Pittsburgh School of Law. In that course, Bell and Taylor walked students through the political theologies of enslavers and segregationists along with the visions and analytical insights of Howard Thurman, Martin Luther King Jr., Gustavo Gutiérrez, Vine Deloria Jr., Lucia Silecchia, Joan Didion, Paula Fredriksen, Cornel West, and James H. Cone. The course represented a homecoming of sorts for Bell, returning not only to his alma mater but to his and Jewel's hometown and neighborhood. One thing a person learns when studying Bell's life is that he was fiercely loyal, always returning to the places and communities where he was rooted.

Bell's Black (Male) Heroes

In 1954, as he wrote his law school application essay, Bell was keenly aware of the "shortage of capable Negro attorneys."[24] He listed several Black heroes he wished to emulate: "In the constant battle for true equality which the Negro has fought in America, Negro law men have done more than their share. The William

Hasties, the Wendell Greens, the Ralph Bunches, are by their stirring achievements in the legal field winning more and greater respect for both themselves and the race which they represent."[25] The invocation of these great Black men was aspirational at this point in Bell's young life. Wendell E. Green (1887–1959) was the first African American judge in Illinois. Soon after Illinois governor Adlai Stevenson appointed Green to the bench in 1950, he presided over a case in which prosecutors charged a Chicago police officer with murder for shooting and killing a Latino teenager. Green's steadfastness in the face of threats from supporters of the police officer and his fair sentence once the jury returned a verdict had brought him national prominence.

More so than Green, Bell's appreciation of Bunche and his relationship with Hastie would prove pivotal to him personally and to the historical development and contemporary shape of CRT. Ralph Bunche (1904–71) is an anomaly in Bell's list because unlike the others, Bunche was not a lawyer. In 1950, however, Bunche received the Nobel Peace Prize for his role in negotiating the 1949 armistice lines between Israel and its Arab neighbors. While Bunche's international success led to some perceiving him as a token who somehow transcended race, Bell's 1954 essay claimed him as a significant Black leader.

Prior to his work in the international arena, Bunche was a significant academic race theorist whose ideas still resonate today. In his 1936 book *A World View of Race*, Bunche put forth his view that "race is a social concept which can be and is employed effectively to rouse and rationalize emotions" and that "race, having no scientific definition, is sufficiently flexible in its social meaning to make it an admirable device for the cultivation of group prejudices."[26] His description, of course, presages the CRT tenet that race is a social construct.

Bunche went on to work closely with Swedish economist Gunnar Myrdal, whose 1944 study, *An American Dilemma: The Negro Problem and Modern Democracy*, argued that American racism was an anomaly the United States would eventually overcome. Nearly half a century later, in his 1992 book, *Faces at the Bottom of the Well: The Permanence of Racism*, Bell would argue directly against Myrdal. Rather than an incongruity that would fall by the wayside, Bell argued that race is a permanent feature of the United States, woven into its foundations.[27] This insight, which would become a key tenet of contemporary CRT, will be discussed in more detail in chapter 3.

In 1946, Bunche was part of the US delegation to the first United Nations General Assembly. As head of the organization's Trusteeship Division, Bunche helped several countries transition from colonization to self-government. His engagement in Arab-Israeli peacemaking and decolonization provides a pathway that became a model for later efforts, by critical race theorists and others, to dismantle entrenched material inequities built to preserve the social construct of race. Through Bell's recognition of Bunche's international work toward decolonization and conflict negotiation, we catch a glimpse of CRT's international horizons. Through pioneering theorists like Palestinian American legal scholar Noura Erakat, for example, we see tireless efforts to reframe and re-envision interpretations of international law. CRT, alongside other theoretical contributions, carries promise for confronting neocolonial structures of domination.[28]

Of the three heroes Bell names in his law school admissions essay, he would become most closely connected to William H. Hastie (1904–76). Bell met Hastie, the first Black federal judge, in 1957, his final year of law school.[29] When the eager student informed the seasoned judge and civil rights activist of his intent to become a civil rights lawyer, the optimism of *Brown*, decided in 1954, informed Hastie's response: "Son, I am afraid that you were born fifteen years too late to have a career in civil rights."[30] Hastie was a graduate of Harvard Law School and had become dean of the law school at Howard University where his students included Thurgood Marshall. But his career was not without challenges.

In 1941, during WWII, Hastie was hired as a civilian aide to Henry Stimson, the US secretary of war. In a later reflection, Bell notes that Hastie was wary of the position since his presence could be "used to legitimize the segregation of black soldiers."[31]

Hastie pushed for integration, protesting against segregated and substandard training for Black pilots. Unable to make progress on these issues during wartime, he resigned his position in January 1943, feeling he could be more useful as a private citizen.[32] Hastie's resignation caught the attention of the Black press; the resulting attention forced the Defense Department (previously the Department of War and renamed by President Truman following WWII) to adopt many of the policies Hastie had promoted. After his service as governor of the US Virgin Islands, President Truman appointed Hastie to the United States Court of Appeals for the Third Circuit.

Judge Hastie has a far-reaching legal legacy. Long after his promotion of racial desegregation during WWII, a highly promising Harvard Law School graduate would become the 1984–85 William H. Hastie Fellow at the University of Wisconsin Law School: Kimberlé Williams Crenshaw. Established in 1973, the Hastie Fellowship program provides aspiring scholars some of their first significant opportunities to prepare for a career in law teaching.[33] During her Hastie year, Crenshaw worked on her LLM thesis under the supervision of critical legal studies (CLS) founder David Trubek.[34] In a September 1986 letter to Crenshaw, Bell urged her to prioritize publishing during her first year of law teaching, stating she should send her essay to "eight or ten" law reviews. Bell suggested that UCLA might be particularly interested because they failed "to get Chuck Lawrence's piece which will go to the *Stanford Law Review* and thus [UCLA] might be particularly interested in another innovative article on the issue of race." In a handwritten postscript to this letter, Bell writes, "Saw Trubek in hall yesterday. Gather he urges you to wait to improve your piece in the spring. Very few in this field recognize perfection—especially when race is involved. They all recognize two publications. Pay your money & take your choice. D."[35] By 1988, Crenshaw had published "Race, Reform, and Retrenchment: Transformation and Legitimation in Antidiscrimination Law" in the *Harvard Law Review*.[36] The essay has since become one of CRT's canonical texts.

Returning to the University of Wisconsin in 1988 as a visiting fellow, Crenshaw and her successor Hastie fellow, Stephanie L. Phillips, coordinated with then Wisconsin Law School faculty member Richard Delgado. Together, they approached Dave Trubek, then director of Wisconsin's Institute of Legal Studies, to seek financial, intellectual, and administrative support for a workshop they titled "New Developments in Race and Legal Theory." This workshop, held in July 1989 at a convent on the shores of Lake Mendota in Madison, Wisconsin, is widely regarded as the founding meeting of CRT.[37] Judge Hastie's legacy of critical protest thus informed the movement long before it received a name.

A Good Lawyer

Bell's law school application essay was explicit in his intention to contribute to "the constant battle for true equality which the Negro has fought in America." He was aware of "a shortage of capable Negro attorneys," making it difficult for Black people who "would like to take their cases to Negro lawyers but are unable to do so." Because leaders like Hastie, Green, and Bunche had been so successful, "in the near future, other young Negroes will because of the record of these men be expected to accept ever increasing responsibilities in the judicial affairs of our nation. I hope, no more than this, I intend [he added for emphasis] to be one of these men." Bell was confident in his abilities: "I feel moreover that I have the ability to further advance both America and the Negro in America. A knowledge of the law will be the foundation used in carrying out this undertaking. To this end, I have definitely decided to first become a good lawyer."[38]

In the first law review article Bell published while teaching at Harvard Law School, "Black Students in White Law Schools: The Ordeal and the Opportunity," a draft of which he shared with Judge Hastie, he recounted the stress of "beginning my legal education in a school that usually failed one-third of its first-year class." That general anxiety was augmented by "the necessity of keeping one's temper during property classes where (according to the briefings I had received from the two black upperclassmen in the school) the professor would 'test' black students by sprinkling his hypotheticals with 'negras' whose craving for watermelon induced entrance on property not their own."[39] Bell was frustrated again when during his third year, white classmates to whom he had generously offered insights on Black culture received job offers while he did not. Finding no local prospects, Bell followed the advice of his professors and gained a US Department of Justice position through the Attorney General's Honors Program, established in 1953.

Once in DC, where he would reconnect with Jewel Hairston, Bell initially worked in the Conscientious Objectors Section of the Department of Justice, assessing appeals from men seeking to avoid military draft. In 1958, he received a transfer to the Civil Rights Division, which had gained recognition the year before. His time in that office was short. His supervisors determined that Bell's membership in the NAACP constituted a conflict of interest and demanded he resign from the organization. Bell reached out to friends and mentors for advice. Most counseled him to give up the NAACP membership so he could work on the inside, effecting change within the system. Judge Hastie, however, gave different advice. "In the end," Bell later recalled, "Hastie emphasized that I should do what I felt was right. He did not mention it, but his own life gave meaning to what he viewed as right."[40]

With Hastie's example, Bell decided not to give up his NAACP membership. Rather than firing him or transferring him to another office, his supervisors moved his desk to a hall and barred him from working on any race-related projects, filling his time with busy work. Taking the hint, he soon resigned but not before he composed a poem:

IN MEMORIAM
Ring the Church Bell, Sound the Death Knell,
Drape in Black both old and young;
Gather, Gather, Brother, Sister
While my tale of toil is sung.

Come still nearer, You, my hearer,
Come, my voice will fail me soon;
Shadows fading in the gloaming
Herald night's oncoming gloom.

I was young once, young and pretty,
I had hope then, Just as you;
But I entered Civil Service;
Oh, if only then I knew.

All the tiresome, tedious typing,
Filing papers, memos, drafts,
Making phone calls, citing old laws
Bickering with the office staffs.

Ambitions dead now, dead and buried,
My woe increases day by day;
The future holds but one thing for me,
Greater work for no more pay.

"Find new work," cried both my parents,
"Leave the old job," my friends pled;
Useless warnings, Useless pleadings,
Courage long before had fled.

Murder talent, Kill Incentive,
Bury skill 'neath time and grade,
Shackle faith and hope to payday;
Thus does Man become a slave.

Useless efforts, wasted motions,
No need now to push or strive;
My life's schedule clear before me,
Mortal Hell from 9 till 5.

Ring the Church Bell, Sound the Death Knell,
Five years gone is what we mourn;

Repeat the ancient ceremony,
Pin on my breast your badge of scorn.

Hear my words, my youthful mourners,
There's moral in my sad lament;
Better sell your Soul to Satan
Than spend your life in Government.

Written by Mr. Bell.[41]

In 1959, Bell headed back home to Pittsburgh, where he headed up the local branch of the NAACP. There, in addition to learning just how much fundraising and administrative work went into grassroots civil rights organizing and inspired by Martin Luther King Jr.'s work in the South, he attempted to organize a sit-in. It failed dramatically. One evening in 1959, several Black friends agreed to join him at a de facto whites-only bar in downtown Pittsburgh. When none of them showed up, Bell, dressed in a suit and tie, sat at the bar by himself, where he succeeded only in being ignored. "When the civil rights sit-ins began on a national scale the following year," he later wrote, "my respect for their courage was based firmly on my experience."[42]

After a few months in that job, Bell met Thurgood Marshall, then serving as director-counsel of the NAACP Legal Defense and Education Fund (LDF), who came to Pittsburgh on a speaking tour. Judge Hastie had already mentioned Bell in conversation. In addition to being an instructor of Marshall's at Howard Law School, Judge Hastie was a cousin of Charles Hamilton Houston, first NAACP general counsel, and had worked closely with Marshall to develop precedent-changing legal theory. As Judge Constance Baker Motley later recalled, "Hastie thought highly of Derrick and recommended him to Thurgood Marshall. I think Hastie never gave Marshall any advice with respect to staff appointments that Marshall did not follow."[43]

But Marshall was no fan of civil disobedience. Motley would also recall that Marshall nearly had a stroke when he learned about the first arrests resulting from lunch counter sit-ins. At this point, the NAACP had not yet endorsed civil disobedience, especially since there was no guarantee such actions could receive judicial protection.[44] Had Bell's sit-in been a headline-garnering success—if more people had participated, generating violence or arrests—Marshall might have thought twice about Judge Hastie's recommendation. Luckily for Bell, Marshall came to town ready to offer him a job with the LDF in New York City, working civil rights cases alongside Motley, Jack Greenberg, and James Nabrit III. Although Bell had been working in a non-lawyer capacity in Pittsburgh following his debacle with the Department of Justice, he must have made a good impression. He accepted the position on the spot. The pieces of his life were coming together. Jewel and Derrick would marry on June 26, 1960.

Justice for the People

Throughout 1960 and into 1961, Derrick and Jewel adjusted to married life, including an eventual relocation for Jewel, who joined Derrick in New York to set up house and home in Harlem at the Riverton Houses while continuing to pursue her career as a psychiatric social worker and community organizer.[45] Derrick began his work with the Legal Defense Fund, assisting the NAACP's general counsel, Robert L. Carter. Within a few months, he was assigned the role of assistant counsel to the sole woman on the LDF legal staff, Constance Baker Motley. The case was *Meredith v. Fair*.[46]

Memphis, Tennessee—nestled along the Chickasaw Bluffs—is home to the National Civil Rights Museum. This museum is a national memorial and pilgrimage site because it stands at the location of the once-operational Lorraine Motel where Martin Luther King Jr. was assassinated on April 4, 1968. As museum patrons are led through the chronology of the US struggle for rights and equality, sections of the museum detail the events of *Brown* and the 1961 *Meredith* case in which a young Black Air Force veteran, James Meredith, attempted to enroll at the University of Mississippi, becoming the first Black person to legally desegregate the school.

The museum tells an important story but gives scant attention to a central character—Constance Baker Motley. Motley had written the original complaint in *Brown*. She also led legal efforts to desegregate universities in Florida, Georgia, Alabama, South Carolina, and Mississippi. Later, after King was jailed in Birmingham, Motley became his lead attorney. In 1965, King himself noted the importance of lawyers in creating the conditions for social change. Among those "leaders of great renown," King listed "Clarence Darrow, Wendell Willkie, Thurgood Marshall, Charles Houston, Jack Greenberg, and that Portia, Constance Baker Motley," alluding to the heroine of *The Merchant of Venice*.[47] For all this, the National Civil Rights Museum at the Lorraine Motel barely mentions Motley in a video playing in the *Brown v. Board* room, a significant oversight.

In January 1961, Thurgood Marshall, then director-counsel of the LDF, stormed into assistant counsel Motley's office and threw a letter down on her desk. It was from James Meredith appealing to the organization for help with anticipated difficulties he would encounter as he sought admission to the University of Mississippi. Letters of appeal like this were not uncommon in the LDF offices; Black youth activists were constantly floating ideas for cases that could advance the cause of civil equality and desegregation on behalf of themselves and their communities. Meredith stated that he was writing at the suggestion of Mississippi NAACP field secretary Medgar Evers, with whom he had discussed the matter. Evers himself had applied for admission to "Ole Miss" in 1954 and had been denied when he was unable to furnish the additional alumni certificate that the institution, knowing that such a certificate did not exist and therefore could not be produced, demanded as a condition of his acceptance.[48]

"This man has got to be crazy," Marshall declared.

With this definitive statement and the letter informally pitched onto Motley's desk, she had come to understand this as Marshall's way of saying this was her case if she wanted it. After all, "all white men had black Mammies," as Marshall put it, to explain why Black women fared better in the South than Black men. But Motley didn't have to deduce much beyond Marshall's dark humor.

"That's your case," he concluded, and that was that.[49]

Within that same month—January 1961—a Black high school student in Birmingham, Alabama, U. W. Clemon, appealed to local attorney Arthur D. Shores, known as the Dean of Black Lawyers in the State of Alabama.[50] In a manner similar to James Meredith, Clemon was interested in generating a desegregation-oriented test case by attempting to enroll at the University of Alabama. This effort would require the support of the NAACP and the LDF. Shores, licensed to practice law in Alabama in 1937, had cemented his national reputation in his work with NAACP counsel Charles Hamilton Houston when they successfully argued a workplace discrimination case (*Steele v. Louisville & N.R. Co.*) before the US Supreme Court in 1944.[51]

"I went to Mr. Shore's office in downtown Birmingham. I told him I wanted to apply to the University of Alabama," Clemon shared in an interview.[52]

Clemon, who would be appointed in 1980 by President Jimmy Carter as the first Black federal judge in Alabama, recalls that Shores was interested in the idea but said he would have to talk with Thurgood Marshall first. Shores assured Clemon that he would immediately call the LDF office in New York.

"A week went by and I didn't hear back," Clemon said. He visited the office again. "Shores said the LDF didn't think the time was right at the University of Alabama."[53]

The time for desegregation at the University of Alabama was right two years later. Neither Shores nor Clemon knew that the LDF was already preparing to enter a legal battle, representing James Meredith in the neighboring state of Mississippi. What Clemon also couldn't have known at the time was that, by September 1965, when Meredith and Clemon both enrolled as students at Constance Baker Motley's alma mater, Columbia Law School, Clemon and Meredith would become best friends.

In 1998, Motley published her autobiography, *Equal Justice Under Law*, detailing key moments in the life of the first Black woman to sit on the federal judiciary. The book cover, which she probably chose, is telling; in the historic photo of her walking

Figure 1.4. Derrick Bell, James Meredith, and Constance Baker
Motley. AP.

shoulder to shoulder with James Meredith, dressed for trial, a
bemused and determined slight smile illuminates her face. Reflecting in the autobiography on this moment in her life, Motley
states, "I could not have made it through the *Meredith* trial, with
all its pleadings, briefs, and trips to Mississippi, without Derrick's
able assistance."[54]

By the summer of 1961, Motley and Bell arrived in Jackson, Mississippi, for the preliminary injunction hearing in

the *Meredith* case. Medgar Evers, in his capacity as Mississippi NAACP field secretary, would meet them at the airport countless times throughout the duration of this eighteen-month trial, shuttling them all around the state in his distinctive powder-blue 1962 Oldsmobile 88. He coordinated with local community leaders to make sure outside visitors had places to eat and sleep—one of those places sometimes being the Evers' own home.[55] Mississippi during this time was an all-out war zone, and community organizers such as Evers—whom everyone knew and admired—were regarded as serious enemies by those determined to resist racial change.

The Mississippi summer of 1961 was a frenzy of activism. During one of his many visits to Jackson, Bell first met Winson and Dovie Hudson, two sisters he described as "pillars of the all-black Harmony community," in rural Leake County, Mississippi. With "purpose in their eyes," they traveled the hour or so—on Evers's advice—into Jackson to seek the help of the two lawyers from New York. The white school board closed their beloved Harmony School as a means of intimidating and suppressing community activists like the Hudson sisters who used it as both a school and a community meeting space.[56]

Meanwhile, Motley was approached by the Jackson branch of the NAACP to bring a lawsuit against segregated local bus and train terminals. The Freedom Riders, in their staunch belief that activist pressure would end segregation, kept riding into Jackson and getting thrown into jail but nevertheless declined to file suit, believing their acts of civil disobedience would eventually wear down local policymakers and law enforcement to make the necessary change. In contrast to Thurgood Marshall's skepticism, Motley had always admired the gumption and bravery of the civil rights youth, led by MLK in his nonviolent, civil disobedience campaign. She knew they were willing to violate segregation laws and go to jail "and even die, if necessary, to change our segregated society." She reckoned that the country had not experienced such passionate protest and rejection of law, custom, or practice that were the bus boycotts, lunch counter sit-ins, and freedom rides

Figure 1.5. Winson and Dovie Hudson. Photograph by Brian Lanker. National Portrait Gallery, Smithsonian Institution; partial gift of Lynda Lanker and a museum purchase.

"since the last century, when slave revolts occurred and runaway slaves and former slaves joined the Union forces."[57]

What would finally solve the problem of segregated spaces and services? Would it be civil disobedience or victories in the courts? In the end, it would be a combination of both. And white folk were resentful.

The eighteen months during which the *Meredith* case dragged on saw so much violence that some refer to it as the "last battle of the Civil War." In an attempt at Ole Miss to prevent the enforcement of the *Brown* decision, the Ku Klux Klan committed at least "a dozen murders, thirty church burnings, and seventy bombings."[58] When James Meredith was finally able to enroll on September 30, 1962, he felt such fear for his life that he stayed in a dormitory room with a US marshal as his only roommate until he graduated the following June.[59] The entire Black community was under constant threat. Motley recalls staying one night as a guest in the home of a fearless Jackson lawyer, R. Jess Brown, who acted as local counsel on the *Meredith* case. When Motley, a born and bred Connecticut girl and New Yorker, got up to go to the bathroom, she was startled to meet her pistol-wielding host in the hall. Upon realizing who it was, Brown joked, "Thought it might be a burglar," and she scolded him for so quickly brandishing a gun.[60]

On another visit to Jackson, Motley was the guest of Doris Green, a neighbor of Medgar Evers's. One afternoon, during the *Meredith* trial, Motley was sitting in Green's living room with Bell, Green, and Evers. She looked out the living-room window at Evers's house and saw "overgrown bushes on the ground that created the fork in the road."

"Medgar," she said. "Those bushes would provide perfect cover for anyone who wanted to get you. You have to be careful when you come home at night because someone could be crouching behind those bushes."

He said, "Oh, yes, I know, I know. I always stop and wait a minute before I get out of the car."[61]

As Bell recalls, Medgar Evers "did not carry a gun and refused bodyguards. He was a man of peace and urged against violence in retaliation for violence." After his work on the *Meredith* case, Bell spent many more years going back and forth from New York to Mississippi litigating desegregation cases and doing community organizing with Medgar Evers. At times he would stay in the Evers home and have dinner with Medgar's wife, Myrlie, and their children. He often marveled at their ability to maintain a sense of normalcy in the face of so many threats, so much danger. If racial confrontations broke out, Evers was either already there or racing there as fast as his Oldsmobile could go. He was seemingly tireless, somehow everywhere all at once through the chaos of that hectic period.

In early June 1963, Bell and Evers were still litigating to deseg-regate public facilities. Bell was one among several lawyers filing suit, and Evers was organizing protests and sit-ins on behalf of the NAACP and with local community leaders. It was summer, and these efforts had begun in the spring, with no real end in sight. Bell suggested he might cancel his trip home one weekend in early June, just to wrap up some rounds with Evers and con-tinue to offer legal advice he might need. Shaking his head, Evers said, "No, Derrick. You get back to New York and spend a few days with Jewel and your kids."

Bell followed his advice. Two nights later Jewel answered a late-night call and then handed Derrick the phone.

"Derrick. Tonight, as he was getting out of his car in his drive-way, someone shot Medgar from ambush. He's dead."[62]

Mrs. Behonor McDonald of Harmony, Mississippi, had been listening to her radio that humid June evening when she first heard the news. She immediately called her cousins, Winson and Dovie Hudson. "Everybody loved Medgar," Winson recalled. "When he was assassinated in 1963, we didn't care any more. We were so angry. We just walked the roads and hollered and cried and cried and hollered. Then we met in my house, and we felt like just taking guns and shooting up everything. I was nonviolent, but my husband was not. He always said if he got killed, he was taking someone with him."[63]

Despondent, traumatized, and grief stricken, Motley could not get out of bed for weeks following Evers's death nor bring herself to attend his funeral in Jackson. In fact, after having made twenty-two trips to Mississippi for the *Meredith* case alone, with Evers meeting her at the airport each time, she decided the price ev-eryone was paying to end segregation there was too high. Motley quit Mississippi and did not return until 1983 for a reluctant visit commemorating twenty years since the *Meredith* victory.

The price had indeed been high, for Evers, his wife Myrlie, their children, and all the Mississippi community he had brought into the movement for desegregation. "It's been a long hard fight for so many things," Winson Hudson said. "My husband, and my friend Behonor McDonald, and some others, just fell dead, and one of these days, I'll do just that. My husband was under so much pressure, and Behonor too until it just finally got 'em."[64] The flip side of the coin to harassing white folks is the wear and tear on your body and soul.

A journalist once praised Thurgood Marshall for being courageous. His response was withering: "You forget just one little fucking thing. I go into these places, and I come out on the fastest vehicle moving. The brave blacks are the ones who have to live there after I leave."[65] Marshall once told *Time* magazine about his admiration for local Black NAACP attorneys such as R. Jess Brown, Arthur Shores, and, eventually, U. W. Clemon, leading the struggle for civil rights. "There isn't a threat known to men that they do not receive," he said. "They're never out from under pressure. I don't think I could take it for a week. The possibility of violent death for them and their families is something they've learned to live with like a man learns to sleep with a sore arm."[66]

Motley turned her attention elsewhere but never lost her focus on civil rights. In February 1964, she was elected to the New York State Senate, the first Black woman in that body. Although Bell left the LDF in 1966 and eventually became the first Black tenured professor at Harvard Law School, his ties to Mississippi remained strong. Throughout the 1970s, he remained in steady correspondence and collaboration on various post-*Brown* projects with Winson Hudson, who continued to organize in Harmony, as well as with the LDF luminary Jean Fairfax. In coalition with community-based organizers and activists throughout the United States and the world, Bell's formative experiences and relationships in 1960s Mississippi do much to explain his foundational contributions to the critical race theory movement many years later, laying a foundation for the CRT tenet of commitment to social justice.

A single bulletin for Evers's funeral rests in box 36, folder 3 of Derrick Bell's NYU archive. A "hymn of assurance" called "Be Not Dismayed" was sung that day. Although this hymn carries a message of hope for the suffering Mississippi community, even within this message many questions remain. What is to be done in the continued work toward justice? For whose benefit? And at what cost? What confidence can we have that real change will come, that the dream of equality can be realized?

These questions haunted Derrick Bell as he moved on from his work in Mississippi. Like Constance Baker Motley, his life had become interwoven with the people there, his roots entangled with theirs.

2

Richard Delgado and Jean Stefancic

"People on a Parallel Way"

CRT TENETS COVERED: Accessibility; Centrality of
Experiential Knowledge and/or Unique Voices of Color;
Interdisciplinarity; Challenge to Dominant Ideologies;
Commitment to Social Justice

> The marriage,
> Not the month's rapture. Not the exception.
>> The beauty
> That is of many days. Steady and clear.
> It is the normal excellence, of long
>> accomplishment.
> —Jack Gilbert, "The Abnormal Is Not Courage"

On June 30, 2022, Ketanji Brown Jackson made history as the first
Black woman sworn in as a US Supreme Court justice. Before
that momentous achievement, her journey to this highest judicial
bench required that she face the Senate Judiciary Committee for a
confirmation hearing in March of the same year. US Senator Ted
Cruz (R-TX), who attended Harvard Law School and served on
the *Harvard Law Review* with Judge Jackson, seized on her hearing as an opportunity to demonstrate his devotion to what had
become the Republican Party's hardline anti-CRT stance.[1]

After a series of initial questions in which Senator Cruz demanded Judge Jackson define critical race theory (CRT) and explain why she made reference in one speech to the 1619 Project
and the project's creator, Nikole Hannah-Jones, Cruz eventually
produced a poster-size quote from one of Judge Jackson's speeches

as evidence. The poster, composed of all black text on a dramatic red backdrop, concluded with the words "Critical Race Theory" in bold-face font. This is it. He had her. Caught her red-handed. However, when discussion of this accusation ended in frustration and confusion for both parties, Senator Cruz jumped to another subject.

"Let me ask you a different question," Senator Cruz began. "Is critical race theory taught in schools? Is it taught in kindergarten through twelfth grade?"

Pausing, in a moment of stunned silence, Judge Jackson shook her head.

"Senator. I don't know. I don't think so. I believe it's an academic theory. That's it. It's law school level—"

Furrowing his brow in consternation, Senator Cruz paused a bit himself, seemingly for dramatic effect.

"Okay, as you may recall during the confirmation hearings of Justice Amy Coney Barrett, there was a great deal of attention paid to the fact that Justice Barrett served as a board member of the board of trustees for a religious private school, and the press focused very intensely on the views of that school. In your questionnaire to this committee, you disclose that you are similarly on a board, specifically the board of trustees for the Georgetown Day School. And that you've been a board member since 2019 and you're currently still a board member. Is that correct?"

At the mention of Georgetown Day School, Judge Jackson's face lit up in a smile.

"That is correct."

Flipping the page of his loose-leaf binder and furrowing his brow even deeper, Senator Cruz feigned resignation, reminiscent of a doctor giving a bad prognosis.

"Ah. Well, in regard to the Georgetown Day School, you've publicly said, 'Since becoming a member of the GDS community seven years ago, Patrick and I have witnessed the transformative power of a rigorous progressive education that is dedicated to fostering *critical* thinking, interdependence and *social justice*.' When you refer to *social justice* in the school's mission—on '*social justice*' [using air quotes], what did you mean by that?"

Visibly steeling herself and looking like someone who had prepared a lifetime to answer a question like this, Judge Jackson squared her shoulders, smiled, and confidently leaned over the microphone.

> Thank you, Senator for allowing me to address this issue. Georgetown Day School has a special history that I think is important to understand when you consider my service on that board. The school was founded in 1945 in Washington, D.C., at a time in which, by law, there was racial segregation in this community. Black students were not allowed in the public schools with white students. Georgetown Day School is a private school that was created when three white families—Jewish families—got together with three Black families. They said that despite the fact that the law requires us to separate, despite the fact that the law is set up to make sure that Black children are not treated the same as everyone else, we are going to form a private school so that our children can go to school together. The idea of equality, justice [said with emphasis] is at the core of the Georgetown Day School mission, and it's a private school such that every parent who joins the community does so willingly with an understanding that they are joining a community that is designed to make sure that every child is valued—every child is treated as having inherent worth and none are discriminated against because of race.

Seemingly unmoved by Judge Jackson's unflinching speech in support of Georgetown Day School's mission, Senator Cruz proceeded.

"So, Judge Jackson, all of us will agree that no one should be discriminated against because of race. When you just testified a minute ago that you didn't know if critical race theory was taught in K through 12, I will confess, I find that statement a little hard to reconcile with the public record, because if you look at the Georgetown Day School's curriculum areas, they are filled and overflowing with critical race theory."

Figure 2.1. Senator Ted Cruz waves copy of the third edition of *Critical Race Theory: An Introduction* during the confirmation hearing for Judge Ketanji Brown Jackson before the Senate Judiciary Committee on March 22, 2022. Saul Loeb/AFP via Getty Images.

Reaching under his desk, Senator Cruz produced a stack of books.

"Among the doctrine," Cruz continued, "the books that are either assigned or recommended include," and fishing a book from the stack, Cruz held up a slim black book with a thick red stripe through the center of the cover. Waving it at Judge Jackson for emphasis, Senator Cruz pronounced triumphantly, "*Critical Race Theory: An Introduction*."

CRT Accessed

The first of the books Senator Cruz highlighted that day, *Critical Race Theory: An Introduction*, written and first published by Richard Delgado and Jean Stefancic in 2001, is easily the most accessible way to learn about the history, commitments, and current practices of CRT. Angela Harris, in her preface to the slim book, describes it as "a primer for nonlawyers that makes the now sprawling literature of critical race theory easily accessible to the beginner."[2] It's also a popular bestseller. Ted Cruz only helped its numbers. As *Vanity Fair*'s Caleb Ecarma observed, "Ted Cruz thought he had a slam dunk when he asked Ketanji Brown Jackson to answer for some anti-racist books taught at her daughter's school. Now, those books are top sellers."[3] Delgado and Stefancic got to work producing a new edition of the book (the fourth), which was published to wide acclaim by spring 2023, including a feature on *Literary Hub*.[4]

Intended for a new generation of critical race scholars beyond the scope of legal studies alone, Delgado and Stefancic's book employs "reader-friendly language" without buzzwords and jargon to cover CRT's central themes, critiques, and implications. The book embodies the CRT tenet of accessibility, offering teachers and students/learners classroom exercises for practical application and a glossary of key terms.[5] The conclusion of each chapter provides discussion questions and short lists of suggested readings.

While the book's accessibility makes it useful for learners, it also provides an entry point for CRT's opponents, especially in times of political scrutiny. Justice Jackson's confirmation hearing coincided with a period of growing political controversy over conservative perceptions of CRT and related concepts (including everything from diversity, equity, and inclusion to affirmative action and vague notions of social justice). By emphasizing concepts such as "social justice" and "critical" as potentially problematic commitments for a Supreme Court Justice to hold, Cruz placed himself squarely in the mainstream of that political season's right-wing attack on CRT, informed by commentators like academic hoaxer James Lindsay and Southern Baptist minister Voddie Baucham.

For Lindsay, a perpetrator, along with Helen Pluckrose and Peter Boghossian, of the so-called grievance studies hoax that sought to humiliate progressive social science researchers, anything considered "critical" implies that "its intention and methods are specifically geared toward identifying and exposing problems in order to facilitate revolutionary political change."[6] In other words, anything critical—thinking skills, for instance—is code for Marxism and, potentially, communism. That cynical construction of postmodern thought has been mainstreamed through evangelical Christian discourse by writers such as Voddie Baucham, whose book *Fault Lines* was published by Salem Media Group, the largest evangelical media conglomerate in the US. Although Lindsay is an atheist, Baucham chose to emulate him to the point of plagiarism. Curiously, that plagiarism occurred while Baucham was summarizing key points from *Critical Race Theory: An Introduction*, which he inaccurately (and misogynistically) cited as being written by Richard Delgado alone.[7]

Ted Cruz acknowledged in the hearing that he, along with Ketanji Brown Jackson, attended Harvard Law School in the early 1990s and presumably learned first-hand about the content and controversy of the legal movements known as critical legal studies and critical race theory.[8] He chose to adopt the recent right-wing construction of CRT cobbled together by writers like Lindsay and Baucham to inform his attack on the first Black woman Supreme Court nominee, someone who is at most only circumstantially related to those movements. Although neither Cruz nor Jackson studied under Derrick Bell, who had accepted a visiting professorship at NYU School of Law in 1991, they were at Harvard during the aftermath of Bell's protests against the Law School's hiring practices. While Bell wasn't the sole cause of controversy during their time at Harvard Law School, Cruz and Jackson could not have escaped debates generated by Bell's writing, classroom teaching models, and methodological commitments, especially in their overlapping periods of service on the *Harvard Law Review*.[9] Given his evident familiarity with that school of scholarship, why did Cruz wave a copy of Delgado and Stefancic's *Critical Race Theory* at Judge Jackson? In a word, accessibility. For people who did not attend Harvard Law School (but arguably even for those who did!), it is still the best entry point into the topic.

But how did this book, now in its fourth edition, come about? How did Delgado and Stefancic first decide to coproduce research and writing? How did the unique combination of backgrounds and interests of this pair—people are generally unaware that they are a married couple—both of whom can be understood as founders of the movement known as critical race theory, leave an indelible, humanities-based, and storytelling-infused mark on CRT itself? Let's take a look at their foundations. What we will see, no less than Derrick Bell's encounters with the Hudson sisters in Leake County, Mississippi, is a consistent commitment to what would be CRT's insistence on accessibility, challenging dominant ideologies, interdisciplinarity, and commitment to social justice.

Running for Justice—Running for Resistance

In the early 1950s, the House Un-American Activities Committee (HUAC) was nearing the height of its powers. In tandem with the demagoguery of Senator Joseph McCarthy (R-WI) and with the encouragement of FBI director J. Edgar Hoover, the HUAC sought to root out disloyal and subversive people within American society. In this early period of the Cold War, the surest evidence of disloyalty was association with the Communist Party or sympathy with socialist or Marxist ideas.

In 1947, following a smear campaign launched by *Hollywood Reporter* founder and publisher William Wilkerson, the HUAC called several prominent Hollywood figures, including Walt Disney and Ronald Reagan, president of the Screen Actors Guild (SAG), to testify about communist elements in the movie industry. Nineteen were suspected of being members of the Communist Party. Of those, ten refused to testify, citing their First Amendment rights. The consequences were swift. In November of that year, SAG, under Reagan's leadership, made its officers swear a loyalty oath pledging they were not communists. The next week, the US House of Representatives charged the group, now called the Hollywood Ten, with contempt of Congress. The next day, November 25, film industry executives issued the Waldorf

Statement declaring that the Ten would not be employed until they were cleared of contempt charges and swore they were not communists. This first Hollywood blacklist would remain in effect for decades.[10]

The Hollywood Ten were all convicted of contempt in 1948. After the US Supreme Court refused to hear their appeal, they began serving one-year prison sentences in 1950.[11] Following their year in federal prison, several of the ten, including Albert Maltz and Dalton Trumbo, along with their friend Hugo Butler, who had been blacklisted after refusing to appear before the HUAC, moved to Mexico.[12] Eventually, they settled with their families in Mexico City, enrolling their children in the American School, where those children would meet and grow up with a young Richard Delgado.

Richard was born in Chicago in 1939. In 1952, when Richard was twelve, his father, an immigrant to the United States from Mexico, moved his family to Mexico City to start a branch of a Philadelphia-based company. Along with his younger siblings, Richard attended the American School, since, as he said in an interview, "I didn't speak a word of Spanish." About half the children at the school were from wealthy Mexican families who wanted their kids to learn English and have access to US culture. The other half were sons and daughters of families from the United States. In that mix, according to Richard, were "the sons and daughters of American screenwriters and producers who were escaping the US from McCarthyism."[13]

The American School and the families surrounding it made for a heady environment. Mexico's tradition of providing political asylum was attractive to people associated with the Hollywood Ten. "There is in Mexico great respect for people of the arts," Albert Maltz, one of the Ten, said in an interview in the mid-1970s. "I learned as I was learning Spanish that I was not to tell people I was a writer because that meant that I was a journalist: I was to say I was an author because that was the word that was used. And introducing me also as one of the Hollywood Ten was a factor that gave me sympathy in Mexico." Although he initially moved with his family to Cuernavaca, Maltz recalled that in "August of 1952, my family and I had moved up to a rented house in Mexico City because we wanted to put our children into school."[14] He was impressed with the school's reputation: "When I was living in Mexico City, some young friends of mine who were going to what was called the American School there, everyone was bilingual. They were already reading things in literature that I was not assigned until I came into college."[15]

The expatriate environment of an international school provides students with opportunities to cross class and ideological boundaries in ways that can scarcely be imagined in one's home environment. Through friendships with their children, Richard was present in the homes set up by famous Hollywood personalities like Maltz, Trumbo, and Butler. Their homes, much like what Derrick and Jewel Bell experienced with Jefferson and Mary Grace Rogers, were intellectual parlors of creativity and resistance, a space charged with experiences of imprisonment and exile for the sake of free thinking and free speech. With everyone out of place, living as expatriates, whether by choice or by exile, relationships are freer of barriers of class and celebrity. A relatively middle-class person, for instance, can enter the homes of the super-wealthy by virtue of friendship alone. "That was an intellectual hothouse for me," Richard said. "It was only later that I found out their parents were world famous!"[16]

After graduating from the American School, Richard stayed in Mexico City to attend community college alongside Americans funding their studies through the GI Bill. He was so adept at algebra that his teacher, another expatriate exiled from the United States, hired Richard as a teaching assistant. In 1958, Richard transferred to the University of Washington, where he studied mathematics and philosophy while honing his skill as a future nationally ranked middle-distance runner.[17] Within a few years of graduating, he was running two-mile races at nine minutes, twenty-nine seconds. With the US military draft, begun in 1940, still in effect, Richard decided to enlist in the US Marine Corps because, as he says, "they had the best track and field program."[18] Richard's time in the Marine Corps (1961–63) overlapped with Oglala Lakota Olympian gold medalist Billy Mills. "Half my duty was on the track team," Richard says of his time in the Marines. "The other half was teaching Spanish to Marines to help the effort of spreading imperialism."[19] He hated it.

Once he left military service in 1963, Richard began teaching high school in Marin County, California. When President Johnson made the fateful decision to increase US military engagement in Vietnam and began ramping up conscription, Richard put his body on the line in opposition to the war. In 1965, after his application for discharge from reserve duty as a conscientious objector was denied, Richard, alongside two other objectors, headed out from San Francisco on a three-thousand-mile Run for Peace against the war.[20] Though they had some mishaps along the way, including a pace-car collision in Kansas, the group made it to Washington, DC, where they handed their message of peace to a representative of the Johnson administration.[21] Along with his high-profile protest efforts, Richard became "an expert anti-draft counselor." In addition to teaching mathematics and history, he would meet with students, collaborating with lawyers in their offices. "I met the first lawyers of my life there. We used their offices after hours. Kids who had bad numbers would come in for advice on how to stay out," Richard said.[22] One term, "the local draft board failed to get any of our young men."[23] Seeing that legal training was a path toward making a material difference in people's lives, Richard began his studies at the University of California-Berkeley School of Law in 1971—but not before another cross-country trek back East.

As Richard tells it in his Kafka-inspired counterstory, "Metamorphosis," he was eager to start law school. He had been accepted to several but chose Harvard because of its august reputation.[24] The problem was that Harvard's financial aid offer was insufficient. "I had a wife and an infant child at the time, and despite having saved up some money from my teaching career, was hardly flush," Richard writes.[25] When he arrived in Cambridge, he took this financial question to the dean of admissions, whose response still rings in Richard's ears.

"Delgado, I want you to know that your counterparts have accepted our offers of admission this year at a slightly higher rate than usual. In short, our yield rate is greater than expected."[26] The dean explained that if Delgado and a few other ingrates decided not to attend Harvard, the first-year class would be smaller and the professors happier.

That was bad news for people like Richard who wanted to be public interest lawyers and did not want to take on high educational debt. The dean was not moved.

"Delgado, I want you to know that my wife is a Latina like you—a Mexican American, in fact. So, I am fully acquainted with the problems of your people. If you really want a Harvard law degree, I suggest you talk to a loan officer at a bank of your choosing who will know the value of one, even if you seem not to."[27]

Richard wasn't convinced by the advice from this dean and self-appointed expert on Latino financial planning. Berkeley, which he had recently turned down to accept admission at Harvard, agreed to let him in.

"I and my small family turned our car around, filled up the gas tank, and headed back West. I never got my deposit back from Harvard."[28]

A Writing Partner

On July 16, 2023, the *New York Times Magazine* interviewed writer Joyce Carol Oates. Reflecting on her eighty-five years of life and literary output that includes a staggering sixty-two novels, forty-seven short-story collections, sixteen collections of nonfiction, nine collections of poetry, plays, and books for children and young adults, Oates also discussed threads that weave together the tapestry of her life. She married twice, first to Raymond J. Smith, then to Charles G. Gross, ultimately outliving both men. She has served on the faculty of many universities and has thus encountered, engaged, and influenced many students, some of whom she truly loved. The details Oates has on recall from fond moments within her marriages, or about treasured students, live on within her writings. As she put it, "It's a kind of devastating fact. Everything that you think is solid is actually fleeting and ephemeral. The only thing that is quasi-permanent would be a book or work of art or photographs or something. Anything you create that transcends time is in some ways more real than the actual reality of your life. . . . I am a person who was married, and was very happily married. Yet, that's all gone now. Where is it?"[29]

One life is generally more than enough for most people to live; Jean Stefancic says she's lived two. Each life has been connected to a significant love, a significant husband. Each of these relationships betrays a unifying thread: both husbands are ardent social justice activists and leaders within their professions. You might say Jean has a type. Jean is a feminist who negotiates her identities at a volume and pace that are, for most people, formidable. The undiscerning observer may easily mistake her demeanor and approach as reticence, but don't be fooled. She is not and never has been some woman in the shadow of the great men in her life. Sure, her story includes many instances in which she has stood beside her partner, but at many times, Jean has also stood in front, launching out to do her own work, to make her own contributions on behalf of women, immigrants, librarians, and the humanities.

If one were to compare the life and career of Jean Stefancic to the supernova moments of Derrick Bell's or Richard Delgado's, the most notable difference lies in volume and pace. Jean Stefancic's life has included major contributions to CRT, including over seventy articles, twenty books, and multiple awards, fellowships, and faculty appointments, all composing a tapestry of texts that transcend time "in some ways more real than the actual reality" of life.[30] Delgado and Bell were both rapid writers. But if you take Jean's output on a pages-per-year basis, she matches both supernovas and, like Joyce Carol Oates, could easily outlive them both.

Don't All Immigrants Dream?

When Jean's mother died, she left a cloth bag of things she had saved for her daughter. One of the most surprising finds was Jean's WWII ration book, a memento of difficult years during the war.

Jean was born in Cleveland, Ohio, in January 1940, and thus grew up during a time of anxiety for her parents and grandparents. She was an only child until her sister came along in 1947. All four of their grandparents had immigrated from Croatia to the Midwest, mainly landing in Illinois and Ohio. Their paternal grandfather was a steelworker; their maternal grandfather a factory worker. Growing up in Cleveland, Jean was immersed in ethnicity and her family's struggle to fit into America. As acculturating Americans, her family spoke English, but at family gatherings almost all would lapse into Croatian. Jean thought of herself as American, but her Croatian identity was an undeniable part of her makeup and experience while growing up.

Cleveland at this time was a beehive of immigrant activity. In the late nineteenth century, 75 percent of the city's population was foreign born or born of foreign parents. Jean's early schooling included classmates of many nationalities and descriptions. When Jean, in the first grade, tested at a very high level, the public school system sent her to a special program for kids like her. At the age of seven, she took two streetcars to her new school and joined the small group of "lunch kids" who lived too far away to go home at noon for lunch. Her grade school years were spent with smart Black, Jewish, Puerto Rican, Greek, and white kids who were voracious readers and confident oralists. Some went on to become scholars, lawyers, or journalists. Jean credits the Cleveland public school's Dewey-inspired Major Work program with endowing her with a fierce belief in democracy and the ability of each person to succeed if given a chance.[31]

At a large public high school in an Italian neighborhood, Jean met a boy who would alter the course of her life. Stan Stefancic was a few years older than Jean and beginning to discover his own path. His father was a carpenter, and a bricklaying apprenticeship was arranged for the tall, strongly built teenager. Stan began working during the day and attending evening classes in civil engineering at what is now Cleveland State University. Around this same time, he also attended a Presbyterian church and met an Oxford-trained minister who mentored him and eventually convinced Stan that he had a good mind and should go to college fulltime. For Jean, a high school valedictorian, her family's plan for college was always the next step in her education, so she readily signed onto Stan's new ambition. She had already begun studying at Western Reserve University in Cleveland.[32] She and Stan began to make plans for marriage. So it was that during the summer of 1958, when he was twenty-one and she eighteen and a half, the Stefancics married and soon thereafter enrolled in a small private college near Knoxville, Tennessee.

A surprising detail about Jean, especially when presenting her work to respectful audiences of lawyers and legal scholars, is that she is multiply degreed in English and American literature, creative writing, and poetry. Maryville College was a perfect learning environment for the Stefancics. They took several classes together and lived in a cozy apartment above the garage of a house owned by the college engineer. He and his wife were generous toward their tenants, inviting them to their mountain cabin for Thanksgiving and into their home downstairs to watch the inauguration of John F. Kennedy on their television.

During their college years in east Tennessee, the young Stefancics were confronted with issues surrounding the Cuban revolution, lunch counter sit-ins in Greensboro, North Carolina, school desegregation in New Orleans, resistance raging throughout the South, and the onset of civil disobedience and freedom rides. Jean recalls Maryville College hosting an all-campus event in 1960 to show a film, *Operation Abolition*, praising the work of the HUAC.[33] During that time, images sprang up around campus of Stan made up to look like Fidel Castro. The HUAC had previously indicted the Hollywood Ten in 1947. Shortly afterward, nearly a continent away, Richard would find himself going to high school in Mexico with children of those blacklisted parents.

After Maryville, although both Stan and Jean had been admitted to University of Iowa graduate programs, they headed to
Cambridge, Massachusetts, where Stan studied at Harvard Divinity School and Jean became an intern in the Harvard University
Library while earning her degree in library science at Simmons
College. Few other careers were open to women then, and Simmons had developed unique graduate programs so women could
gain access to careers such as librarians, social workers, and
teachers, ensuring they could support themselves. During Jean's
time at the Harvard Library, the poet Archibald MacLeish was
invited to give a talk. "I was so taken by this person who made a
great impression on me," Jean said in an interview. "When you're
a twenty-four year old at Harvard and you meet a person whose
work you admire, it stays with you."[34] As the reader will see, it
very much did.

MacLeish had also lived many lives. He had been the librarian of Congress between 1939 and 1944, leaving that post to become the first ever assistant secretary of state for public affairs,
along with various other governmental positions. Between 1949
and 1962, MacLeish was the Boylston Professor of Rhetoric and
Oratory at Harvard.[35] Early in that tenure, he was criticized and
investigated by anticommunist politicians, primarily because of
his associations with leftist writers. MacLeish had spent much of
the 1920s in Paris seeking to gain approval from other poets like
T. S. Eliot and, especially, Ezra Pound, leaders within a group of
poets, some of whom must have struck HUAC members as having leftist inclinations.[36]

At the time Jean met MacLeish, just at the end of his tenure at
Harvard, he spoke with the gravitas and distinction only age and
long service can provide. "Being in that community connected
me, for the first time, to the world of scholarship and writing,"
Jean said. "When I look back on it, it was a deep and rich experience. When you get to meet and hear the voice of the person
who wrote the work you so appreciate, it brings home that they
are a real person, a human who lived these experiences. It is a
different way of being attached to academic content. Otherwise,

it might not seem that it is for you, or something you have access to."[37] Little did Jean know that her star, too, would soon begin rising.

The World of Work

Travel for further graduate education took Jean and Stan to Dallas in 1965, eighteen months after President Kennedy's assassination. The country was in turmoil, and President Johnson was deploying an increasing number of troops to Vietnam. "Dallas was a stronghold of resistance to the ongoing civil rights movement; it was a soul-wrenching time," as Jean puts it. "We lasted two years and had to get out of there."[38]

They landed in the first of two Birminghams, the first in Michigan, between Pontiac and Detroit, in early 1967. Soon after they arrived, Detroit exploded with the Uprising of 1967, a response to police brutality and the collapse of inner-city conditions. Stan's responsibilities, as a Unitarian associate minister, included counseling and finding runaway teenagers, locating abortion help, and most importantly, performing social outreach to the Black communities in Pontiac and Detroit. Suddenly, he found himself thrust into the position of being a white man in a Black milieu, striving to build relationships and trust necessary for joint problem solving. In February 1968, Jean recalls, he participated in community meetings and strategy sessions twenty out of twenty-nine nights. And then, on April 4, the civil rights community, stricken by grief over the murder of Martin Luther King Jr., accelerated the Black Power movement.

By the end of 1969, a small Unitarian church in Birmingham, Alabama, the only one in the state, was seeking a minister. "They asked Stan and me to visit to get to know them," Jean recalled. During their stay, in December 1969, the Stefancics turned on the television in their hotel room, only to see "an agitated man standing in front of a big Confederate flag making a campaign speech. We just stared at each other. It was a different world down there."[39] But the church, founded in 1954, the year of *Brown*, was home to people with stories about their reaction to the Ku Klux Klan bombing of the Sixteenth Street Baptist Church just a few years earlier and the security measures the Unitarian church had taken shortly afterward with the advent of bomb threats. One person Jean and Stan encountered was U. W. Clemon, a young civil rights lawyer who had returned to his hometown in 1968 with support from the LDF's Earl Warren Scholarship, "a stipend that, at the time, helped young civil rights lawyers establish their own offices." In 1969, Clemon rose to prominence with a lawsuit against famed Alabama football coach Bear Bryant, who had refused to recruit Black players.[40]

Nevertheless, Jean and Stan soon felt at home and stayed in Alabama for several years. Jean, who has lived in many different parts of the United States, looking back on her time in the South, comments, "There's something fascinating about the region that most Northerners don't understand at all. To be sure, there's a lack of equality; it's very hierarchical, in terms of both class and race. But a quality of relationship and compassion among beleaguered people makes it different than other parts of the country."[41] After seven years in Birmingham, Stan and Jean moved with their young son to churches in Seattle in 1976 and San Francisco in 1980. Stan began serving the second largest Unitarian congregation in the United States, immediately becoming engaged in many forms of activism. This did not sit well with a number of elderly members of the congregation. When the HIV/AIDS crisis began in 1981, communities of gay men in New York and California were the first to experience the effects, including social stigmas, of this new plague. Stan helped gay men in the church form a caucus, 140 strong.[42]

The following year, he led a group of congregants to El Salvador under the aegis of the Unitarian Universalist Service Committee. It sponsored a fact-finding congressional delegation to Central America to meet with human rights activists and bring six tons of medical supplies to El Salvador. These delegations were instrumental in changing US aid policy in the region, resulting in Senator Paul Tsongas acting as a broker for peace in El Salvador.

Others in the church became active in the nuclear-freeze movement. When another group began looking for ways for the church to invest its multi-million-dollar endowment to help social justice causes, it stirred consternation.

By the summer of 1984, the Stefancics learned of efforts to push Stan out of his position. Although he received strong support from a vote of confidence, the result was far from uniform, and he resigned in May 1985. During Stan's final service at the church, Jean remembers, "so many of the liberal members came up saying 'I wish I had known. I'm sorry you have to leave.'" The first-hand experience of liberals failing to protect someone facing conservative backlash has stuck with Jean ever since. After Stan's resignation, he made a turn to therapy and counseling, an enthusiasm Jean did not share. The couple sadly but amicably parted ways in September 1988.

Over the years, much criticism aimed at CRT has come from self-identified liberals and echoes the lament of Martin Luther King Jr. when he wrote in April 1963 that "over the past few years I have been gravely disappointed with the white moderate. I have almost reached the regrettable conclusion that the Negro's great stumbling block in his stride toward freedom is not the White Citizen's Counciler or the Ku Klux Klanner, but the white moderate."[43]

While things began falling apart at the church, Jean knew she might need to increase the income she derived from two part-time jobs in order to become the family's principal provider. Perusing the wants-ads in a local newspaper, she saw a job advertised for a librarian at the University of San Francisco (USF). "I didn't know it was in the law library. I made the appointment for an interview and only then found out it was in the law school," she said. "Lucky for me, the job was in the very specialty I had developed at Harvard. I interviewed on a Friday and was hired the following Monday in October 1984. I had never been in a law school before."[44] That brief job search would mark an entry point to a new phase of Jean's life.

Everyone Comes to San Francisco at Some Point

As she familiarized herself with the law library, Jean realized that there was not much to read during her lunch break. She decided to attend a faculty colloquium instead. The speaker, Charles (Chuck) R. Lawrence III, "was discussing his summer experience in China, learning about dispute resolution through communal decision-making," she remembers. "The person who sat down next to me was john a. powell."[45] Jean was glad to meet these Black legal scholars, and they her. Both quickly realized that "I knew something about civil rights. They learned about my life." Reciprocating their interest, "I shared with them articles and notices that I came across. I did this quietly because I didn't want to attract too much attention, inviting envy."[46] Within a few months, powell let Jean know that some members of the faculty were starting a study group on the recently published *Passion: An Essay on Personality*, by Brazilian philosopher and social theorist Roberto Unger, who by that time was a faculty member at Harvard Law School. Coincidentally, Jean was already reading it, so she was happy to join the group.

Whether by design or serendipity, Jean's early experiences at USF illustrate a number of points that would turn out to be vital to the development of critical race theory as a movement, particularly on the role of white people in it. First, she quietly showed up to listen to a Black man share his experience and analysis of non-Western legal systems. In addition to demonstrating her respect for the perspective of a person of color, she implicitly accepted the CRT tenet of the centrality of experiential knowledge and unique voices of color.

She then entered the conversation, sharing her own experiences and perspectives of being a white woman in Black communities committed to working with those communities. When Jean shared articles and other information with Black scholars, she showed how white people can proceed carefully and be welcomed into interdisciplinary organizing spaces like a study group, an intimate space in which a less critically self-reflective white person could be a disruptive source of harm.

One premise of the recent right-wing attack on CRT is that it teaches that "whites are incapable of righteous actions on race."[47] Given a chance to respond to that characterization by critic Voddie Baucham, Jean's husband, Richard Delgado, was clear: "I very much doubt I've ever said anything remotely like it."[48] One need only look to his own spouse and writing partner.

The Back Story

In April 1985, a law professor visiting from UCLA came into the University of San Francisco Law Library, inquiring about reference materials. "He told me he was on sabbatical, so I invited him to the study group," Jean recalled. Then he said his name. "Oh, *you're* Richard Delgado!" Chuck and john—by now she was on a first-name basis with her colleagues—had recommended Delgado's "The Imperial Scholar," a study of how legal scholarship virtually ignores research produced by scholars of color. "I had read it and knew who he was."[49] As with Archibald MacLeish, meeting the person behind the writing has always been important for Jean. Later that year, in October, Derrick Bell visited the USF campus. Bell had just resigned in protest from his post as the first Black dean of the University of Oregon Law School due to the faculty's refusal to hire an Asian American professor, Pat Chew. Later that same year, 1985, the *Harvard Law Review* would publish his pathbreaking foray into fictional legal counterstories, "Foreword: The Civil Rights Chronicles."[50] Charles Lawrence had been quick to invite Jean to hear the talk. The invitation proved consequential. "I went to a building across the street, and who should be standing by the door? Richard Delgado. I ended up sitting between him and Stephanie Wildman, another law professor, who was, I believe, the very first white woman to write about white privilege, along with her Black coauthors Margalynne Armstrong and Adrienne Davis."[51]

USF Law School in the mid-1980s was its own kind of intellectual hothouse. And Jean quickly found herself a part of it. Jean
and Richard both note that many of the ideas discussed at USF
at that time still inform critical legal discourse today. In addition
to Wildman was Trina Grillo, who died of Hodgkin's disease in
1996 and had been working through the implications of multi-
racialism and intersectionality.[52] john powell, who was raised in
Detroit and had traveled to India on a spiritual quest, became the
national legal director for the American Civil Liberties Union and
now teaches at UC Berkeley School of Law.

Lawrence was writing his own seminal CRT article on structural racism, "The Id, the Ego, and Equal Protection."[53] Delgado had offered to read it through. "Richard was known for
his editing skills," Jean says. She also served as their drop box.
Because of her library position, she was easy to find. Richard
would drop off a marked-up manuscript Lawrence would review before sending the piece out for publication. On one occasion, Richard called to say he would be running over to drop off
his latest edit. He arrived, manuscript in hand, when Jean was
in a meeting with other librarians. "Someone told me Professor
Delgado was here," Jean said. "He had indeed dashed over in
his running shorts and a T-shirt and popped his head in. The
cataloguer, an older woman who had been nodding off, suddenly woke up!"[54]

Soon afterward, Richard wrote to Jean about his ideas on the
shape of legal knowledge. Their conversation about how to improve legal scholarship by critiquing the cataloguing systems
through which legal cases and articles were classified and organized resulted in their first cowritten publication, "Why Do We
Tell the Same Stories?"[55] Published in top-ranked *Stanford Law
Review*, the short article was a bombshell and spurred a generation of inquiry into the relation between commercial research
databases and what passes for legal knowledge.

Their collaboration validated and reinforced the growing
interdisciplinary quality of much critical race writing. Jean,
of course, was a humanities scholar before she became caught

up in the world of CRT. Her early work with Richard reveals the potential of that form of work. Indeed, she later became a student in a second study group that few of her readers know about.

In 1987, Jean came to a crossroads when faced with deciding to apply for the evening JD program or a masters-level writing program USF had recently started and which met in the evening. As the mother of a teenage son, she did not want to turn her full attention to law school and was more strongly attracted to the two-year writing program, which she chose. "It was glorious!" Jean remarked in an interview. The students were broadly inter-generational, and the program gave Jean an opportunity to focus on poetry. She was able to study with Brenda Hillman, whom Jean remembers as a careful reader. She also appreciated the opportunity to study with Jack Gilbert, whom Jean describes as "on a parallel track with the beat poets" like Jack Spicer and Allen Ginsberg and in some respects superior to both. "I loved Gilbert's poem 'The Abnormal Is Not Courage.'"[56]

As it turned out, Clark Smith's course on literary biography brought together two strands of Jean's thought. "I wrote the paper for that course on two poets—Ezra Pound and Archibald MacLeish—and sent it to Richard," Jean recalls.[57] He suggested that it could make the basis for a good law review article "since the relationship between these two opposite characters shed light on tensions in the practice of law." The article appeared, with Jean as lead author, in May 1990, in a second top journal, *Southern California Law Review*.[58] A penetrating critique of legal formalism and simplistic reliance on legal precedent, the article, fifteen years later, went on to form the basis of a cowritten book about the legal profession and its discontents.[59] In the meantime, Jean published a number of articles promoting critical legal research, garnering positive attention from her law dean.[60] After more years of scholarly collaboration—mailing and faxing drafts back and forth to each other—Jean and Richard fully became part of each other's lives in Boulder, Colorado, on Valentine's Day, 1993.[61]

Partnership

Through the 1990s and beyond, Richard and Jean have partnered to produce a formidable body of scholarly research. Richard is now the top-cited critical race legal scholar, and Jean isn't far behind. But their scholarship is notable for more than their place on citation lists. Instead, their work has been geared toward providing access points to CRT for learners at many levels and across a diversity of disciplines. As they did in their first cowritten article, "Why Do We Tell the Same Stories?: Law Reform, Critical Librarianship, and the Triple Helix Dilemma," they are committed to finding new ways of sorting through and rearranging knowledge so they can invite other people into the conversation. As a result, law librarians are revisiting the "Triple Helix" article to inform contemporary critical legal research now being taught in many first-year law school curricula. This is true even at the place Jean began her career in legal studies. John Shafer, who worked directly with Jean at the University of San Francisco School of Law in 1986, now serves as a research librarian and assistant professor of law at USF's Zief Law Library. "I still have my students read the 'Triple Helix,'" he said, recalling his deep respect for Jean's work. He wonders, if Jean and Richard had a chance to revise the article, what they might have to say about the rise of artificial intelligence.[62]

Jean and Richard have never settled for producing scholarship solely based on existing theories, analytic frameworks, or precedent. Instead, they theorize, they demonstrate methodology, they reimagine systems, and they communicate these findings accessibly so others can understand as well. As such, their work is both analytical and interdisciplinary—as is their partnership.

Richard's approach to legal storytelling, which he was the first to call "counterstory," is experiencing a revival of interest in legal studies. As we will see in the next chapter, Derrick Bell was one of the first to use counterstory as a CRT methodology. In Richard's article "Storytelling for Oppositionists and Others: A Plea for Narrative," he demonstrated but was also the first to theorize the method so others could participate in the practice.[63] Richard published "Rodrigo's Chronicle" soon afterward, embarking on a counterstory journey that continues to this day.[64] As Richard has said, "*The Rodrigo Chronicles* are intended to appeal to undergraduates. The imaginary characters discuss things. They eat things; they drink coffee."[65] But most of all, Rodrigo and the Professor discuss matters of law and society in a way that is conversational and intended to be accessible to general readers. For Richard, story never diminishes the analytical rigor of his legal writing: "The storytelling aspect of CRT greatly enhances and strengthens the analytical part."[66] Even when Richard is writing solo, his pieces always pass through Jean's watchful, editing eye. "I have never sought advice or criticism from strangers," Richard has said, "just people like Jean or law review editors who I know genuinely like my stuff and only want to make it better."[67]

Critical Race Theory: An Introduction is the apex of their collaborative work. Richard identifies Jean as the "major force" behind the book's form and style. He credits Jean as key to their ability to craft a well-written product.[68] The accessibility of the text that invites all audiences in—even opponents who would attack CRT and neglect to cite her as a coauthor—owe their appreciation to Jean.

Jean doesn't see herself as a founder of the CRT movement and points out that the movement's earliest scholarship was well underway when she joined forces with it at USF in 1985. At the time of this writing in 2024, Jean and Richard are still working, teaching, mentoring, and writing. They have things to say, new insights to share. They are moving discourse forward, within and beyond legal studies, reflecting on their extraordinary writing and teaching partnership and questioning even their own established categories and forms, going so far as to question if race still needs to be the center of social inquiry or if it's time to examine more deeply questions of class.[69]

When given the opportunity to reflect on their lives and contributions to legal scholarship, Richard said he's never stopped long enough to identify major themes. Given the pace at which he has run his life, looking back hasn't been a priority.[70] Nevertheless, Richard can be pressed to consider the sources of the

Figure 2.2. Jean Stefancic, Derrick Bell, and Richard Delgado in 2000. NYU Archive.

materialist commitments that shine through in his work. When asked whether his time in Mexico City spent in the homes of the Hollywood Ten may have influenced him toward these ideas, he paused, thought for a moment, smiled, and said, "Hmm. You may be right."[71]

For Jean, looking back has been a constant part of her life. She is grateful to teachers and friends who inspired her to think and write, and to poet William Stafford, who wrote

> *There are people on a parallel way. We do not*
> *see them often, or even think of them often,*
> *but it is precious to us that they are sharing*

the world. Something about how they have accepted
their lives, or how the sunlight happens to them,
helps us to hold the strange, enigmatic days
in line for our own living. . . .
here is a smoke signal,
unmistakable but unobtrusive—we are
following what comes, going through the world,
knowing each other, building our little fires.
    —William Stafford, "Smoke Signals"

3

Finding Geneva

A Composite Choir Sings

CRT TENETS COVERED: Permanence of Race and
Racism; Interest Convergence; Intersectionality and
Anti-Essentialism; Interdisciplinarity

Singing a Civil Rights Hero's Song: In Three Scenes

Scene I

At about ten in the morning, the phone rang in Constance Baker
Motley's New York home. It was June 7, 1962, and she was deep
in the throes of the *Meredith* trial to desegregate the University
of Mississippi. Motley, still making her way through her mid-
morning routine, answered the phone. It was Medgar Evers.[1]

"Mrs. Motley, they're gone arrest Meredith, today if they can
find him."

"What are Mize and Shands trying to land on him this time?"
Motley asked, angry, exasperated.

"They say he voted in the wrong county," Evers replied.

"Right," Motley said, nodding. "The Fifth Circuit is in New
Orleans now. I'll need to make an application to Judge Wisdom
under the All Writs Statute to enjoin the Mississippi attorney general from arresting him. Meet me at New Orleans International?"

"Jumping in my car now, I'll see you there," Evers said, determined, with one foot out the door. With several thousand miles
on the odometer from developing connections between NAACP
chapters across Mississippi, Evers knew his 1962 Oldsmobile 88
could get him to the Crescent City well before Motley landed.

By three in the afternoon New Orleans time, Motley and Evers had Judge Wisdom's order in hand, enjoining Mississippi officials from arresting James Meredith. Knowing full well the entire trial—all fifteen months of labor to this point, not to mention Meredith's personhood, life, and future—all hinged on their next move, Motley and Evers had to think quick. Time was not on their side.

"We have to serve this writ to the Mississippi attorney general today, before they can find and seize Meredith," Motley said, taking long bounding strides toward Evers's Oldsmobile.[2]

Keeping pace, Evers looked at his wristwatch, furrowed his brow a bit, then shook his head, a smile spreading across his face. Motley and Evers stopped to face each other on either side of his powder blue car, him standing on the driver's side, she on the passenger's.

"You do know Jackson is about a hundred miles from New Orleans?" Evers began.

"I do," Motley affirmed with a curt nod.

"And you know the courts close in Jackson at five, and seeing as it's now three . . ." Evers continued.

"Yes," Motley said. "And I also know what this car can do."

"Yes ma'am," Evers said with a chuckle, a twinkle illuminating his eyes. He had purchased the car specifically for its power and speed. Evers had often been followed by groups of hostile whites while investigating incidents like the lynchings of Emmett Till and Mack Charles Parker. His best nonviolent defense was to outrun his pursuers, leaving most other cars in the dust, the speedometer changing from green to red and finally black as he passed 100 mph.

"What I suggest," Motley continued, "is that we get in this car and risk a speeding ticket to save Meredith from prison."

Shaking his head again and laughing a bit, Evers said, "Okay, then let's go, Mrs. Motley."

By some miracle, Motley and Evers arrived in Jackson and the attorney general's office at precisely five, unscathed and without incident, just as a man was locking the front door. They served him with the writ and marveled at their luck.[3]

Scene II

Constance Baker Motley stared at the mural behind Judge Mize's bench. In more ways than one, the scene loomed large over the courtroom, located in the James O. Eastland Federal Building. The center of the painting featured a white family receiving advice and guidance from a white judge. To the right, white men were busy planning and building the future of the state. On the other side, "Black folks picking cotton, women dragging cotton sacks and down on their knees picking cotton and having the sacks weighed in," labored under a sweltering sun. The coincidence could hardly escape Motley as she was seated on the side of the courtroom directly facing the Black field workers while opposing counsel, Mr. Dugas Shands, Esq., sat on the other side directly facing the hardworking white citizens assumed as the builders of Mississippi's future.[4]

When it came to skill and dramatic flair, Shands and Motley were fiercely matched. Motley's litigation heroics were by this point well known throughout the South, especially when she faced off with old Shands, transforming courtrooms into "places of rich racial drama."[5] Courtroom observers reported that Motley was better prepared for cases than her white opponents, speaking firmly and with full knowledge of her case. This irked Shands to no end. During the *Meredith* arguments, when Derrick Bell served as Motley's assistant counsel, he would dash back to the New York LDF offices and excitedly regale the team with tales of her litigation prowess. Simultaneously, embellished stories about Motley spread like wildfire into the Mississippi streets through "barbershops and beauty parlors for weeks to come."[6] Here was a courtroom with "whites on one side, exhibiting silent hostility, and blacks on the other side, barely able to restrain their pride" at the priceless scenes in which, time and time again, this strong, educated, Black woman stood up and pushed back.[7]

At fifty-five-years old, Dugas Shands, tall, thin, white-haired, and with a slow southern drawl, embodied a cultivated anti-Black hostility. He made a great show of his racial hatred and personal bigotries, aiming them directly at his opposing counsel: this six-foot-tall Black woman from New York, out of place with her strength, dignity, and lack of deference. Shands was named for his grandsire, G. Dugas Shands, a veteran of the "War of Northern Aggression" who taught at Ole Miss's Law School, serving as its first dean. The younger Shands was a proud defender of white supremacy, segregation, and his generations-deep legacy institution, Ole Miss.[8]

Motley, on the other hand, was descended from generations of West Indians, a people famous for their pride. Her mother and father were immigrants to New Haven, Connecticut, from the Caribbean Island of Nevis. Motley's parents maintained a tight circle of West Indian friends, preferably Nevisian, "all properly educated in the English Standard Schools of their island."[9] Motley's self-confidence from her upbringing meant she "never had to fight off the inner demons of fear and inferiority sometimes instilled in southern Black people by the deprivation and violence of segregation."[10]

As Mrs. Constance Baker Motley, Esq., readied herself to square off with Mr. Dugas Shands, Esq., she knew she would require the strength of her West Indian forebears to become the lightning rod necessary to battle this opponent representing the virulent interests of white resistance to school desegregation. The taunting mobs, the verbal abuse from the demonstrations outside the courthouse—these white faces contorted with riotous anger supporting Shands's cause—swirled fresh in Motley's mind. Evincing a calm demeanor, she made a slight adjustment to her strand of pearls, dislodged her gaze from the mural and looked through Shands with her practiced thousand-mile stare.[11]

As arguments proceeded for the day, Shands attempted any number of maneuvers to throw Motley off balance. Attempting to assert his racial worldview on this Black woman lawyer, Shands refused to address what he perceived to be his subordinate as "Mrs. Motley," opting for "she" and "her" flicked in Motley's direction. His opposing counsel took these jabs in stride, her infuriating air of aristocracy still intact, unshaken. Shands would have to change tactics.[12]

"Constance—" Shands began.

At the mention of her first name, the unearned familiarity and lack of regard of this unrepentant racist, Motley's defenses were piqued. Jumping to her feet she shot back.

"Your Honor, I object. I would like for Mr. Shands *not* to call me by my first name."[13]

Judge Mize sustained Motley's objection and put Shands on notice about his display of disrespect and lack of professionalism. But Shands was on a mission to preserve "segregation through legal obstruction, social and economic intimidation, and violence."[14] He would go to any lengths to stand between Mississippi and integration. Beholding his opposing counsel with contempt running at least three generations deep, through gritted teeth he addressed Motley as "New York Counsel" for the remainder of the trial.[15]

Scene III

Evers drove Motley and Bell to Hawkins Field in Jackson, Mississippi, for yet another flight back to New York. They chatted about the courtroom showdown and Dugas Shands's despicable yet predictable behavior.

"He's a member of the White Citizen's Council, you know," Evers said.[16]

"Which is what exactly?" Bell asked.

"It's still the Klan, no doubt about that," Evers said over his shoulder to Bell in the back seat. Motley, in the passenger front seat, nodded her agreement.

"The Council sprang up after *Brown* passed. It's all upper- and middle-class types who have hate for the Negro in their hearts but the resources to fight integration too!"

"And Shands, being a government man, having worked for the state attorney general's office as long as he has—how long, Medgar, almost twenty years?" Motley asked.

"Yes, ma'am, old Shands has been with the AG for going on eighteen years," Evers affirmed.

"Right. Men like that, government men, politicians, professionals, and clergy, are exactly the type you'll find are card carrying Council members," Motley finished.

Bell let out a low whistle. "So then why do you think someone like Judge Mize was pushing back on Shands and insisting he use your proper titles and names? Wouldn't you guess he's a Council member too?" Bell asked.

"Mize may be a lot of things—and a defender of white supremacy is high on that list—but he is an educated and civilized man. Decorum and professionalism in his courtroom rank high on that list as well," said Motley.[17]

"Ah," said Bell. "So in Mississippi courtrooms, at least, people like us can demand the respect and dignity we deserve."

Evers and Motley exchanged a glance and a smile.

"To a degree," Motley affirmed.

When they arrived at the airport, Motley and Bell exchanged "thank yous" and "see you laters" with Evers and headed into the terminal. As they walked toward their gate, distracted by double-checking the boarding time and gate number, Motley and Bell walked directly into the path of none other than opposing counsel, Dugas Shands.[18]

Startled by the encounter, all parties halted on the spot, momentarily stunned. As everyone regained their composure, Shands's eyes darted from left to right. Motley's face softened to a mask of benign neutrality, and Bell glanced at his mentor, then her opponent, and back again as if waiting for a cue. Encountering each other in the wild of the Jackson airport as opposed to the structure of a well-ordered courtroom was akin to encountering an escaped zoo animal outside its habitat—only who was the zoo animal to whom?

Squaring her shoulders, Motley extended her hand. Yet there Shands allowed her hand to hang, suspended in space between them. Dropping his eyes to her hand, Shands's face contorted in sneering revulsion. His head snapped up in shock at her gesture, clear hatred and contempt burning in his eyes. Motley's expression remained impenetrable. She was a fortress of composure and dignity.

Calmly retracting her gesture, she said, "Oh, you don't shake Black people's hands. Very well, then."

Motley looked at Bell, made a slight directional nod toward their gate, and off she glided to her flight.[19]

The Foreword

The Harvard Law Review is a student-run organization sourcing from, yet independent of, the Harvard Law School. The main goal of the group is to publish eight issues a year. A major accolade offered by the *Review*, arguably the top academic legal studies journal, is the invitation to write the Foreword to the journal's Supreme Court issue published early each November. Accordingly, *Law Review* editors develop "a preliminary list of persons whose contributions to legal scholarship have been consistent and important, whose writing evidences both comprehensive research as well as synthesis and critique, and whose past work has been on the cutting edge of his subject area."[20] The key phrase here is "his subject area." Although the author selected may be very well established in their own specialty, their name or work may be little known elsewhere. The opportunity to write the Foreword blasts all this possible anonymity into oblivion.

During the spring of 1985, newly elected *Law Review* president Carol Steiker, now the Henry J. Friendly Professor of Law at Harvard Law School, invited Derrick Bell to write the Foreword.[21] This was an historic move by the *Harvard Law Review* staff, the first such invitation to a Black legal scholar. What no one could have anticipated was the riot Bell and his team of energetic, skillful, and enthusiastic *Law Review* editors—Carol Steiker, supervising editor Elena Kagan, now US Supreme Court Justice Kagan, and Stephanie Y. Moore, now chief of staff to Rep. Maxine Waters (D-CA)—would cause when they published Bell's "unorthodox" epic narrative. This narrative consisted of four sci-fi/

Figure 3.1. Carol Steiker speaks upon being elected president of the *Harvard Law Review*, 1984. Photo courtesy of Stephanie Y. Moore.

fantasy chronicles featuring intense debates between a fictionalized version of Bell and his newly debuted heroine-protagonist, Geneva Crenshaw.[22]

In Bell's foreword, Geneva Crenshaw is introduced as "a highly respected civil rights advocate, well known for her willingness to represent blacks in the rural South, where living conditions were poor and personal risk was considerable." The fictional Bell meets Geneva in New York City in 1960; soon after, he joins the NAACP Legal Defense Fund. Geneva is described as "strikingly tall, well over six feet" and "as proud of her height as she was of her ebony complexion."[23] In a 1986 reflective essay, Bell recounts the time he was staying in the NYC home of his brother Charles Bell, a jazz musician and college teacher. Bell was "worried to death" about the looming deadline for his *Law Review* contribution. Producing

a foreword places considerable strain on an author's schedule because the timeline is linked to that of the US Supreme Court.[24]
Generally speaking, the most interesting decisions are not handed
down until the end of their term in June or July, and forewords
are published by November. The invitation to write a foreword
is an honor, yes, but also a major source of anxiety, stress, and
sleepless nights.

Bell was tossing and turning late one night in his brother's
guest room. He could feel the panic growing in his chest. Suddenly, he was startled upright to see *her*, sitting there on the edge
of his bed. She was a Black woman, clearly tall, slender, with a
regal bearing, "and the tough mind rendered alternately cutting
or smooth by her quick wit delivered in that quintessential black
woman's voice."[25] She was at once very familiar to Bell—jogging
every memory of many Black women in his life all at once—yet
she also slightly scared him. She was formidable—perhaps a
specter? To Bell, her apparition seemed a haunting yet cathartic
manifestation and outlet for stories too long suppressed. Whether
Geneva Crenshaw was real or a dream mattered not. When Bell
woke the next morning, he noticed a yellow legal pad filled with
notes lying on the floor. He finally knew what to do.[26]

Surveying the "project" of *Harvard Law Review* forewords,
Mark Tushnet and Timothy Lynch reason that although prestigious, time constraints often lead to intellectually disappointing
forewords since authors resort to recycling "the one really good
idea of their careers." One possibility is that "the editors might,
almost by chance, catch an author just at the point when he or
she is having the second really good idea of his or her career."[27]
By 1985, Bell was ahead of the curve, having articulated at least
two really good ideas, both of which would later be identified as
tenets of CRT.

Bell's first good idea, the permanence of race and racism, had
been put forth in his 1976 article, "Serving Two Masters: Integration Ideals and Client Interests in School Desegregation Litigation." Bell had seen too many children sacrificed during his
work with the LDF.[28] He argued against the trend of civil rights

litigators serving the interests and idealism promised by integration. "The great crusade to desegregate the public schools has faltered," Bell argued, because "civil rights lawyers . . . have not wavered in their determination to implement *Brown* using racial balance measures developed in the hard-fought legal battles of the last two decades. This stance involves great risk for clients whose educational interests may no longer accord with the integration ideals of their attorneys."[29] It was a shot across the bow of his former LDF colleagues, particularly Director-Counsel Jack Greenberg.

The second of Bell's big ideas, racial interest convergence, was closely related to the first. In its most distilled form, the idea had been launched in his landmark 1980 *Harvard Law Review* commentary "*Brown v. Board of Education* and the Interest-Convergence Dilemma." There, he argued that the "principle of 'interest convergence' provides: The interest of blacks in achieving racial equality will be accommodated only when it converges with the interests of whites." In the specific case of *Brown*, the convergence occurred within a Cold War moment that lent "credibility to America's struggle with Communist countries to win the hearts and minds of emerging third world peoples."[30] Bell argued that *Brown* should be interpreted less as a blow to American racism than as an ideological rocket launched by the United States in its Cold War posturing against communism. That argument was confirmed later with the release of previously classified US government documents.[31] In an important forerunner to CRT's tenet of interdisciplinarity, Bell's refinement of interest convergence was cultivated within the context of a 1978 symposium at Harvard Law School featuring legal scholars like Bell, Robert L. Carter, Alan D. Freeman, and Charles Lawrence III, alongside education scholars Ronald R. Edmonds, Diane Ravitch, and Sara Lawrence Lightfoot.[32]

By 1985, Bell's reputation within his area of expertise in legal academia was fully established. His "good ideas" were known, if not always appreciated. By the mid-1980s, Bell was ready to unleash his long-standing interest in sharing legal ideas through stories. In a January 1984 speech he gave at the University of California, Davis, School of Law to mark Martin Luther King Jr. Day, Bell decided to do just that. Inspired by a literary favorite, Langston Hughes, Bell crafted what would become his first published composite character, Jesse B. Semple. In a footnote to the published version of the speech, Bell explained that his character, Semple, was based on Hughes's own Jesse B. Simple, whom Bell describes as "a composite of people [Hughes had] met and known in Harlem."[33] The speech and the subsequent article are made up of an anti-essentialist (another tenet of CRT) dialogue between two Black perspectives: the working-class Semple and the "bourgeois" Bell, now dean of a predominantly white law school.

The dialogue opens with Semple's rejection of MLK Day as a token, a symbol intended to placate Black American anger. Semple argues that this is akin to "a bunch of bogus freedom checks" given only after "you work, plead, and pray for them," and then, "As a matter of fact, regardless of how great the need is," the Man gives them only "when it will do *him*, the most good."[34] The hard-hitting exchange between his composite characters is an effective illustration of Bell's ideas of the permanence of race and racism and interest convergence; it also served as a precursor to what would come next.

The invitation to produce a *Law Review* foreword provided Bell an opportunity, a featured platform, to do something different, something *big*. Derrick Bell had a poet's heart and soul; his archive evidences that he was a creative writer through most of his life. Before his 1984 speech, Bell composed poems, short stories, and creative nonfiction.[35] He even attempted to publish stories about his time in Mississippi that addressed questions about *Brown* and its effectiveness following the success of his first legal textbook, *Race, Racism and American Law* (1973). He approached the casebook's publisher, Little, Brown, in 1975 with a new idea for a trade publication intended for a broader audience. The working title, based on an allegory he crafted, was *Still Looking for the Pony*.[36] Although very pleased at the sales and success of his casebook, the publisher was not interested in Bell's idea for a collection of "stories."[37] This did not deter Bell from continuing to write creatively.

In 1979, Bell drafted a short story titled "Dependent Status," attempting to publish it in *Essence* magazine.[38] The story's main character, Martin Motley, has a message for the broader public about a manuscript he is preparing to publish:

> It was good. I had certainly put everything I had in it. It would be controversial. White liberals and the higher-up blacks in the national civil rights groups would not like it at all. But my hope was that black community leaders as well as black academics would read it and start thinking about some of the programs and remedies it contained. That was a large hope, but it was my message and I was trying to communicate it in the only way I knew.[39]

The only way he knew. With the invitation to write a *Harvard Law Review* Supreme Court foreword, Bell knew what ideas he wanted to communicate. In an oral history interview, Bell recalled, "They asked me to do it and I thought—what's that old spiritual? [singing] 'Sinner, Please Don't Let This Harvest Pass'— this is an opportunity to write about race and bring all of [my] experience and insight" to "what I thought race in America was all about."[40] The question was *how*, what method would he use? The answer was story. He went for it.

On April 25, 2012, *Breitbart News* published a sensationalized report on "previously unknown handwritten notes from Elena Kagan to radical professor Derrick Bell, sent to Bell as Kagan worked on his seminal 1985 article on Critical Race Theory." The report is aghast at the discovery of this previously undisclosed relationship between the Obama-nominated Supreme Court candidate and the "radical" professor who influenced them both. In the offending note, Elena Kagan provided a comment on one of the more prophetic stories within the Foreword, the "Chronicle of the Slave Scrolls." Within this chronicle, Bell sends a haunting message that resonates with today's sometimes invigorating and often menacing political dynamics:

> Virtually every state enacted what were called Racial Toleration Laws. These Measures severely restricted—and, in some states, banned outright—public teaching that promoted racial hatred by focusing on the past strife between blacks and whites. Penalties were severe for leading or participating in unauthorized healing sessions, or for publicly wearing what the law termed "public symbols of racial hatred." State officials enforced these laws with vigor, severely hampering the ability of blacks to carry out their healing campaign. Whites whose fears were not allayed by the government's actions organized volunteer citizens groups to help rid their communities of those whose teachings would destroy the moral fabric of American society.[41]

One of the notes emphasized by *Breitbart*, in an attempt to somehow discredit Kagan's Supreme Court nomination, focused on what even the investigator described as "minor editorial comments": "As Carol and I told you [Bell] on the phone, we're a little bit concerned at the focus on this part of the piece," Kagan wrote. "The doctrinal section centers on the idea of creating a substantive due process right to racial healing. But the reader is left wondering: why wouldn't the Court strike these laws down on first amendment grounds?"[42] Nothing earth-shattering. But the exchange illustrates a few points.

First, it's clear that Bell was in collaborative relationship with the student leaders of the *Harvard Law Review*. He was open to feedback and often revised accordingly. Second, the editors, at least at this point, had no objections to Bell's choice to communicate his ideas through story. Instead, they recognize the "doctrinal" points being made through storytelling, tacitly accepting that the method of counterstory in no way diminishes the intellectual rigor or academic value of Bell's contribution. As Richard Delgado noted in his history of the origins of CRT, "The young seem, by nature, particularly receptive to new ideas, especially when the person in front of the classroom offers provocative insights."[43]

The four tales of the Foreword, told by Geneva Crenshaw, are a blend of genres, including science fiction, speculative fiction, and Afrofuturism. They present interpretations of America's racial past and possible racial futures. The "Prelude to the Chronicles" offers a commentary on the foundations of the US Constitution itself, suggesting that "the framers made a conscious, though unspoken, sacrifice of the rights of some in the belief that this forfeiture was necessary to secure the rights of others in a society embracing, as its fundamental principle, the equality of all." The result is a fundamental contradiction in which "the framers, while speaking through the Constitution in an unequivocal voice, at once promised freedom for whites and condemned blacks to slavery."[44] Instead of limiting himself to a commentary and assessment of just the 1984 US Supreme Court session, Bell focused his attention on the foundation of their work, the US Constitution itself. He did so in the way he had developed in his classrooms, both at Harvard Law School and, by that time, the University of Oregon School of Law. Bell told stories because he taught through story.

In a 1992 interview following the release of his bestselling collection, *Faces at the Bottom of the Well*, Bell said, "Many of those stories were initiated as challenges in the classroom."[45] Those classroom experiences, infused with story, were electrifying for students. Like many casebooks, Bell's *Race, Racism, and American Law*, first published in 1973, contained hypothetical cases and trials. From the beginning, and expanded through ongoing revisions, Bell's "hypos" were stories with developed characters and community-based settings. Robert A. Williams Jr. (Lumbee, Harvard Law School '80) said in an interview that being in Professor Bell's classroom in the late 1970s reminded him of being back home: "My Lumbee grandmother was a Baptist. It was really just preaching," he recalled. "You'd read the case and he'd ask one of the students to recite facts. And then he'd go off on it. Students were raising their hands and asking questions about race. We didn't know it was CRT. It was usually just stories."[46]

The platform offered through *Harvard Law Review* and the Foreword extended Bell's classroom to new audiences, new students. He used the Foreword to introduce the broadest swath of learners yet to his two really good ideas of the permanence of race and racism and interest convergence. With the support of enthusiastic young editors willing to take risks, Bell pushed past formalism and precedent into uncharted waters with the new CRT methodology of composite counterstory as expressed through dialogues with the composite character, Geneva Crenshaw.

The Chronicles: Triumph and Scandal

It is no overstatement to say that Derrick Bell's foreword marked an historic moment for the *Harvard Law Review* and, arguably, US legal studies as a whole. Not only was Bell the first Black person invited to write a foreword, he was the first to write the entire contribution as story. Bell's radical departure from traditional "doctrinal analysis," paired with his decision to pointedly focus on the constitutional contradiction that created and maintains the permanence of racism in the United States, caused an uproar.[47] As if anticipating the Foreword's possible negative reception, the final sentence Bell wrote is a question spat in anger by a white male colleague at Geneva Crenshaw: "By what right have you come here, taken our time, and had the effrontery to try to teach us anything?"[48]

There was also great praise and celebration surrounding Bell's risky venture. In 1986, the *Harvard BlackLetter Journal* convened a forum of comments by Regina Austin, Paul R. Dimond, Jane DeGidio, Linda S. Greene, Joel F. Handler, Hank McGee, Daniel J. Monti, Patricia Williams, and Bell himself expressing interdisciplinary reactions to the Foreword. Austin pointed out that the scholarly rigor of Bell's writing, combined with its readability, "subverts the law review format by conveying the message that Black people ought to be giving more thought to extralegal liberation strategies."[49] Greene said that while the honor of being selected to write a foreword belongs to the author, Bell's selection as the first Black legal scholar enriches and empowers a different group of people who meaningfully share in his experiences.[50] In the form of a footnote as counterstory, Williams "calls on her own considerable skill as a writer of fantasy to make several sensitive points about the significance of Geneva in the Chronicles" through the introduction of the stories of her enslaved great-great grandmother and her slave owning great-great grandfather.[51]

As word spread about the triumph/scandal of Bell's ingenious/ disastrous writing with the Foreword, letters spilled in from friends and fans, not regularly subscribed to the *Harvard Law Review*, begging Bell for offprints.[52] Requests reached such a clamor that Bell exhausted his own set of offprints and had to tell his eager audience he had nothing left to send. Bell's long-time friend and collaborator, Diane Ravitch, who he says "disagreed with some aspects" of his thesis, was nonetheless caught up in the fervor. She recommended the work to her own publisher, Martin Kessler, president and editorial director of Basic Books.[53] By 1986, Bell secured his long-desired trade book contract for a collection of stories first titled *The Civil Rights Chronicles*, later *And We Are Not Saved*, all centered on his heroine-protagonist Geneva Crenshaw.

Many Facets: Who, Exactly, Is Geneva?

Many have attempted to pinpoint the identity or inspiration of Bell's Civil Rights super lawyer/supernatural Black woman hero. In 2021, for instance, Jelani Cobb reported that Bell "told Kimberlé Crenshaw that he had 'borrowed' her surname for the character who was a composite of Black women lawyers who had influenced his thinking."[54] If you ask longtime national director of Head Start, Ron Herndon, a close friend and collaborator of Bell's in Portland, Oregon, he'll tell you that Geneva Crenshaw's "first name and much of her persona were taken from Northeast Portland's own Geneva Knauls,"[55] a local business owner, community organizer, and, for lack of a better word, legend. "Derrick told me that's where he got the name and some of her characteristics," Herndon said in an interview. "He was impressed with her elegance, intellect, and common sense. That came from his mouth."[56] The key word to keep in mind about the identity of Geneva Crenshaw is *composite*. As modeled by Langston Hughes with Jesse B. Simple and then by Bell, composite characters represent more than any one individual and are sourced from personal experiences, literatures, and research data. Because composite characters are informed by many sources, they do not have a one-to-one correspondence to any one individual.[57]

Bell was well known for telling Black women he held in high regard that they inspired the character Geneva. His long-time development editor and very dear friend, Stephanie Y. Moore, was an integral part of Bell's writing process as he crafted Geneva through the Foreword and beyond, revising this law review essay toward his mass market bestseller, *And We Are Not Saved*. Like Bell's father's family, Moore is from Alabama, raised in Birmingham. As they worked together and as Moore offered thorough and honest Black feminist feedback toward the cultivation and growth of both Bell's craft and Geneva's complexity, Bell told Moore about the character: "You're in there."[58]

In fact, Bell credited Moore with his receiving the invitation to write the *Harvard Law Review* foreword in the first place. His exact words? "I had no thought that I would ever be offered" the chance to write a foreword, "and I kid a Black woman, one of my former students, that she had threatened [the *Law Review* staff] and that's what got them to do it. She denies it."[59] To this day, Moore says Bell gives her too much credit and denies she did any such thing.[60]

Bell nods to another likely influence for Geneva in the Foreword's acknowledgments. In addition to CRT founder Charles Lawrence, Bell thanks his former student Karl Klare (Harvard Law '75), who would go on to be a well-known figure in the critical legal studies movement alongside Duncan Kennedy, Peter Gabel, and Mark Tushnet. He also acknowledges the research

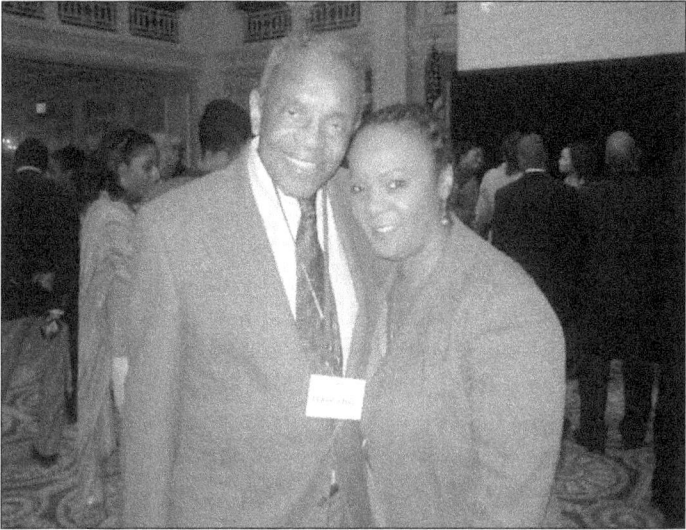

Figure 3.2. Derrick Bell and Stephanie Y. Moore at an event celebrating the election of Barack Obama as president of the United States, 2008. Photo courtesy of Stephanie Y. Moore.

assistance of a then current student at Oregon, Barry Kemp. Beyond the field of legal scholarship and the counsel of men, Bell thanks poet, writer, and professor Sonia Sanchez.

Sanchez, like Moore, is originally from Birmingham, Alabama. She was a leader in both the civil rights movement and within the Black Arts movement. Demonstrating Bell's commitment not only to interdisciplinarity but also to engagement with literary luminaries, in 1985 Sanchez received the American Book Award for *Homegirls and Handgrenades*, her collection of prose, prose poems, and lyric verses published the year before. Many years later, in a 2018 Martin Luther King Day keynote address at Amherst College, Sanchez called on students to "speak up and speak out," by invoking the names of outspoken Black leaders: "Derrick Bell. Maya Angelou. Alice Walker. June Jordan. Audre Lorde."[61]

In a 1992 interview, Bell was asked about the true identity of Geneva Crenshaw. "Geneva is a consolidation or a fictional product of many Black women I have known: my mother; my late wife, Jewel Bell, who died two years ago after 30 years of marriage; Constance Baker Motley, the now federal judge who I assisted in some of the early cases in the early 1960s, a number of Black women. I think that they are a marvelous group, very strong, very persevering," Bell responded. The interviewer pressed further, wondering if it's really Bell speaking when his stories quote Geneva. "Oh, it's always me," Bell confessed. "And it reflects the ambivalence . . . I feel and I think that a lot of Blacks feel."[62] Using composite characters like Geneva Crenshaw allowed Bell to accept his own ideological and practical ambivalence, his sympathy for multiple perspectives and possibilities. This dialogue-centered approach helped him avoid a stridently doctrinaire or overly ideological perspective on a topic as complex as the liberal, color-blind perpetuation of racism.

It is easy to think that the most obvious source code for Geneva Crenshaw is Constance Baker Motley. Even she thought so. "I don't know that it's written any place, but . . . Connie Motley says, 'Oh Geneva's *me*,'" Bell once recalled with a chuckle. That's not wrong. But Geneva reflects far more than a single source. As Bell told his mentor directly, "I said, 'Well, Connie, you're part of it.' But it's the sort of strong Black women I have known and that I've been married to."[63] Even more than that, as Bell admitted, Geneva is him as well! But how does he pull it off? How does Bell, a Black man, speak through the character of a Black woman without alienating the very people he is seeking to represent?[64] Part of the answer to that question is that he solicited critical feedback on his writing from a tremendous number of Black women. Another fact is that throughout his life, Bell consistently cultivated deep community with Black women, identifying them as mentors and leaders. Together, they make up various facets of the gem that is Geneva Crenshaw.

The Ada Childress Bell Facet

Bell often told the story about his mother, Ada Childress Bell, challenging their family's landlord during his early childhood.

"We were just barely above welfare. My father worked as a laborer," Bell recalled. "I remember [her] taking my brother and I to the local rent office . . . a short walk from our home, going into her pocketbook, bringing out the rent money and waving it at the man behind the little cage, and saying, 'I have my rent and you will get it when you send somebody out to fix the back stairs so my kids won't fall and hurt themselves.'" It was a risk. The family could have been evicted for nonpayment. "But that didn't happen. Rather, the man sent somebody out and fixed our back steps and fixed the back steps of everybody along that row of houses."[65]

Several years after the incident, Bell asked his mother if the neighbors ever knew why their back steps were fixed, what risk had been taken. "Not from me, they didn't," she replied, adding, "Many of those people were friends. I didn't want them to feel beholden to me for something I did for my family, something I did for myself."[66]

Bell carried that story with him. "She took the risk; she confronted [the landlord] with what she thought was clearly a wrong, a danger, and it worked."[67]

The Jewel Hairston Bell Facet

Derrick, Bell's first wife, Jewel Hairston Bell, was for many decades a vital presence in his life. After Bell left the LDF in 1966, he worked briefly as deputy director of the Office for Civil Rights in the US Department of Health, Education and Welfare (HEW, now Health and Human Services), a brief stint back in government that sent him toward an academic career. In 1968, after being assured he could teach at least one course, Bell headed west to direct the newly formed Western Center on Law and Poverty at the University of Southern California.

In her January 1968 recommendation letter supporting Bell's candidacy for the position in California, Constance Baker Motley included a surprising mention of Jewel Hairston Bell. Along with Jack Greenberg and Robert Carter, Motley had been writing letters supporting Bell's job search and admission to various state bars.[68] Motley's letter stands out for its personal touch. "For several years he worked very closely with me on school desegregation and other cases, most notable among them being the fourteen months proceeding to secure the admission of James Meredith to the University of Mississippi," she wrote. "Mr. Bell is not only exceptionally competent in the law but also creative. He is a man of unusual integrity. He is strengthened in his personal and social life by an extremely mature and intelligent wife."[69] Here, we see one source for Bell's composite character of Geneva Crenshaw acknowledging the strengths of another.

We catch a sense of that maturity and intelligence in the description of Hairston Bell provided by Sara Lawrence Lightfoot, an educational sociologist who collaborated with the Bells. "It was not just Jewel's courage, her insights, and her generosity that made her a precious friend to all of us. It was also . . . Jewel's sense of herself as an African American woman that brought us comfort and strength," Lightfoot remembered after Hairston Bell died in 1990. "She was so firm in her identity as a black woman. So fierce in her commitment to our liberation. So wise in her understanding of our vulnerabilities. So witty in her view of our pretension. So proud to be one of us. It was that certain clear black woman identity that allowed her to be so loving, so devoted, so enduring a wife to Derrick. . . . So much to celebrate and so much to miss."[70]

In 1969, following the societal upheavals caused by the April 1968 assassination of Martin Luther King Jr., Bell was invited to join the Harvard Law School faculty. He was tenured in 1971, but the process was anything but smooth. Hairston Bell was by her husband's side every step of the way. As Bell's tenure review drew near, a member of the law school's Appointments Committee offered benevolent counsel and concern—a move many tokenized faculty will recognize as gatekeeping by their white mentors. Bell was advised that since his criminal law course "needed more work," he should consider postposing tenure review for a year.[71]

"Tell them no!" Hairston Bell was furious. "You've worked hard for two years and kept your part of the bargain. Now they have to decide what to do after which *we* will decide what to do.

Remember, dear," she added firmly, "Harvard needs us. We do not need Harvard."[72] With that encouragement, Bell stood his ground. Within a few weeks, the Law School faculty voted to tenure the first Black professor in their school's history.

Although Bell had achieved the status of being the first tenured Black faculty member at Harvard Law School, he remained acutely aware that he didn't come from the same socioeconomic class as his colleagues. "They had all gone to prestigious colleges where they'd done extremely well, and then on to top-line law schools where they won academic honors and edited their schools' law journals," he once wrote.[73] Jewel Hairston Bell wasn't so moved by the status of her husband's colleagues. Remembering a faculty dinner they attended, he could hear how "Jewel would be arguing with this one over here, arguing with that one over there and holding her own."[74]

Afterward, on the walk home, Jewel turned to Derrick and said, "You know your colleagues are smart, but many of them are not impressive."[75]

Hairston Bell's insight was a source of strength. Bell had been "almost blown away with their credentials and what have you . . . but she saw through all of that," he remembered. "I was stronger as a result of her insight about individuals [and] about that school, which she never loved."[76]

Stephanie Y. Moore was a student at Harvard Law School in the early 1980s. Bell had already moved to Oregon to be dean of the University of Oregon School of Law but was traveling back and forth before his family followed. Moore met Hairston Bell for the first time when the visiting professor invited leaders of the Black Law Student Association to the Bell home for breakfast. "As a shy student, the thing that impressed me so much about Jewel is that she came downstairs in a housecoat with her hair in a night scarf," like Hairston Bell was communicating "This is my house. I'm not dolling up for you guys!" Moore recalled in an interview. "I loved that about her. She was amazing, an academic in her own right. She supported Derrick. I was impressed by the genuine and beautiful relationship they had. She was his Rock of Gibraltar."[77]

Derrick Bell later shared how a Black female student, pondering Hairston Bell's legacy, observed that she "seemed to be the archetypal STRONG BLACK WOMAN" while wondering "how women like Mrs. Bell maintained their feminine strength in the face of the struggle." For Bell, this question contained "implications larger than gender and of special importance to those of us who would continue that struggle without Jewel's unique insight and understanding which bordered on the divine."[78] Here again we catch a glimpse of Geneva Crenshaw.

When a group of their friends gathered for a remembrance of Jewel Hairston Bell soon after her death, Bell reflected on her centrality in his life: "I am sustained by the kindness of friends, the challenge of my work, and the knowledge that I am one of Jewel's life products. Make no mistake. Jewel moved many people. She made me."[79]

The Mississippi Leaders' Facet

Given their importance every time Bell told stories about his life, there's no doubt women on the ground in Mississippi contributed some attributes to the composite character of Geneva Crenshaw. Especially when it came to the perseverance of standing strong in the face of violent, white supremacist opposition to voting rights and integration, women like Winson and Dovie Hudson, along with their neighbor, Behonor McDonald, stood as beacons of inspiration. These women did it *all* in their community of Harmony, Mississippi: they organized their county chapter of the NAACP, petitioned for the reopening and racial integration of their school, and made many trips to Jackson to meet lawyers and statewide organizers, linking their local activities to broader efforts.

Their collective effort was put to the test during the Freedom Summer of 1964. The coordinated effort unified the Freedom Rider movement, begun in 1961, with the local priority of voter registration. Within the first week of the summer program, three civil rights workers—CORE employees James Chaney and Michael

LEAKE COUNTY MASS MEETING ≈ July 19, 1964

Citizens of four of the five precincts (beats) in Leake County had a mass meeting Sunday afternoon, July 19, in the Galilee Baptist Church. Representatives were present from all except beat 4.

The meeting was called to order by Chris Rainone, COFO volunteer. He introduced Mrs. Winson Hudson, who introduced James Collier, CORE, for an inspirational talk.

Rainone then explained the purpose of the meeting and the procedure to be followed. He said all beats would attempt to elect precinct officers and delegates to the county convention of the Freedom Democratic Party next Sunday, July 26. Since most representatives at the meeting live in Beat 5, other beats would be consolidated for the election of delegates. Beats 1 and 2 would elect their delegates together. Beat 3 would elect its delegates later. Beat 4 was without representation at this meeting.

The following officers and delegates were elected from Beat 5.

Officer or Delegate	Nominated by	Seconded by
Cleo Hudson, chairman	Olan Dotson	Mrs. Clyde Harvey
Mrs. Winson Hudson, secretary	Jim Dotson	Mrs. Luella Sanders
Jim Dotson, delegate	Olan Dotson	Joe C. Hudson
Clyde Harvey, Delegate	Anne Lindsay	Johnny Hudson
Johnny Hudson, delegate	Olan Dotson	Jim Dotson
Olan Dotson, delegate	Johnny Hudson	Jim Dotson
Willie Earl Lewis, delegate	Olan Dotson	Mr. Luella Sanders
Joe C. Hudson, delegate	Willie E. Lewis	Olan Dotson

Jim Dotson moved that the chairman and secretary also be delegates to the county convention. Mrs. Luella Sanders seconded the motion. It passed.

The following officers and delegates were elected from Beat 1-2.

Officer or Delegate	Nominated by	Seconded by
Choice Collier, chairman	Louis Dotson	Cleveland Henry
Mrs. Lilliemae Bounds, secretary	Choice Collier	Willie Campbell
Benny Lee Bounds, delegate	Willie Campbell	William Lefler
William Lefler, delegate	Cleveland Henry	Prebt Lefler
Mrs. Rebanor McDonald, delegate	Cleveland Henry	Prebt Lefler
Barton Gray, delegate	Willie Campbell	Choice Collier

Mr. Rebanor McDonald moved that chairman and secretary also attend the county convention. Benny Lee Bounds seconded the motion. It passed.

Mrs. McDonald moved that the meeting be adjourned at 5 p.m. Seconded by Mrs. Luella Sanders and passed.

Dorothy Teal,
Communications Volunteer
Carthage-Harmony Project

Figure 3.3. Meeting minutes from Leake County Congress on Racial Equality planning meeting (July 19, 1964), documenting involvement of the Hudson, Dotson, and McDonald families. Image courtesy Wisconsin Historical Society.

(Mickey) Schwerner and Queens College student volunteer Andrew Goodman—were murdered by the Ku Klux Klan. Thirteen of the Freedom Summer volunteers came to Harmony. Winson Hudson recalled that "Theodis Hewitt, married to Dovie's daughter, Jean, was the coordinator for the work, and I was the director of the summer project here. James Chaney stayed with us on and off and Michael Schwerner stayed with Dovie a while, before they was killed in June."[80] Their bodies weren't found until August 4, just before the final push for desegregation of the state's public schools.

The crucible of Mississippi in the Freedom Summer of 1964—the same context in which Bell's composite character, Geneva Crenshaw, is run off a rural road, leaving her in a coma until she startles him awake many years later to deliver her "Chronicles"—provided the context of Bell's life motto. During one of his visits to Harmony, he was staying in Mrs. Behonor McDonald's home, even as she was housing other Freedom Summer volunteers. As they walked up the unpaved road, Bell asked, "Where do you and the other black families find the courage to continue working for civil rights in the face of so much intimidation? . . . You told me shots were fired through your windows just last week."

Bell (as previously noted in chapter 1) remembered her words coming with slow seriousness: "I can't speak for everyone, Derrick, but as for me, I am an old woman. I lives to harass white folks."[81]

The Jean Fairfax Facet: Singing an Unsung Civil Rights Hero's Song

"Your sense of direction sure is better than mine, Ms. Fairfax," Bell said. He and Jean Fairfax (1920–2019) were once again driving the rural road between Jackson and Harmony. After Medgar Evers was assassinated, Constance Baker Motley couldn't bring herself to come back to Mississippi, and Bell was now leading LDF desegregation efforts in the state. "Oh, Derrick," Fairfax sighed, her hands on the wheel and eyes on the road. "That's no compliment. Anyone's sense of direction is better than yours!"[82]

Fairfax directed southern civil rights programs for the American Friends Service Committee.[83] She was a veteran activist, but the white supremacist violence they faced in the summer of 1964 was harrowing. Bell once asked her if she was afraid of what could happen to them if they took a wrong turn. "No," she said. "That's what God is for."[84]

Fairfax had traveled more than a few roads by the time she got to Mississippi. After graduating with honors from the University of Michigan in 1941, she earned a master's degree in comparative religion through a joint program administered by Columbia University and Union Theological Seminary. She had gone to the South to work as dean of women at Kentucky State College and then at Tuskegee Institute. In both places, she became involved with the Fellowship of Southern Churchmen, a forerunner of church-based civil rights efforts. The group was founded after a 1934 gathering in Monteagle, Tennessee, "after hearing a rousing call to action by the Christian Socialist Reinhold Niebuhr."[85] Niebuhr (1892–1971) was Fairfax's primary professor at Union.

"He was by far the best professor I ever had," Fairfax once recounted. She began her studies at Union in the fall of 1941, just before the Japanese attack on Pearl Harbor, Hawai'i. Although Niebuhr was very critical of pacifists, Fairfax, a principled pacifist in the Quaker tradition, found him "a very caring and warm professor. . . . Niebuhr was a teacher and a professor to everybody. And I have always been grateful for that. His concern for the social issues and his public position against repressions of all kinds is something that made a big impression on me."[86]

By the time Fairfax came to study with Niebuhr, his own thought had undergone a thorough transformation sparked by his struggle, alongside theologians like Karl Barth and Dietrich Bonhoeffer, against the rise of fascism in Europe and North America.[87] Active throughout the 1930s in the Socialist Party of America, Niebuhr in 1941 helped found the Union for Democratic Action to support US participation in WWII. His critiques of liberal idealism led to his development of Christian realism, a school of thought that influenced the shape of US foreign policy during the early years of the Cold War.[88] Niebuhr's is a complicated and multifaceted legacy. There is no doubt, however, that his influence on Jean Fairfax left a lasting impression on Derrick Bell, whose concept of racial realism—so often misunderstood as mere pessimism—hews closely to the pragmatic, non-idealistic tenor of Niebuhr's insights into human nature and social structures.

When she arrived in Mississippi, Fairfax was well acquainted with white supremacist violence. In the summer of 1946, after being turned away from Blue Ridge Assembly YMCA in North Carolina for planning a multiracial camp meeting, Fairfax, then serving at Tuskegee Institute, was part of a team that leased a campground near Henderson, North Carolina. "Word of the gatherings found its way into the nearby town; rumor spread quickly that the Ku Klux Klan would raid the camp and punish the participants." Neither local clergy nor local police were of any help. "We sat up all night, singing and praying, waiting for the assault," Fairfax later recalled. "It was a terrifying experience." After the group endured that night without incident and ended their meeting on schedule the next day, that evening "a caravan of cars brought more than a hundred Klansmen with guns and torches to the empty campground. Apparently, the hooded men had targeted the wrong date for their invasion."[89]

Through the American Friends Service Committee, Fairfax had led several international humanitarian efforts. In Austria, she connected with Catholic anti-Nazi resistance leaders. In Israel, she led a work camp and, drawing from experience with Jewish neighbors, operated a Kosher kitchen.[90] In 1956, "she set off for a year-long tour of the African continent, visiting seventeen countries."[91] She joined the LDF in 1965. Extolling her legacy, LDF director-counsel Jack Greenberg recalled:

> Jean forged new links between LDF and the black community, organizing community groups to demand desegregated education and fair employment, and published influential pamphlets dealing with the school lunch program, busing, treatment of Native

Americans, federal policies affecting elementary and high school education, and exclusion of women from private clubs. She became the most influential single staff member in determining the direction we took on such issues as integration of black colleges and which industries we should target in employment cases.[92]

In short, Fairfax was a powerhouse, a true civil rights hero.

Like Constance Baker Motley, Thurgood Marshall, and Bell, Fairfax insisted that although she was in leadership positions, she was not the center of the civil rights struggle. "Very often the civil rights revolution was initiated by the most vulnerable black persons. Many of them were women and many of them were children—tough, resilient, hopeful, beautiful children," she said in 1984. "The greatest experience of my life was standing with them as they took the risks."[93] In a 2005 interview with historian Jill Titus, Fairfax said she believes "we all have to be the vehicles that disrupt the lives of others. That's why I believe in litigation, sometimes demonstrations, the wonderful Quaker phrase 'speaking truth to power.' It's not just speaking the language of truth, but demonstrating that there are people who can trouble the waters."[94]

The Patricia Williams Facet: Embodying Geneva

Patricia J. Williams is someone used to being accused of troubling the waters. Her writing gathers the ghosts of her family's stories and interprets how those testimonies illuminate truths concerning the nature and development of law in the United States.[95] Her most well-known book, *Alchemy of Race and Rights*, generated over sixty reviews in both law reviews and the popular press, a polarizing response in which Williams was accused of being "unhinged, or playing at being unhinged," in a way that put "her style . . . at odds with her credibility."[96] Williams first met Derrick Bell in 1970 as a nineteen-year-old undergraduate. Near the beginning of Bell's time at Harvard Law School, she was invited by a friend to sit in on one of Bell's classroom lectures. What she

Figure 3.4. Jean Fairfax at Howard University, November 1963. Photo courtesy of Rowland Scherman and University of Massachusetts Amherst Archive.

encountered there shaped her career trajectory. "He had that class divided into interest and advocacy groups, taking various sides in the Supreme Court cases they were studying," she recalled in her tribute to Bell following his death in 2011. "The teams were arguing with each other like mad, and the passion and purpose flying around that room were like tangible objects. You had to duck to avoid getting laser-beamed by the sharp, whizzing commotion of high-octane ideas." She quickly realized that Bell "made ideas come alive. He made the dry pages of treatises vivid; he never let us forget the human stories behind every tract, every suit, every appeal."[97]

Once she became a student at Harvard Law School in 1972, Williams found her relationship with Bell and his family a source of strength and protection from the school's otherwise "intimidating and unfriendly atmosphere." In that time, "Derrick and his entire family really intervened in not just my life, but everybody who was dealing with that sense of loneliness, that sense of outsiderness."[98] Eventually, Williams became Bell's research assistant, helping edit the first two editions of *Race, Racism and American*

Law. During that time, Williams found herself being treated like a daughter among extensive and extended family. At the Bell home, Williams was welcomed to Jewel's spaghetti dinners; she would babysit their sons—Derrick, Douglass, and Carter—and sometimes even walk their prized Weimaraner dogs. For Williams, this psychologically comforting atmosphere gave her "a family within the law school and the occasion for the kinds of conversations I never had with any other professor from the beginning to the very end of my law school career."[99]

Williams and Bell encouraged and developed each other's craft of legal storytelling, before it was called counterstory. In October 1985, Bell wrote to Williams, telling her, "The Foreword is finishing its 4th edit, [and . . .] should be in page proof in the next few weeks. It has been a long labor and I only wish I had been able to get more help and advice from you. But your writing was a part of my inspiration and your encouragement was most welcome." He also reports forwarding a developing piece of hers—an early version of what would become "Alchemical Notes"—to *Harvard Law Review* editors.[100] This draft would develop into a paper presented at the January 1987 critical legal studies conference, "Sounds of Silence." On one undated memo titled "Critical Legal Mythology," Williams scrawled a handwritten note on the top-right corner—"Dear Derrick, See what you have wrought? Your form inspires."—above the title of what appears to be an early draft of her celebrated allegory, "The Brass Ring and the Deep Blue Sea."[101] Bell "convinced me that I was a good writer, and that writing was something I needed to find space for. . . . I started writing in a genre that used the first person and was playfully fictive, not fiction but fictive," Williams later stated. "I am completely indebted to him, always shall be."[102]

Bell introduced his first book-length collection of counterstories, *And We Are Not Saved*, on September 17, 1987, the bicentennial anniversary of the founders' signing of the US Constitution. The joint commemoration took place during an event at CUNY Queens Law School, where Patricia Williams was then a professor. Geneva Crenshaw was present as well.

For his presentation at the bicentennial event, Bell chose to perform a dramatized version of "The Chronicle of the Constitutional Contradiction," the first counterstory in *And We Are Not Saved*. The story is an expansion of ideas Bell articulated in his introductory and concluding remarks in the 1985 foreword, specifically the idea of a Black time-traveling interloper interrupting the Constitutional Convention. In the chronicle, Geneva Crenshaw speaks to a room full of white "Founding Father" delegates on the historic consequences of their pragmatic decision to not forbid slavery, even while propounding liberal ideas of equality and freedom. Using Bell's fully documented research, the framers—once recovered from their shock at being challenged by a Black woman—debate Geneva on the point, illustrating the intentionality with which racial contradictions were woven into the document itself. The script for the performance lies in Bell's archive with a cover letter addressed to Patricia Williams, who on that day would perform a key role, appearing as the embodied manifestation of Geneva Crenshaw.[103]

Enduring Relationships, Haunting Remembrance

In late 1985, when Derrick Bell published "The Civil Rights Chronicles," he introduced the world to Geneva Crenshaw. Legal studies circles buzzed, both at the daring method and form of the "Chronicles" and about the question of who this protagonist, Geneva Crenshaw, actually was. Was she a real person? While Bell all but shouts from the rooftops that Constance Baker Motley was a primary model for Geneva Crenshaw, he insisted that she was a composite character representing a multitude of women leaders.

Bell's second wife, Janet Dewart Bell, to whom he was married for twenty years before his death in 2011, shares Bell's priority of gathering the wisdom and insight of Black women. The couple came together through story. In the early 1990s, Janet contacted Bell to request permission to include one of his stories in the National Urban League's annual publication, *The State of Black America*. Their relationship bloomed over an exchange of ideas and edits.[104] Her own books, *Lighting the Fires of Freedom* and *Black-birds Singing*, tell stories that share perspectives and insights from Black women throughout US history.[105] Geneva is a composite of a multitude of Black women, including Constance Baker Mot-ley, Ada Bell, Jewel Hairston Bell, Jean Fairfax, and so many oth-ers. Moreover, editors and others who provided feedback on the stories—Jewel, Janet, Patricia Williams, Stephanie Moore, Elena Kagan, Carol Steiker—left their traces within Geneva as well.

Geneva haunted Derrick Bell. She was a specter who appeared to offer new insights and to argue points of legal theory and US history through many sleepless nights. Geneva—comprising the many women whose stories are highlighted in this chapter along with many others—is a source of constant pressure. Just as Mrs. Behonor McDonald said that she "lives to harass white folks," Ge-neva exists to harass Derrick Bell. He worked to get Geneva right, constantly soliciting feedback from a multitude of Black women. From close associates and relative strangers alike, he received many edits and advice for further reading and reflection, particu-larly to read Black feminist theorists like bell hooks.[106] He took much of this feedback seriously as he refined both the character of Geneva Crenshaw and readjusted his intersectional framework for comprehending the specific challenges Black women face. Bell consistently made a choice to open his writing and his actions to critique. He opened himself to harassment, even to the point of welcoming memories of uncomfortable truths.

When he decided to use the platform provided by the invi-tation to write a *Harvard Law Review* foreword comprising composite counterstories, Bell embarked on his long-held plan of accessing audiences of learners outside legal academia. In an interview at a Dallas restaurant, Mrs. Emma Scruggs Rodgers, a student at Spelman College in the early 1960s who participated in "sit 'n' runs" before sit-ins were more widespread, shared how Bell cultivated commitments to Black community leaders throughout the United States.[107] Rodgers cofounded Black Images Book Ba-zaar in 1977 in Dallas, Texas, because she "couldn't find African American books for her son's birthday."[108] The bookstore served a

Figure 3.5. Emma Rodgers, Derrick Bell, and Ashira Tosihwe at Black Images Book Bazaar, Dallas, Texas, 1992. Courtesy of Emma Rodgers.

community need. It soon became a destination for Black authors; the shop hosted, among others, Maya Angelou, Edward P. Jones, Terry McMillan, E. Lynn Harris, and Derrick Bell.

"He came to the shop several times," Rodgers remembers. One of Bell's most memorable visits to Rodgers's bookstore was in 1992, when he was promoting his second bestselling collection of stories, *Faces at the Bottom of the Well*.[109] Unfortunately for the evening event, Bell's plane was delayed by weather. People gathered at the shop at the advertised time. Rodgers and her business partner, Ashira Tosihwe, urged attendees to go grab a bite to eat in their Oak Cliff neighborhood and come back; people were so committed to his work that they *all* showed up a couple hours later. "He read 'The Space Traders,'" a story in which visiting aliens offer the United States wealth and the solution to all its problems in exchange for every Black citizen. "My absolute favorite!" Rodgers exclaimed.[110]

At that evening's event, Bell was introduced by Bernestine Singley (Harvard Law '76); Bell had been Singley's LLM thesis advisor at Harvard Law School; she was also, alongside Patricia Williams, a research assistant for the 1975 supplement for his casebook, *Race, Racism and American Law*.[111] "She was our Geneva," Rodgers says of the group of friends she shared in common with Singley.[112]

"I raised hell in law school and suffered the consequences, which is why I spent much tissue time at the Bells' kitchen table," Singley wrote in her tribute to Derrick Bell after he died. "Derrick and Jewel Hairston Bell, his fierce, brilliant, perfect partner . . . embraced me as family. Derrick and Jewel were a gleaming example of what life could be like inside a committed, healthy relationship of loving independence and reciprocity. The blessing of my life and marriage today are a direct outcome of what I learned there."[113]

Bell's presence in Dallas, in addition to adding another "Geneva" to a well-stocked list, confirms Jean Fairfax's observation that Bell "was very personally involved with [the people]. This was not just a New York lawyer who breezed in and left."[114] Bell's

Figure 3.6. Bernestine Singley introducing Derrick Bell in 1992. Photo courtesy of Emma Rodgers.

plans for what would become CRT always included storytelling and always included engagement with community spaces created and led by people of color, particularly Black women. Mrs. Rodgers's treasured snapshot of Bell standing in her independent bookshop with a room full of Black Dallas citizens willing to return after a delayed flight provides proof of that.

In 1986, Carol Steiker, president of the *Harvard Law Review* when Bell's foreword was published, sent a handwritten letter updating him on receiving a Supreme Court clerkship with Justice Thurgood Marshall, based in part on Bell's recommendation. She was thrilled to be co-clerking with Elena Kagan. At the time, Bell was making his way back to Harvard Law School following a disastrous stint at Stanford. "I hope this summer has given you more time to spend dreamin' with Geneva than your term at Stanford did. I'd love to read whatever you've done."[115]

More than just a memory, remembrance actively brings the past into the present for the purpose of shaping the future. Derrick Bell's central character, Geneva Crenshaw, is a vehicle of disruptive remembrance, a near-divine time traveler transcending past, present, and future. She came to Derrick Bell's rescue through dreams.[116] She is a specter, a ghost who doesn't let him go. Bell was haunted by memories of Mississippi and the question of whether civil rights law had best served the interests of Black children and families. His experiences within communities of color, Black communities in particular, goaded him, leading him to new insights and legal theories. Through Geneva, Bell sings the praises of the multitude of women he counted among his heroes, many of whom are otherwise unsung or forgotten altogether. Through Geneva Crenshaw, the polyphonous choir continues to sing.

4

Clash of the Titans

The Many Paths to Critical Race Theory

CRT TENETS: Centrality of Experiential Knowledge and/or Unique Voices of Color; Interdisciplinarity; Intersectionality and Anti-Essentialism; Challenge to Dominant Ideologies

"You're not going to be one of those students protesting my dad, are you?" Josiah Greenberg asked, a bit of a smile discernable from his profile.[1]

It was 1982. Stephanie Y. Moore and Josiah Greenberg were sitting side by side, highlighting briefs. Moore, an intern, and Greenberg, a clerk, were working that summer under Judge U. W. Clemon, the first Black federal judge in Alabama. Through years of civil rights law practice and five years (1974–80) as one of two Black leaders elected since Reconstruction as an Alabama state senator, Judge Clemon had gained a reputation for challenging every aspect of racial segregation. His efforts in *Singleton v. Jackson Municipal Separate School District* had set a precedent for national efforts for school desegregation.[2] Appointed to the federal bench in 1980 by President Jimmy Carter, Clemon was in a position to nurture the next generation of LDF-related lawyers.

For some people, the Legal Defense Fund (LDF) was less an office than a family. Stephanie Moore, for instance, happily identifies as an "LDF baby," the product of generations of leaders who worked to improve legal conditions for people of color in the United States. This was especially true of LDF efforts in the Deep South where LDF and NAACP support for lawyers like U. W. Clemon and his forerunner in Alabama, Arthur D. Shores, had brought real change to people's lives. In January 1961, the LDF chose to desegregate the

Figure 4.1. Judge U. W. Clemon in 1980, immediately following his appointment as the first Black federal judge in Alabama. Photo courtesy of Stephanie Y. Moore.

University of Mississippi with James Meredith rather than the University of Alabama with Clemon. Clemon stayed up to date with progress in that case as he completed undergraduate studies at the historically Black Miles College, in Birmingham.

Clemon kept busy during his undergraduate years at Miles. In 1962, he helped organize a "selective buying" campaign to boycott segregated stores. In 1963, when Martin Luther King Jr. launched the Birmingham Campaign, Clemon was assigned the task of desegregating the Birmingham Public Library. He graduated from Miles College as valedictorian in 1965.[3] From there, Clemon went to Columbia Law School. Since law schools in Alabama remained closed to Black people, the state paid part of his tuition. While in New York, his relationship with the LDF would deepen.

At Columbia in the mid-1960s, Clemon came to the attention of Professor Walter Gellhorn, by then a longtime LDF board member and a close friend of Thurgood Marshall. Marshall was known to hire staff on the recommendation of trusted advisors. "In February 1966, Professor Gellhorn invited me to the men's faculty club at Columbia for lunch, a big deal," U. W. Clemon recalled in an interview. Gellhorn was his academic advisor. "He said he knew I was from Alabama and wondered if I wanted to go back. If so, he [Gellhorn] wanted to tell me about a program at the LDF that might be of interest." The Earl Warren Scholarship program enabled law students to set up a law practice in the South by paying a diminishing salary over a five-year period and providing for an administrative assistant, a small law library, and assistance toward office rent. At the time, Marian Wright, later founder of the Children's Defense Fund, was utilizing the program to do innovative work in Mississippi. "He told me that if I was interested, he would set up an appointment with Jack," Clemon recalled. Just as Thurgood Marshall had done with Derrick Bell when recommended by Judge William Hastie in 1959 and with Jack Greenberg when recommended by Gellhorn in 1948, Greenberg, emulating his predecessor, hired Clemon in 1966 as a part-time intern at the Fund.[4]

In the fall of 1982, Clemon's intern, Stephanie Moore, would begin her first year at Harvard Law School. Moore's father, a professor at an historically Black College in Alabama and former high school teacher, had taught many of Clemon's siblings and was a good family friend. Clemon's law clerk, Josiah Greenberg, was son of the legendary attorney, human rights advocate, and LDF director-counsel Jack Greenberg. Josiah's question about the student protest and threat to boycott his father's winter 1983 course at Harvard Law School hung in the air. Moore shrugged her shoulders and, smiling, shook her head. "As a first year I don't think I even qualify to take the course he's teaching and that the students are protesting."[5]

The course in question was "Racial Discrimination and Civil Rights" offered in the winter of 1983. It was a replacement to mollify students disappointed over Derrick Bell's 1981 departure from Harvard Law School. Bell resigned in protest over the school's sustained refusal to meaningfully recruit and hire faculty of color beyond his own hire twelve years earlier in 1969.[6] Bell had consistently advocated for additional permanent hires since his first moments at the school.[7] When the opportunity to serve as dean at the University of Oregon School of Law came about, Bell accepted. Perhaps the opportunity to work in higher administration would be the route toward realizing his goal of creating a more diverse faculty through reformed hiring practices.

When the fall 1981 term began at Harvard Law School, first year students like Kimberlé Crenshaw "who had chosen Harvard because the renowned Derrick Bell was there, [were] disappointed to find that he had departed a few months earlier."[8] Bell's work, however—especially his casebook, *Race, Racism, and American Law*—remained influential. Students like Crenshaw still purchased Bell's book and were confident that their school's administration would move quickly to provide curricular and faculty offerings to fill the sizeable gap Bell's departure had created. No such plan materialized. In fact, Bell's course "Constitutional Law and Minority Issues" was dropped from the course offerings altogether, and there seemed to be no hiring plan to replace him. The students were stunned.

The goal of encouraging Harvard Law School to hire and tenure more minority faculty members was "endorsed by over 500 Harvard Law students, most of them white, in a petition to the law school administration in the fall of 1981."[9] Student organizing made some headway. In mid-December 1981, Harvard Law School dean James Vorenberg invited a small delegation representing Harvard's Black Law Student Association (BLSA) to his office for an afternoon meeting.[10]

Looking up from their list of demands and pointing to the section on curriculum, Vorenberg said, "What I simply don't understand is, what is so unique about 'Constitutional Law and Minority Issues' that it requires such a specific course?"[11]

BLSA president, Muhammad I. Kenyatta, sighed audibly in exasperation. He was an older student, nearing forty, who had been a civil rights activist in the 1960s and was harassed by the Counterintelligence (COINTEL) Program of the US Federal

Figure 4.2. Muhammad Kenyatta, president of the Black Law Student Association at Harvard Law School and leader of the boycott against the Greenberg/Chambers mini-course in the winter term of 1983. Photo courtesy of Stephanie Y. Moore.

Bureau of Investigation.[12] He was fed up with Vorenberg's Socratic interrogation games.

"How's it fair that you make students justify the necessity of what we might learn in a course we haven't been offered? You're stacking the deck in the school's favor when you play that way and you know it."[13]

The other BLSA students nodded and murmured their assent. Nearly all students in Vorenberg's office that day arrived at Harvard with solid backgrounds in activism and a commitment to pursuing a legal career in social justice. Donald Christopher Tyler, from Cheyenne, Wyoming, was dedicated to becoming an impact advocacy litigator like Thurgood Marshall. He had just been awarded a Harvard Public Interest Fellowship to spend the summer interning for the NAACP Legal Defense Fund, with the goal of gaining employment there once he graduated.[14] Kimberlé

Crenshaw's parents were ardent activists. Cecelie Counts protested for Black studies and other curricular demands in East Orange, New Jersey, before moving on to protest the Vietnam War and colonialism in Africa. Ibrahim Gassama was involved in democratic struggles in Sierra Leone.[15] These students were deeply connected to curricular dimensions of racial justice, battles for ethnic studies, and global efforts to provide educational alternatives.[16]

Vorenberg tried again in a hopeful tone. "What I mean is, couldn't you all just distill what you wanted from existing courses—say, just regular 'Constitutional Law' in conjunction with a legal-aid placement?"[17]

"No!" "It's not the same!" "Not at all!" erupted a chorus of impassioned replies from the BLSA group, heads shaking "No."

Vorenberg slumped back in his seat, seemingly deflated and at a loss. What did these students want? What would work? How could they possibly move forward? He tried again.

"Wouldn't it be preferable," he began tentatively, searching for the right way to phrase what he was going to say next, "that we hire an excellent white legal scholar over a mediocre black one?" he finished, evincing a cajoling smile.[18]

The BLSA students stared at Vorenberg in stunned silence. "Did he just say what I think he said?" was etched across each of their faces.

Tyler, easily recognizing one of the familiar insults that propelled him to Harvard Law School, responded, "There are plenty of excellent Black legal scholars. You're just not looking for them."[19]

Vorenberg glared. "Really?" he responded. Pushing on with anxious chatter, Vorenberg continued: "For instance, wouldn't it be outstanding to be taught by a leading white civil rights lawyer, instead of me pulling someone from just a nameless mass of unqualified minorities, someone like Jack Greenberg, for example?"[20]

"No!" the students said, almost in unison. Clearly this meeting was going nowhere. Clearly this meeting needed to end.

The BLSA students were unaware that Vorenberg's hypothetical comparison was not hypothetical at all. Their dean was confident he knew the right man to invite for the job of visiting lecturer: the legendary attorney, human rights advocate, and LDF director-counsel Jack Greenberg.[21]

The Right Man for the Job

In 1961, President John F. Kennedy nominated Thurgood Marshall as a judge for the United States Court of Appeals for the Second Circuit. This nomination could not have come at a more inopportune time for the LDF. The high-profile *Meredith* trial was in full swing, as were many other desegregation suits throughout the South. This was no time for the Fund to lose its charismatic leader who had become a face and spokesperson of the civil rights movement.[22]

The LDF would need a successor immediately, but who could fill Marshall's shoes? Based on Marshall's past NAACP and LDF landmark court victories, two Black leaders within the organization seemed logical choices: NAACP general counsel Robert L. Carter and LDF assistant counsel Constance Baker Motley. To the astonishment of many in the civil rights community, Marshall chose Jack Greenberg, a white man, as his successor.[23] Writing for the Black newspaper *Amsterdam News*, columnist Jimmy Hicks best said what many at the time were thinking: "I think somebody goofed on this one. . . . 'Wha' Hoppen?'"[24]

There was no doubt Greenberg was technically qualified; his credentials as a litigator were impeccable. Greenberg had joined the LDF in 1949 as a Columbia Law School graduate and was eventually part of the team of lawyers that brought the *Brown* school desegregation cases to the Supreme Court. By the time of Greenberg's promotion, he was serving as one of Marshall's senior assistants. When it became clear to Marshall that a Kennedy nomination was imminent, the outgoing director-counsel began to delegate more and more responsibility to Greenberg.[25]

As far as Greenberg was concerned, there was never any "serious" opposition to his succession. According to Greenberg, Marshall discussed his decision with the LDF board members,

Figure 4.3. Constance Baker Motley, attorney for James Meredith, reads a prepared statement alongside Medgar Evers and Jack Greenberg in New Orleans, September 27, 1962. Courtesy of Library of Congress.

claiming that "race shouldn't be an issue—after all, that was what our fight was about, a country with no racial distinctions."[26] Echoing his mentor in 1962, Greenberg told Louis Lomax, the first Black television journalist, "Civil rights is not a *Negro* cause; it is a human cause, a serious problem in world society. True, our organization is designed primarily to aid Negroes in their push for equality, but the cause is human, not *Negro*."[27] Nevertheless, mainstream papers made racial distinctions. On October 5, 1961, the *New York Times* crowed "N.A.A.C.P. Names a White Counsel" on its front page. "The *Times* choose to focus on the least relevant aspect of my persona," Greenberg would comment, irritated.[28] In fact, Black opposition to Greenberg was widespread. In an essay titled "The White Liberal," Lomax shared that "many Negroes feel that the presence of white people in 'Negro' organizations inevitably leads to 'go-slowism.'" This is especially true, he said, "when white people rise to positions of leadership within Negro organizations."[29]

In her autobiography, Constance Baker Motley—a member of the LDF team marginalized by race and gender—cast doubt on Greenberg's tale that his ascension to head the LDF was colorblind, based on merit alone.[30] Within NAACP and LDF leadership circles, desire for the spotlight sparked resentments and jealousies.[31] Marshall had grown to mistrust Carter, while Motley herself was well aware of the era-specific sexism limiting Marshall's imagination when it came to women in executive leadership roles.[32] When Greenberg was elevated, Motley received a promotion—to second in command.[33] Motley's unique perspective as a Black woman, something Mari Matsuda would characterize as "looking from the bottom," provides an illustration for what Kimberlé Crenshaw would eventually coin as the CRT tenet intersectionality.[34]

Motley's minor promotion did not meet expectations down in Jackson, Mississippi. There, Medgar Evers had been so confident Motley would succeed Marshall that he printed celebratory posters for a public meeting at which Motley would be the main speaker. As Motley herself later reflected, "Greenberg's installation came with such swiftness there was no time for the opposition to mobilize."[35] Evers didn't have time to change his posters.

Motley wasn't the first person of color to have a white person she trained be promoted as their supervisor. In Motley's view, even when Greenberg was appointed to lead the LDF in 1961, "he had to learn about ordinary black people, particularly Southern black people, in the same way that a Jewish man appointed to head an Asian organization would have to learn about Asians."[36] A moment Greenberg himself recounted from when they were young lawyers together illustrates Motley's concern.

"Did we remember to pull the statement from the Negress from Topeka?" Greenberg asked, sifting through an array of papers fanned out on the desk in front of him.

Motley's head snapped up at his use of the term, but Greenberg seemed not to notice, so immersed in his search for this Black woman's statement.

"Jack, that term is offensive, and should not be spoken," Motley said, her voice steady and firm, a bit parental.

Noticing the gravity in her tone, Greenberg's head jerked up from his search, a dumbfounded expression on his face.

"I didn't mean anything by it . . . it's just something commonly said . . ." he sputtered.

"Be that as it may," Motley cut in, "that term is akin to calling a Black woman a lioness, or a tigress, a jungle or zoo animal for that matter, and it's offensive," she finished.

Motley said this without anger or really any sort of discernable emotion in her voice. She was cool and calm and she shot straight. She simply let him know how it was.

"I see. Thanks for letting me know, Connie. I appreciate it greatly," Greenberg said sheepishly.

"Yes of course, never mind" Motley said, with a nod. The two colleagues got back to work.[37]

In Constance Baker Motley's estimation, Jack Greenberg never prepared himself to lead a major civil rights organization: "He was not like the white liberals who were committed body and soul to advancing the cause of Black Americans."[38] Greenberg himself recalled that he was often asked how he, a Columbia-educated man from a neighborhood in the Bronx where "no blacks lived anywhere nearby," came to be so devoted to the rights of Black people.[39] Nevertheless, Jack Greenberg's idealistic, colorblind liberalism came to be rejected by the likes of Derrick Bell and students at Harvard Law School. CRT's challenge to liberalism helps expose what Eduardo Bonilla-Silva calls colorblind racism, even among those who identify as "leftists" or "progressives."[40] The tenet of challenge to dominant ideologies can be misunderstood as promoting critique of "conservative" or right-wing ideologies alone. CRT, however, understands itself as challenging *all* ideological manifestations of abstracted Enlightenment liberalism regardless of partisan political affiliation.

Dean Cuisine

In 1990, Jack Greenberg and James Vorenberg published a cookbook titled *Dean Cuisine: Or the Liberated Man's Guide to Fine Cooking*. Positively reviewed by the *New York Times*, the book's back cover features an endorsement from Julia Child, who says, "The male approach to cookery, in my observation, is much freer, faster, more daring, and more casual than the female, and it would seem to me that this book . . . is indeed '*The Liberated Man's Guide to Fine Cooking*.'"[41]

In the late 1960s, LDF director-counsel Jack Greenberg was reorganizing his board. He invited Harvard Law professor Jim Vorenberg to join. Together, they worked on various civil rights matters and formed a profound friendship they characterized as "twinned."[42] In 1970, only months apart, "Jim married Betty and Jack married Debby. Betty and Debby had been friends since the 1950s" and were accomplished civil rights professionals and advocates in their own right.[43] These were second marriages for Jack and Jim who each started to learn step-parenting together. Both men would become law teachers. Both would eventually develop Parkinson's disease. And they both very much enjoyed "many activities together, particularly working in the kitchen."[44]

As the 1970s progressed, the Greenbergs and Vorenbergs began vacationing together in France, renting a house for a month at a time in Eze Village on the Côte d'Azur (the French Riviera).[45] The husbands would do most of the shopping and cooking. In general, this was a breath of fresh air and a nice escape from their demanding jobs. Greenberg was still director-counsel of the Fund. In addition to his professorial duties at Harvard Law, Vorenberg had served as principal assistant in the Watergate Special Prosecutor's Office; he would step into the role of dean of Harvard Law School by 1981.

The idea for the cookbook launched during one of their annual French Riviera vacations in August 1977 but would take more than ten years to complete—after all, how can a book be titled *Dean Cuisine* when only one of its authors is a dean? In 1984, Jack

Greenberg left the LDF to become a professor and vice dean at Columbia Law School.[46] However, a defining moment of their friendship and careers occurred in the preceding years when Vorenberg asked Greenberg to teach a civil rights course during the January 1983 three-week winter term.[47]

Into the Fray

With Greenberg at the helm, Jim Vorenberg was confident that he had hired an outstanding white civil rights lawyer instead of having to pull someone from "a nameless mass of unqualified minorities." The resulting uproar from the students, led by Muhammad Kenyatta and the BLSA, shook the dean's confidence. On April 26, 1982, Vorenberg received a letter initially drafted by Kenyatta and Donald Tyler expressing "outrage at the uniform racial and gender composition of the ten new faculty listed in the April 9, 1982 *HLS Advisor*." The letter was signed by BLSA leadership, joined by six additional law school student organizations. Dean Vorenberg quickly added to the teaching roster a very accomplished and qualified Black civil rights lawyer, Julius LeVonne Chambers, a former president of the Legal Defense Fund who was then in private practice. Vorenberg hoped this would stave off student protests and threats of a boycott. It didn't.[48]

Jack Greenberg had flown for about sixteen hours from New Delhi to Boston to meet Chambers for the first day of class on January 5, 1983. Greenberg had been lecturing for the past two weeks in India but wasn't going to let his good friend Jim Vorenberg down, especially after that last phone call.[49]

"Jack, it's absolute mayhem here. I swear the level of acrimony reminds me of the student takeovers during Vietnam," Vorenberg said, clearly tired, clearly tense.[50]

"What exactly is going on?" Greenberg asked, concerned about the hollowness in his friend's voice.

"The noise is unbearable. The chanting, the constant chanting. Seas of students have invaded the faculty library wearing t-shirts saying 'Desegregate Now!' And my desk, Jack! I can't tell you how many times security has been called to remove students who insist on barging into my office to stand on top of my desk, shouting their protest and demands. It's like all hell's broke loose!" Vorenberg finished, desperation in his voice.[51]

"I see," Greenberg said, nodding curtly, trying to imagine what he would do if anyone barged into his office and stood on Thurgood Marshall's massive old desk.[52] "No worries, Jim, I'll be there soon."

"The students are planning a picket line protest, Jack." Vorenberg said tentatively. "You and Julius will have to be escorted across an angry mob on the first day of class. Are you scared? I won't fault you if you decide this isn't worth the trouble."[53]

"Scared?" Greenberg interjected. "No," he scoffed, sounding annoyed. "I was on the beach at Iwo Jima."[54]

Eventually, Greenberg took the student protests personally, blaming the entire unhappy incident on his former LDF colleague turned critic, Derrick Bell. Greenberg and Bell had clashed in the past, standing on opposite sides of several controversies within the NAACP and LDF on the question of how the organizations should navigate between liberalism and the challenge of race consciousness, most often expressed in terms of Black nationalism and separatism. For decades, Greenberg and Bell had stood on opposite sides of that divide.

In 1956, when the Nation of Islam (NOI) first burst onto the scene, the emergence of this new Black nationalist organization demanded response. "The Hate That Hate Produced," a major documentary produced by Louis Lomax and Mike Wallace (later known for *60 Minutes*), framed Black nationalism as little more than the reactionary flipside of violent white supremacy. The NOI, in other words, was comprehended from its inception as a violent, militant organization. The documentary featured denunciations of the NOI from several civil rights leaders, including "the NAACP's Roy Wilkins, Arnold Forster of the Anti-Defamation League, and Anna Arnold Hedgeman." As Garrett Felber puts it in his excellent study of this period, "A year before the Greensboro Sit-ins sparked a movement of young, college-aged activists . . . , the old guard distanced themselves from a rising tide of black nationalism which was vocally critical of nonviolence as a means—and integration as a goal—of the civil rights movement."[55]

Derrick Bell, then a representative of the younger generation ready for direct action, was not so quick as the "old guard" to dismiss the radicalism of the NOI. While some NAACP leaders wanted to engage in an anti-NOI campaign, Bell, then heading the NAACP field office in Pittsburgh before joining the LDF staff in New York, argued that preventing the publication of Hon. Elijah Muhammad's articles in the *Pittsburgh Courier*, a major Black news outlet, would be ineffective. "The remedy for this problem is not to urge the *Courier* to discontinue a column which thousands of its readers find of interest," he said in an August 1959 NAACP radio broadcast. "The Muslims would simply find another medium to disseminate the same material."[56]

Within the context created by the April 1962 police killing of Ronald Stokes in Los Angeles, Bell would again have a chance to offer comment. Malcolm X seized the opportunity to direct his critical lens on the US justice system and the scourge of police brutality, publishing his landmark essay, "The Crisis of Racism," the next month and leading several rallies throughout the United States. In October 1962, Loren Miller, a longtime legal colleague of Thurgood Marshall and champion of fair housing access who had been a fraternity brother of Stokes, penned his pathbreaking article, "A Farewell to Liberals." Miller offered a strong critique of white limits on Black radical trajectories in the struggle for racial equality—what Lomax called "go-slowism." But this was not a severing of all ties: "Rejection of liberal leadership does not mean that Negroes do not want, and expect, continued liberal aid." White allies, rather than being in leadership positions, should join Black Americans as "foot soldiers and subordinates in a Negro-led, Negro-officered army under the banner of Freedom Now."[57] As Felber unearthed in Miller's archive, the article received praise from several quarters, including from Bell, who wrote that through Miller's insights, "all of us will more easily recognize the liberal in our midst who is not truly in our family but in our way."[58]

Jack Greenberg's reputation as a stalwart liberal was confirmed in 1970 with his decision to not put LDF resources toward the defense of Black intellectual militant leader Angela Y. Davis. After President Nixon described Davis as a "terrorist" for her tangential relationship with a militant incident earlier that year, the FBI eventually arrested Davis in October 1970. The case drew the attention of all civil rights organizations, including the NAACP and the LDF. A week after Davis's arrest on October 13, Greenberg received a memo from one of his younger staff lawyers, Margaret Burnham, informing him that she was actively representing Davis, fighting her extradition from New York to California. The resulting crisis nearly destroyed the LDF.

The day after Burnham's memo arrived, the LDF staff "voted unanimously, with the exception of Jim Nabrit, that [Greenberg] should authorize LDF to take on significant black militant cases as a matter of general policy and that we should represent Angela Davis."[59] Greenberg rejected the staff's recommendation. A week later, Greenberg explained that in the extradition case, "there had not been alleged any denial of legal or constitutional rights" and "that there was no question of racial discrimination apparent." Moreover, Greenberg decided, "the Legal Defense Fund would not identify itself with the politics and ideology represented by Angela Davis."[60]

The disagreement in the 1970s over Angela Davis and Black militancy was a crossroads for the LDF, just as the rise of the Nation of Islam had been for the NAACP in the 1950s. While Greenberg's staff was largely sympathetic to the Black Panthers and other militant efforts, Greenberg found them incompatible with his view of civil rights. "Especially offensive were the separatist beliefs of the new militants, which ran contrary to the views of NAACP, LDF, SCLC, and, during their early history, CORE and SNCC—the latter two having turned separatist—the groups that had made real contributions to the progress of civil rights."[61] Greenberg's confidence was bolstered by the fact that his perspective reflected "the traditional views of LDF and were shared by the board." In conflict with staff members who "wanted to be seen as allies of the Black Panthers, students who tore campuses apart and paraded with rifles, draft resisters, and prisoners who fought jailers," Greenberg took comfort in the unanimous support he received from the LDF's "mostly black board."[62] He never considered that his race, in addition to the age gap between him and his staff, could have contributed to a difference of views. In a review of Greenberg's memoir, another white civil rights lawyer suggested, however, "One cannot help but wonder whether a Black director-counsel might have been more sympathetic toward Black nationalism and therefore taken a different approach to the case."[63]

Conflict between Jack Greenberg and Derrick Bell poured into the open in 1976 when Bell wrote a letter to the ACLU's *Civil Rights Review*. He complained that an interview with Greenberg in the previous issue devolved into a "lengthy and unabashed advertisement for the Legal Defense Fund." There, Bell took Greenberg to task for maintaining an "ideal-oriented approach to racial problems" grounded in "little sensitivity to the real needs of blacks." Given Greenberg's stance of overruling the perspectives of his Black colleagues, with specific reference to the Angela Davis case, Bell labeled the office Greenberg ran a "penthouse plantation." Bell attributed Greenberg's lack of awareness to a "liberal" form of "that special quality of arrogance which is the essence of the racism LDF was designed to combat." Echoing the perspective voiced by Loren Miller in the early 1960s, Bell concluded his letter by saying that

> Mr. Greenberg's dedication to his work should not cause him to mistake his role. He should serve and not try to lead black people. By listening to black critics instead of dismissing them, he might strengthen LDF's program. At the least, he would not evidence that intolerance based on a sense of hereditary superiority that black folks have come to recognize immediately and despise whole-heartedly.[64]

Bell's letter was followed immediately by a missive from Julius Chambers, then LDF president, excoriating Bell's critique and defending Greenberg's contributions to civil rights leadership. The long-simmering conflict between competing ideals for racial justice—represented substantially by disagreements between Bell and Greenberg—would spill over into the Harvard Law School community in the early 1980s.

All Hell Breaks Loose at Harvard Law

On July 26, 1982, Ruth Marcus, then a second-year student at Harvard Law School working a summer job with the *Washington Post*, published a news report titled "Minority Groups Assail Course at Harvard Law." Marcus noted that the "controversy became public last week when Harvard sent a letter to second- and third-year students telling them about the proposed boycott."[65] She went on to quote part of a letter Dean Vorenberg sent to the Law School student body along with protest letters from the BLSA and the Third World Coalition (TWC), a Harvard Law School student group made up of representatives from African American, Arab, Asian American, Chicano, Native American, and Puerto Rican law student organizations.[66] "I believe that to boycott a course on racial discrimination, because part of it is taught by a white lawyer, is wrong in principle and works against, not for, shared goals of racial and social justice," Vorenberg said.[67]

In her recounting of the period, Kimberlé Crenshaw points out that "Marcus failed to interview anyone involved in the boycott, leading to gross distortions in her story" that newspapers, despite pleadings from minority students, subsequently refused to correct.[68] Marcus's article nevertheless sparked national interest, piquing outrage from liberals angry at minority students at Harvard Law School for the audacity of their protest. Mainstream media outlets such as the *New York Times*, the *Boston Globe*, and the *Miami Herald* ran stories harshly criticizing the boycott, praising the manifold heroics of Greenberg and aiming vitriol at the minority students from Harvard Law School's BLSA and the TWC. When the *New York Times* ran its story on August 9, 1982, Donald Tyler was interning with the LDF in New York; he often sat at a conference room table immediately outside Jack Greenberg's office. He immediately felt pressure from his legal heroes, including Greenberg and Lani Guinier. He had been privileged to accompany Guinier while she argued a voting rights case in the Southern District of New York. Not wanting to disappoint her, Tyler set about drafting a letter to the *New York Times*, enlisting another BLSA executive committee member, Cynthia Muldrow, as a coauthor. Guinier added some editing of her own. Before that summer was over, Tyler was interviewed by National Public Radio's legal reporter Nina Totenberg. Tyler's life was soon consumed by the controversy; his third year of law school was taken up with responses to journalists and fellow students who often implied that both affirmative action and the BLSA were racist.[69]

In response to this press campaign against Harvard Law's BLSA and TWC students, Derrick Bell again entered the fray. In September 1982, Bell published "A Question of Credentials" in the *Harvard Law Record* student newspaper. Writing from Oregon, Bell noted that while "there is a tendency to elevate whites who have done substantial service in the civil rights cause to a quasi-sacred status that is beyond criticism, at least by Blacks," the students' demands, although impolitic, should be taken seriously. Bell expressed understanding of the students' suggestion that, "while Greenberg's contributions to civil rights have been great, he should long since have recognized the symbolic value of his position to the Black community and turned over the leadership post to a Black lawyer." Bell contended that the student boycott of the Greenberg/Chambers course, far from being an open-and-shut case of "reverse racism," must be received as "a call for a teacher whose credentials include experiences in and with American racism similar to those the students have already suffered."[70] Although Greenberg long suspected Bell of being the mastermind behind the student protest, this article was subdued compared to previous complaints.[71]

Tales of what exactly happened on January 5, 1983, the first day of the Greenberg/Chambers class, are a study in contrasts. Greenberg, girded to storm the beachhead, reported that "pickets

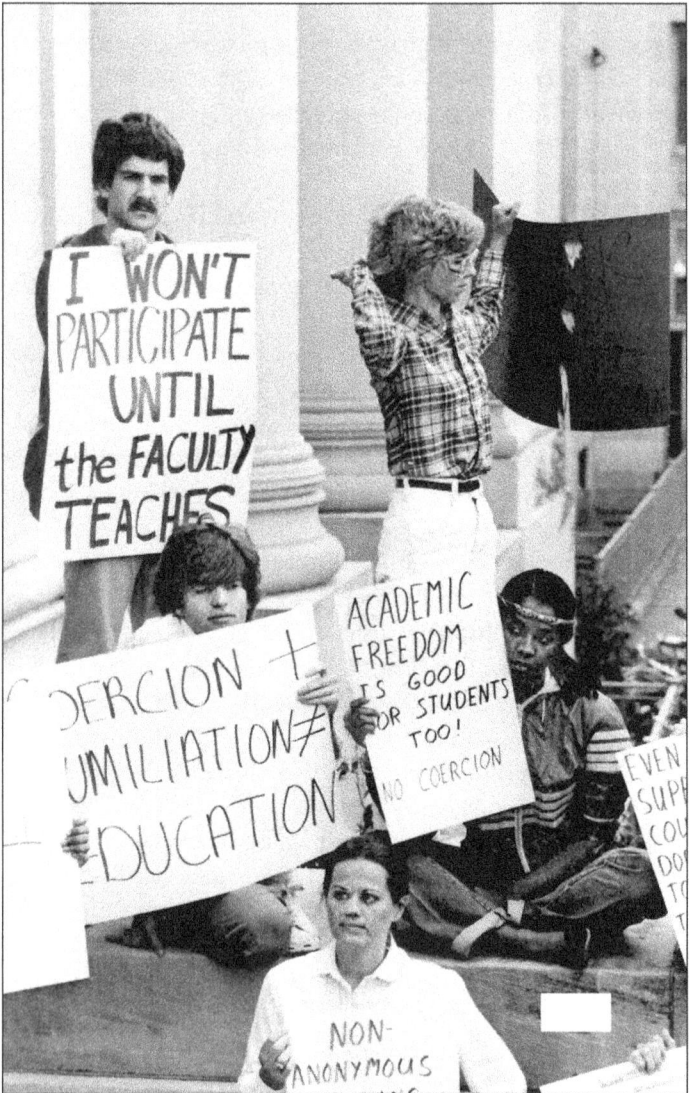

Figure 4.4. Harvard Law School student protest, 1984 Harvard
Law School yearbook. Courtesy Harvard Law School Historical &
Special Collections.

from BLSA and the [TWC] patrolled the building entrance." An associate dean "led Julius and me to the classroom through a line of chanting, sign-holding protesters." From Greenberg's vantage point, "the line quickly dwindled and disappeared," consisting "mainly of gay and lesbian students" who, he surmised, "were so marginalized that any sort of alliance was better than none."[72]

The student protester perspective is different. The coalition organized a silent vigil outside the building. Far from dwindling or disappearing, the group of about forty-five demonstrators, once the class began, made their way to Dean Vorenberg's office where Joseph Garcia, president of La Alianza, the Latina/o group within TWC, read the students' list of demands. Garcia "then proceeded to the steps of Langdell [Law Library], where he presented to reporters the TWC's demands for increased minority admissions and recruitment of minority faculty and administrators, in addition to the development of courses on minority issues."[73] The group announced their intent to organize a fourteen-week civil rights course as an alternative to the three-week Greenberg/Chambers offering. Called "Racism and American Law," it would take place the following spring term. The primary text would be Derrick Bell's *Race, Racism and American Law*. The Alternative Course was born.

As students involved with the TWC planned the Alternative Course, they enlisted help from a broad network of talented and qualified minority faculty across the nation. That network itself was a refutation of their dean's still-offensive "nameless mass of unqualified minorities" comment; it was also in the self-interest of students who wanted to expand their networks while learning about racism and civil rights litigation.[74] As Donald Tyler and Cynthia Muldrow wrote to the *New York Times* on behalf of the BLSA in 1982, the boycott was not motivated by the fact that one of the proposed teachers was white. "Rather, we are protesting the lack of good faith by the law school administration in recruiting and retaining minority tenured professors," they said. "If there is any racism at Harvard, it is on the part of that administration, whose dean expressed a preference for hiring 'an excellent white teacher' over a 'mediocre black one.'"[75]

Every organization involved in the TWC donated their speaker series funds to sponsor the lectures of prominent minority professors and practitioners; La Alianza, for instance, contributed the resources to bring Richard Delgado to campus, even sending a letter to Dean Vorenberg inviting him to Delgado's lecture. That lecture provided the basis for Delgado's influential article "The Imperial Scholar," in which he argues that white liberal civil rights scholars should make room for scholars of color. It is unlikely Dean Vorenberg would have appreciated Delgado's approach, given the context that sparked the Alternative Course in the first place. Other scholars who participated would also become central figures in CRT: Charles Lawrence, Linda S. Greene, Denise Carty-Bennia, and Neil Gotanda participated, along with student organizers like Kimberlé Crenshaw and Mari Matsuda.

As Stephanie Moore recalls, "The protest was, to this day, probably the most powerful by students at Harvard Law School." The Alternative Course provided a showcase of minority legal talent. As far as the TWC was concerned, this course was the perfect opportunity to bring these professors to the attention of the Harvard Law School hiring committee.[76] "That's how I met Linda [Greene]!" Moore fondly recalls, "and she and I became the closest of friends."[77]

At the time of the Alternative Course, Greene was associate professor of law at University of Oregon Law School, where Derrick Bell was dean. An expert in Constitutional Law, civil procedure, and employment discrimination, Greene did indeed come to the attention of the Harvard Law School hiring committee. In 1984, the Law School invited her to become the first African American woman to teach there. She left after just a year. Harvard wouldn't tenure a Black woman as a law teacher until 1998, with Lani Guinier. Also in 1984, student activism eventually resulted in the hiring of a minority faculty member who specialized in civil rights law, a promising young African American man with every establishment credential valued by Harvard Law School's august halls: Randall LeRoy Kennedy. Within the decade, Kennedy would establish himself as a central figure to the development of CRT.

Many Strands, Many Stories

The Alternative Course at Harvard Law School is, as one group of scholars put it, "a useful point to mark the genesis of Critical Race Theory." The course marked "one of the earliest attempts to bring scholars of color together to address the law's treatment of race from a self-consciously critical perspective"; it contested "the terrain and terms of dominant legal discourse" and expressed "dissatisfaction with and opposition to liberal mainstream discourses about race."[78] Other histories, including the broader story contained in this book, identify other key moments that, along with the Alternative Course, create a many-stranded braid of historical origins leading to what was eventually called CRT.

Richard Delgado, for instance, in his effort to disentangle those strands, has identified "liberal McCarthyism" as an effort to protect liberal intellectual spaces from radicalizing influence and as a significant factor contributing to the conditions that gave rise to CRT. Beginning around 1969, ideologically radical professors, "most of them young, talented, and white," were purged from Ivy League universities.[79] As post–civil rights affirmative action practices began to open doors and pathways for people of color, administrators were not eager for these future degreed professionals and leaders to "learn social analysis from far-left professors of law, history, criminology, and political science."[80] As Delgado details, "Having just lived through the turbulent sixties, these visionary figures preferred the new cohort of minorities moderate, responsible, and above all, not angry. Accordingly, the establishment removed the white radical professors in a series of tenure denials that spread across the country."[81] David Trubek, a founder of critical legal studies and eventual financial and intellectual sponsor of the 1989 inaugural CRT conference in Madison, Wisconsin, was one of these professors.[82]

Trubek first arrived at the University of Wisconsin in 1953 when the school was a hotbed of radical thought and political action— particularly among student efforts to recall US Senator Joseph McCarthy. Within this campus swirl of political activist energy,

Trubek met fellow activist-oriented student Louise Grossman. Among many individual activist efforts, the two would eventually work together on a campaign defending the academic freedom and membership list privacy of the communist-identified Labor Youth League. Their collaboration on this ultimately victorious activist experience brought Trubek and Grossman together personally.[83] They married a year later, and Trubek would follow Grossman to Yale Law School (YLS).[84] Years later, Trubek joined the faculty at YLS, where "despite his establishment credentials, [he] provoked the ire of some of the older faculty when he took part in a study group at Yale that included students Duncan Kennedy and Mark Tushnet and led, a few years later, to the formation of the Critical Legal Studies movement."[85] With that student experience at YLS, Kennedy would go on to do much the same as a tenured faculty member at Harvard Law School.[86]

By the early 1970s, Yale law students began a protest, accusing their faculty of being liberal apologists and incremental reformers of an unjust US legal system. The faculty were shocked and taken aback.

"We advocated for civil rights in the South!" some objected.

"We established the Peace Corps!" others proclaimed.

"We have proudly served in liberal administrations!" still others maintained.[87]

The students remained unimpressed and unmoved. Ever the radical activist, Trubek, along with five other young left-leaning faculty members, sided with the students.[88]

Yale, however, like many other institutions in the early 1970s, was in no hurry to host a repeat of civil rights–era protests on their campus. The thought of out-of-control white students, radicalized by their own faculty, and then a wave of minority students also influenced by these white radicals in their ranks created an impossible living situation for equilibrium-seeking establishment liberals at Yale. The Law School dean, Louis Pollak, made the institution's position clear: "Yale must train black leaders, not revolutionaries."[89]

By 1972, Trubek was denied tenure at YLS. Perhaps as fate intended, David and Louise Trubek secured positions back at their alma mater, the University of Wisconsin, setting their political compass back on Madison.

In addition to Delgado's historiographic assertion that "liberal McCarthyism" played a role in preparing the seedbed of CRT, Margaret Montoya, a 1978 graduate of Harvard Law School now retired from the University of New Mexico School of Law, places CRT within a broader sweep of social and legal developments.[90] She understands CRT as an outgrowth not only of critical legal studies but also of broader struggles for ethnic studies, LGBTQ+ rights, and second wave feminism, a clear reflection of the CRT tenet of interdisciplinarity. Moreover, she identifies at least three origin stories for CRT. Along with the "student-centered" story of the Alternative Course at Harvard Law School, Montoya highlights another student-centered story at the University of California, Berkeley. Along with Sumi Cho and Robert Westley, Montoya points out that on the heels of the Third World Strike of 1969, 31 percent of the UC Berkeley School of Law student body were "special-admissions" students resulting from new affirmative action policies. In 1988, the Boalt Coalition for Diversified Faculty succeeded in securing "an unprecedented four diversity hires out of five total hires" at the school.[91] In addition to student action, Montoya identifies a scholar-led movement in the mid-1980s focused on the uneasy relationship between the critical legal studies movement and CRT.

Linda S. Greene's participation in Harvard Law's student-organized Alternative Course was informed by her early 1970s experience as a student leader in UC Berkeley's Black Law Student Association. Because of her participation in various movements and organizing efforts, Greene has been a tireless chronicler of minority law professors' efforts to challenge what she calls "apartheid in legal education." While during the 1960s the Association of American Law Schools (AALS) allowed for a committee addressing minority concerns, "this monopoly was challenged . . . with the independent formation of the Caucus of Black Teachers in 1969 which was led by Derrick Bell of Harvard Law School and Spencer Boyer of Howard University Law School."[92] Although incorporated into the AALS in the early 1970s, law professors of color continued meeting outside the association.

Greene highlights the importance of two meetings of the AALS's Minority Law Teachers Conference, in 1983 and 1985, as vital intellectual forerunners to the founding of CRT. Many of the same people identified as CRT founders—including Mari Matsuda, Charles Lawrence, Neil Gotanda, and Greene herself— were present for both. The 1983 meeting "focused on the development of legal theory challenging the calculus of mainstream jurisprudence and its tendency to minimize or render invisible the interests and needs of minorities." The 1985 meeting, held at the University of San Francisco School of Law, synthesized those elements; it therefore constituted "a watershed event" foreshadowing "the full flower of the Critical Race Theory movement."[93]

This same period, Greene reports, saw the formation of the Northeastern Corridor, a study group of Black women law professors. Meeting initially in 1988 as an informal discussion group, they grew into an important forum "focused specifically on the legal system's marginalization of Black women's experiences."[94] Each of these efforts, Greene says, "highlighted the need to create critical space in which to develop legal theory sophisticated enough to reflect the complexity and multiplicity of minority experience."[95] The question of how to account for anti-essentialist approaches to minority experience would be the decisive factor in minority scholars' work within the critical legal studies movement and the perceived necessity of creating a separate discipline that centered stories of experiences.

A Titan Falls

Derrick Bell's difficult experience at Stanford Law School in the spring 1986 term is an often-overlooked moment within histories seeking to trace the rise of CRT.

"Professor Bell?" The administrative assistant's voice came hesitantly over the intercom. Bell was a visiting professor at Stanford Law School. His assistant was still getting used to Bell's open-door policy for students. "There's a . . . group of students here to see you."

"If I have enough chairs for them, send them right in," Bell responded. Since he had begun his teaching career, he had cultivated a student-centered approach to teaching law informed by the critical pedagogy of his one-time Harvard colleague, Paulo Freire. His approach was unconventional, but no more unconventional than the Foreword published in the *Harvard Law Review* in 1985, just a few months earlier.

When the students entered his office, Bell's welcoming smile was met with faces of sadness and rage. These representatives of the Stanford Black Law Student Association (BLSA) were arriving with bad news.

"Professor Bell, do you recall the invitation you received from Dean Ely to offer a public lecture on Constitutional Law?" Bell certainly did. He was teaching an introductory course on the topic and had interpreted the invitation as a sign of confidence from his new Stanford colleagues. "Well, they're pulling a fast one on you," one student said, shaking his head in dismay.

Bell's smile slightly faltered. "What do you mean?"

"Their invitation to you is a ruse, a sham, a *trick*," another student said, getting worked up.

Bell held up his hand, "I get the picture, I understand. What I don't understand, is *why*?"

"It's the other students," the first BLSA representative replied. "They've somehow convinced the other faculty and now the administration that you don't know how to teach Constitutional Law. That there's no way they'll get what they need from the class if you're teaching it, so they've demanded these 'enrichment lectures' as a supplement to make sure they get a 'real' education and their money's worth. It's pure racism!"

Bell's stomach dropped. For once, he didn't know what to say.[96]

Until precisely that moment, Bell had been flying high. Having secured his scholarly reputation with the Foreword and serving as dean of the University of Oregon School of Law, he had earned a visiting post at Stanford on his own merit. Oregon had been a welcome escape from the urban turmoil of Boston where his children had been caught in another round of white resistance to school desegregation, rocks being thrown at their buses.[97] But Oregon had been filled with budgetary challenges and racial dynamics; Bell's deanship ended when he resigned in protest over the faculty's decision not to hire an Asian woman, Pat Chew.[98] His resignation allowed him to accept Harvard Law School dean James Vorenberg's standing offer for a return to Cambridge.[99]

As many people in multiple-career households can attest, the timing for a cross-country move is not always the same for both partners. Jewel Hairston Bell had put down strong roots in Eugene, Oregon, where she directed the University of Oregon's Council of Minority Education, now the school's Center for Multicultural Academic Excellence. She was also on the boards of the Eugene Symphony Orchestra and the campus Interfaith Ministry.[100]

The offer to join the faculty at Stanford Law School in a short-term visiting position met several needs, allowing Bell to gracefully depart Oregon while remaining on the West Coast nearer his family. More than just convenient, Stanford was prestigious and, he had thought, friendly, with several critical legal studies (CLS) adherents (known as crits) on the faculty. Bell thought he would be spending the spring term of 1986 in paradise.

In this moment, Bell could feel it all slipping away. The BLSA members were in Bell's office to share the statement they intended to read before the first of these "enrichment lectures." The assessment was sharp: "It is clear to us that one of the primary motivations for these lectures is a hostile and racist response to the teaching style of Professor Derrick Bell. . . . That first year law students could pass judgment on such an eminent scholar, when the teaching style of those of similar or lesser achievements goes unquestioned, leads us to believe that the students' response is racially motivated."[101] The situation was compounded further when the administration of Stanford Law complied with student complaints. The BLSA statement succeeded in scuttling the entire lecture series.

For Bell, however, this was a devastating professional blow. His own invitation to participate in the lecture series, far from an expression of confidence, was a ruse designed to hide a wide-ranging conspiracy against his perceived shortcomings. "I was totally unaware of the project's real purpose until members of [the BLSA] came to my office and shared with me the protest statement they planned to read before the first lecture," Bell wrote in an opinion column for Stanford's law student newspaper later that same term:

> Even some weeks after the event, I am unable to rationally express the range of my feelings—from abject humiliation to absolute outrage. Here were black students, some of whom had hailed my visit as a real gain for them, forced to bring me the news that even as I taught my courses, walked through the halls, attended meetings, and generally participated in the life of this community, a large percentage of students knew that the administration had approved a program organized and specifically designed to compensate for student-reported teaching inadequacies. It was by a considerable margin, the worst moment of my professional life.[102]

Student complaints were focused on Bell's teaching style rather than substance. In a *Washington Post* story on the controversy, Jack Friedenthal, a Stanford Law associate dean at the time, while disavowing any institutional responsibility for the lecture series, recalled "'widespread student complaints' about Bell's teaching style" that he had brought to Bell's attention.[103] Curiously, the scholarly content of Bell's course was no different than other sections being taught the same term. They were all using the same textbook.[104] The difference was that instead of rearranging the book's contents to get to the doctrinal principles informing contemporary constitutional interpretation, Bell began with the historical context of the document's framing. As Richard Delgado later recalled, Bell emphasized "the Slavery Compromises—six provisions, still in the document, which guaranteed the continuation of the institution of slavery," showing "how those clauses shaped the American legal system during its formative years, leaving traces even today."[105]

Bell's teaching style that term was no doubt shaped by the research he had conducted to provide the basis of his chronicle of Geneva Crenshaw's time-traveling disruption of the Constitutional Convention, a story-based exposé of those very same compromises.[106] Mark Savage, a student who participated in the class, reported that "on the second day of class . . . he placed us in the role of Supreme Court justices" while Bell, as counsel for Maryland, "reargued *McCulloch v. Maryland*," an 1819 decision defining the scope of federal and state authority. Savage, in contrast to those who complained, "thought this exercise . . . a brilliant pedagogical tool."[107]

Bell could have chosen to frame his humiliating experience at Stanford as little more than an embarrassing personal defeat. As Delgado later observed, anyone else "might have felt like hiding under a rock."[108] Instead, Bell broadcast the news. As he shared in a September 1986 letter to Stanford Law professor Jerry Lopez, "Copies of my Stanford article have been sent to all law school deans under a cover letter signed by 22 minority law teachers."[109] The cover letter urged that Bell's article be posted for all faculty to see and urged discussion concerning the treatment of minority faculty members. The outpouring of response from law school deans throughout the United States and fellow minority law professors is preserved in Bell's archive.[110]

That wasn't all. Over the summer months, before Bell moved back to Cambridge, a small group of minority law professors, including Richard Delgado and Charles Lawrence, met with Bell at his home in Eugene. In an interview, Delgado recalls Bell as "down and vulnerable." They went to Eugene to help "rescue the fallen icon, the fallen giant."[111] As minority law professors, they understood that Bell's experience was proof that they, too, were vulnerable: "Distressed over what had happened to him at Stanford, we wondered, if it could happen to Bell, could it not happen to all of us?" They had all heard anecdotal reports of "rudeness, disrespect, even denials of tenure to well qualified professors of color around the nation."[112] To move beyond anecdotal accounts, they needed data. The result of that insight was a questionnaire, developed by Bell and Delgado, sent to all minority law professors in the United States. Results of that survey, along with insights from over fifty interviews, were published as "The Bell-Delgado Survey" in 1989.[113]

Derrick Bell's terrible experience in the spring 1986 term at Stanford Law School sparked a chain of events leading to the creation of the distinct academic discipline and movement of CRT. The meeting in Eugene sparked a broad effort, still active when José Bracamonte, Richard Delgado, and Gerald Torres offered a statement at the January 1987 CLS annual meeting. This statement called attention to racially insulting language in the group's newsletter and demanded greater space to discuss matters related to race and racism.[114] The content of Delgado's groundbreaking 1989 article, "Storytelling for Oppositionists and Others," which provided both theory and method for critical race counterstory, was directly informed by interviews he conducted to provide qualitative data to supplement "The Bell-Delgado Survey."[115] As we will see, the distinction between critical legal studies and what would be called CRT hinges primarily on CRT's tenet of the centrality of experiential knowledge and/or unique voices of color. Bell's distinct experience at Stanford turned out to be a catalyst few could have predicted.

Racial Consciousness and Critical Legal Studies

"Well, write it then!" Richard Delgado said in exasperation. His younger conversation partner, Randall Kennedy, was no less frustrated.

Delgado and Kennedy were in Los Angeles participating in the January 1987 conference of the CLS movement. Kennedy had joined the Harvard Law School faculty in 1984, in the wake of student agitation to hire a Black scholar likely to be granted tenure. Unlike his predecessor Derrick Bell, Kennedy had the highest of academic credentials: a Princeton undergraduate degree, selection as a Rhodes Scholar, a law degree from Yale, and a Supreme Court clerkship under Thurgood Marshall. He had inherited Bell's course on civil rights law, the one that caused all the furor back in 1983. As Kennedy was quick to point out, he and Bell, though both Black men, were not the same—exemplifying CRT's anti-essentialism.

This 1987 CLS gathering, happening less than a year after Bell's unfortunate experience at Stanford, was the first to focus primarily on the question of race and racism. By the mid-1980s, a small group of legal scholars of color—Bell, Delgado, and Kennedy, among others—had begun regularly attending gatherings associated with CLS. These scholars of color were in basic agreement with CLS's intellectual trends and commitments, including the assertion that the making and interpretation of law can never be considered apart from social concerns. By extension, lawmaking and legal interpretation should always engage the tools of social scientific analysis. Such progressive, leftist commitments provided safe harbor for the growing number of legal scholars of color.

Although CLS-affiliated "crits" had created a progressive intellectual and political space where they could temporarily escape the stodgy law schools where most of them were employed, "crits of color" weren't always comfortable in what was, despite good intentions, still a white-dominated space. That discomfort was compounded for a scholar like Randall Kennedy who didn't identify with the scholarly and political agenda emerging from other crits of color.

"I read 'Imperial Scholar,'" Kennedy challenged Delgado in the hallway. "It's good, but there's a loophole." The article, a component of Delgado's contribution to the Alternative Course at Harvard, eventually published in 1984, criticized white, male legal scholars working on civil rights for mostly citing the work of other white, male scholars.[116] In addition to calling for minority theorists to produce more scholarship, Delgado controversially called for "white liberal authors who write in the field of civil rights to redirect their efforts," to "stand aside," making room for emerging minority scholars.[117]

Kennedy kept up his challenge to Delgado. "Do you somehow believe that, at least with respect to issues involving race relations, there is no need to argue on behalf of the merit of work done by scholars of color? Is their work in this area . . . self-evidently entitled to recognition?" Kennedy didn't believe one could "make an effective argument that work by academics of color is being treated in a racially invidious manner without taking the time, energy, and risk of elaborating in detail the substantive merits of that scholarship in comparison with that produced by white competitors."[118]

"Maybe you're right," Delgado responded.

"I *am* right! Admit you're wrong!"

"Fine," Delgado finally said. "Randy, if you found something wrong with 'Imperial Scholar,' you should write your own."[119] So the younger scholar did.

A conversation about race had been brewing within CLS, eventually leading the "race crits" to organize their own space. As a group of founding CRT scholars put it, "While we shared with [CLS] crits the belief that legal consciousness functioned to legitimize social power in the United States, race crits also understood that race and racism likewise functioned as central pillars of hegemonic power." Up to that point, CLS, founded and led primarily by white men, had not "developed and incorporated a critique of racial power into their analysis." As a result, CLS's "practices, politics and theories regarding race" responded inadequately to the legal and theoretical concerns expressed by emerging race crits.[120]

Discussion about race within the CLS sphere began in earnest during the group's 1985 conference where feminist crits, initiated by Regina Austin, invited scholars of color to facilitate several discussions about race and racism.[121] Those conversations intensified during the January 1987 CLS workshop titled "Sounds of Silence." That gathering centered conversation on the notion of "rights" in legal discourse. CLS contributors had argued that rights, as with other aspects of law, were little more than a validation of current social structure. While "crits of color" fully understood the academic critique, these ideas presented "another dimension of the failure of CLS to reflect the lived experience of people of color."[122] Experiences of racial subordination and keen, embodied awareness of long struggles to transform society in the quest to gain rights appeared increasingly incompatible, academic insights aside, with CLS trajectories.

The 1987 conference provided the first opportunity for race-crits to shape the center of the CLS conversation. As Charles Lawrence recalled a decade after the event, the racial theme of the conference attracted the participation of more crits of color. "The organizers of the conference had decided that the colored people and white folks should meet in separate 'minority' and 'non-minority' caucuses for the opening evening session," and Kimberlé Crenshaw, then in her first year teaching law, asked Lawrence to chair the "colored caucus." While most of that group was Black, Lawrence noted that "the clear and vibrant voices of Native, Latino, and Asian American brothers and sisters presaged the considerable gifts and important work that they represent among us today."[123] A significant plenary panel discussion, including contributions from Harlan L. Dalton, Richard Delgado, Mari Matsuda, and Patricia J. Williams, took on the dominant CLS conception of rights within legal theory.[124] As Crenshaw recalls, the subsequent debate "found its way into off-stage exchanges where the critique of rights sometimes struck CRT folks as manifesting a certain naiveté about race, and the defense of rights struck some CLS types as a manifestation of naiveté about law."[125]

The distinctive nature of what would soon be called critical race theory was beginning to form. Academic rejection of the movement's foundational tenets—particularly CRT's challenge to the dominant ideology of colorblind liberalism—was being articulated at the same time. In addition to critiquing, in side conversations, Delgado's "Imperial Scholar," Randall Kennedy responded publicly to the plenary presentations from Dalton, Delgado, Matsuda, and Williams with "his impression that the absence of much of minority scholarship was attributable to its poor quality and to the lack of productivity of minority scholars. Scholars of color were urged to stop complaining and simply to write." This perspective, which for Crenshaw and others "provides one of the clearest points of demarcation between critical and liberal discourses," was eventually published as Kennedy's 1989 article, "Racial Critiques of Legal Academia," the taproot of liberal critiques of CRT to this day.[126]

5

Open Season

A Movement Gains a Name

CRT TENETS: Challenge to Dominant Ideologies; Centrality of Experiential Knowledge and/or Unique Voices of Color; Permanence of Race and Racism; Interest Convergence

The Paper Napkin

"I still don't think the 'New Developments' tag fully captures our aim," Kimberlé Crenshaw said, a skeptical look on her face.[1] "I think it sounds generic. We should go for something more . . ."—she thought for a moment—"provocatively substantive," she finished contentedly.[2]

The three others chuckled at her bravado. Crenshaw was joined by Neil Gotanda, whom she met years ago through the Harvard Law School Alternative Course, and current Wisconsin Hastie fellows Stephanie L. Phillips and Teresa "Teri" Miller.[3] It was early in 1989, and this particularly miserable winter in Madison, Wisconsin, seemed like it would never end.[4] Thoughts of gathering a motley crew of race-crits to the shores of Lake Mendota that July sounded glorious and too far in the distant future.[5]

"What's the full title again? Maybe it'll help if we all see it written out," Gotanda suggested.

Phillips began scribbling on her yellow legal pad—"New Developments in Race and Legal Theory"—and then swiveled it around so the group could take a look.[6]

"Hm," they each said, looking thoughtful.

"May I?" asked Crenshaw, gesturing toward Phillips's notepad. Phillips, nodding her assent, pushed the pad across to Crenshaw.

"So, what we know," Crenshaw began, "is that we want to at-tract a specific audience—other misfits if you will—who are look-ing for a *critical* space where *race* is the focus . . ."

"But also, a *race* space where *critical* themes are central," Miller finished.[7]

"Yes, exactly," Crenshaw affirmed, nodding and smiling at Miller.

"Okay, I'm hearing critical and race repeated in what the two of you are saying," said Gotanda, "so perhaps write those two words down?"

"Right," said Crenshaw, quickly inscribing the two words, try-ing them out first as:

"race critical," then "critical race," and then a few "???".

"I guess what remains foremost on my mind is, what is that substantive 'thing' that holds us together as a group?" Crenshaw asked. "What constitutes our distinct contribution to the dis-course on race and the law?"[8]

"The critique of liberalism?" Miller suggested.

"CLS does that as well," Crenshaw responded, shaking her head.

"The critique of liberalism plus race theory?" Phillips offered.

"But it's more, something more . . ." Crenshaw said, looking pensive.

"It's the lived experience," Gotanda said matter-of-factly. Miller, Phillips, and Crenshaw all looked at him, as if waiting for him to go on, so he did.[9]

"Sometimes those who love theory get very lost in the clouds of it and seem to forget theory comes from somewhere! It comes from people, the lives we live, the people we meet, the people we help, the people we fight for and fight with. Theory comes from practice. And I think if there is anything that sets what we do apart from what everyone else does, it's our valuing of the lived experience of people of color. Our belief is that our theories come from this experience, not the other way around."[10]

"Well, Neil," Crenshaw said, clearly impressed, "what I heard you say over and over again is the term 'theory,' but theory in the way *we* understand it."

Gotanda smiled and nodded. "Yes. I suggest you write that down." Crenshaw did.[11]

Why Wisconsin?

The July 1989 conference was something new. Legal scholars of color had long been organizing in distinct spaces apart from their white colleagues (see chapter 4). Now, all of those efforts were coming to a head, especially in the possibility of convening race-crits outside the sometimes strained relationship with other CLS-affiliated crits. The 1980s had made it clear that race—specifically, the lived experience of race—needed to be understood as a decisive factor in the formation of legal theory. Ever since the Supreme Court's *Bakke* decision in 1978 had used a colorblind principle to argue that race-based admissions and hiring practices violated the Civil Rights Act of 1964, civil rights laws had been under siege during the Reagan and Bush administrations. When that societal crisis was compounded by Derrick Bell's treatment at Stanford Law School in 1986, race-crits were reenergized. Something new was brewing. As Charles Lawrence recalled in 1997, "Critical Race Theory was born as part of the resistance to retrenchment."[12]

David Trubek, one of the founders of the critical legal studies (CLS) movement, was in many ways a direct participant in the emergence of CRT. As a faculty member and director of the Institute of Legal Studies at Wisconsin, Trubek "provided intellectual, financial, and administrative support for the famous 1989 lakeside conference that launched CRT as a project in its own right."[13] His account, however, differs from Crenshaw's, specifically with her understanding of the necessity of a split from CLS.

By 1989, as Richard Delgado recounts in "Liberal McCarthyism and the Origins of Critical Race Theory," Trubek had been pushed out of Yale Law School in 1973 and welcomed as a professor of law at the University of Wisconsin. He had also been a visiting professor at Harvard Law School when another CLS-related tenure controversy erupted, leading in 1987 to yet another Derrick

Bell protest.[14] Trubek, a visiting professor, was considered for a permanent appointment at Harvard Law School along with an assistant professor, Clare Dalton. Although the faculty rejected Dalton's application for tenure, Trubek's application was approved, only to be overruled by Harvard's president, Derek Bok. Bok had been dean of the Law School when Derrick Bell was first hired in 1969.[15]

In contrast to Harvard Law School, which is about as mainstream and establishment-oriented as one can get, Trubek says, "It was no accident that CRT found its first institutional support in Madison. At least since the 1930s, the University of Wisconsin Law School had followed a different path." In addition to the university's radical tradition—which Trubek and his spouse, Louise Grossman Trubek, had engaged to the fullest as undergraduate students in the 1950s—"Wisconsin also had a tradition of supporting minority legal scholars," including establishing "the Hastie Fellowship in 1973 to support minority scholars who wished to enter law teaching" and of recruiting "minority scholars for the faculty."[16] The Hastie Fellowship was named in honor of William H. Hastie, the first Black US federal judge, former governor of the US Virgin Islands, and friend of Thurgood Marshall who Derrick Bell named as a hero in his 1954 application essay for the University of Pittsburgh School of Law. Two of those fellows, Kimberlé Crenshaw and Stephanie Phillips, planned the 1989 conference with support from Trubek and minority professors, including Richard Delgado.

Trubek's second objection is to Crenshaw's characterization of CLS as an insufficiently race-conscious foil against which CRT had to be developed. "To suggest that CLS was just a group of white males who saw class as the sole source of oppression in the United States and rebuffed minority scholars' efforts to include race as an independent factor would do an injustice to people like Alan Freeman, Karl Klare, Richard Abel, Mark Tushnet, and a host of others," Trubek adds. To do so "would run the risk of stereotyping CLS as vulgar Marxism—that coding was used by CLS's enemies to justify repressive actions and I know Crenshaw does not wish to do that."[17] Indeed, contemporary enemies of

CRT have sought to paint both movements with that same crude brush, impugning CRT through its association with CLS.[18] People who wish to promote CRT, Trubek pleads, should not do so at the cost of denigrating CLS since we all need allies; CRT should not miss the opportunity to "join with other groups to create wider emancipatory networks."[19] It was no accident that the first critical race theory workshop was held under the auspices of the University of Wisconsin School of Law.

Parting of the Paths

Richard Delgado agrees with Trubek that Wisconsin, "a center of left academic legal thought," was "a logical site" for the first CRT conference, both because of the Institute for Legal Studies and the Hastie Fellowship program: "We gathered at that convent for two and a half days, around a table in an austere room with stained glass windows and crucifixes here and there . . . and worked out a set of principles. Then we went our separate ways."[20]

As an academic discipline, critical race theory finds coherence through sets of tenets. The lists, however, can be quite different depending on which scholar you are consulting. As you now know, we have chosen to work with a set of nine (see Appendix 3). As a movement, critical race theory is even more diverse. In addition to various modes of expression in the field of legal studies (ranging from Bell's science fiction narratives, to Delgado's *Rodrigo Chronicles*, to the rigorously theoretical work of Kimberlé Crenshaw), CRT branched out beyond this founding meeting into a variety of academic fields. Although many of the CRT founders had long been engaged in interdisciplinary study and collaboration, the naming and defining of CRT allowed its insights and tenets to be taken up in many disciplines within education, the social sciences, and the humanities.

The academic field of education has been a major space for the uptake of critical race theory. Again, the University of Wisconsin, through the work of Gloria Ladson-Billings and William F. Tate, played a central role. At the 1994 American Educational Research

Association meeting, Ladson-Billings and Tate's presentation identified the tenets of CRT's relevance to the study of race and racism in education. They followed up with a landmark 1995 essay, "Toward a Critical Race Theory of Education," and have remained at the "forefront of engaging CRT and pushing its boundaries in education."[21] In 1993, in the East Los Angeles College Library, Daniel G. Solórzano came across Peter Monaghan's *Chronicle of Higher Education* article "'Critical Race Theory' Questions Role of Legal Doctrine in Racial Inequality."[22] This work introduced Solórzano to the emerging field, frameworks, and leading legal scholars such as Derrick Bell, Richard Delgado, Linda Greene, Lani Guinier, Mari Matsuda, and Patricia Williams. Solórzano "put the CRT literature in conversation with the fields of Race, Ethnic, and Gender Studies and the work of Paulo Freire" to examine educational research and praxis and has blazed the CRT in Education trail in California ever since.[23]

Most CRT is found within the pages of law reviews and other academic journals. One of the highest profile expressions of CRT with opportunities for engagement with the broader public is the CRT Summer School organized by the African American Policy Forum, a nonprofit organization cofounded in 1996 by Kimberlé Crenshaw and Vassar professor Luke Charles Harris. Each year, the summer school brings together a broadly interdisciplinary array of scholars and activists, showcasing the breadth of what CRT has become since its branding in 1989.

Contemporary Attacks on CRT

The academic world of CRT was caught flat-footed when political controversy about the movement broke suddenly in 2020. Until then, debate surrounding CRT had been mostly theoretical, almost philosophical. The eruption of political controversy—CRT was suddenly a kitchen-table issue—made things more visceral. While something was clearly at stake, it wasn't a debate, since the people leading the attack were loudly exclaiming that they were operating in bad faith.

On March 12, 2022, president Trump told South Carolina rallygoers that they must "lay down their very lives to defend their country" against CRT.[24] This battle cry extended a culture war theme he had launched in September 2020 with Executive Order 13950, "Combating Race and Sex Stereotyping."[25] Until the Biden administration overturned the order in January 2021, it severely limited diversity, equity, and inclusion efforts throughout the US government. The oft-named target of the executive order was a new/old bogeyman of American racial ideology—CRT. According to the UCLA Law School's CRT Forward Tracking Project, from September 2020 to the time of this writing (November 2024), a total of 247 local, state, and federal government entities across the nation have introduced 861 anti-CRT bills, resolutions, executive orders, opinion letters, statements, and other measures.[26]

Trump's ongoing attack on CRT was fueled by conservative media, especially Fox News, following the May 2020 police murder of George Floyd in Minneapolis along with the resulting street protests calling for structural changes to American society.[27] In his post-administration memoir, Trump's former chief of staff, Mark Meadows, detailed how Executive Order 13950 resulted from a September 1, 2020, *Tucker Carlson Tonight* appearance by right-wing media strategist Christopher Rufo. Before becoming engrained with the DeSantis political machine in Florida, Rufo was part of several thinktank operations like the Heritage Foundation and the smaller Manhattan Institute.[28]

CRT was such a problem, Rufo insisted on Carlson's show, that the president should "immediately issue" an "executive order and stamp out this destructive, divisive, pseudoscientific ideology at its root."[29] President Trump took note. The next morning, Meadows got Rufo on the phone. "In a few days," Meadows later recalled, Rufo was "flying out to Washington to help us fine-tune the wording, along with a few other respected scholars and journalists. It would be done and ready to sign by the end of September."[30]

In March 2021, Rufo launched a tweet that reverberated throughout the CRT world: "We have successfully frozen their brand—'critical race theory'—into the public conversation and are steadily driving up negative perceptions. We will eventually turn it toxic, as we put all the various cultural insanities under that brand category."[31] He continued in an additional tweet, saying, "The goal is to have the public read something crazy in the newspaper and immediately think 'critical race theory.' We have decodified the term and will recodify it to annex the entire range of cultural constructions that are unpopular with Americans."[32] The strategic playbook revealed in those tweets would be enacted over the coming months.

Rufo's tweet heard 'round the CRT world was, in fact, a response to someone else, a video blogger named James Lindsay. @RealChrisRufo was responding to @ConceptualJames in an effort to build an alliance. Earlier that day, Lindsay had tweeted "Critical Race Theory is falling. It's end, but not THE end, is coming."[33] Rufo's responses show his gameplan for attacking CRT; they are, at the same time, an intellectual courting ritual, a Twitter-bro mating dance. By August 2021, Rufo and Lindsay appeared together on right-wing podcast conversations. "James and I have been really tag-teaming on this because James is really the theory expert," Rufo said. "I mean James is an encyclopedia of theory connecting all the dots laying out the case making the kind of argument, creating this great content to guide all of us into this world."[34]

After earning his PhD in mathematics at the University of Tennessee, Lindsay published several books supporting the "new atheism" movement and then founded a business combining martial arts and massage therapy.[35] Along the way, Lindsay partnered with Helen Pluckrose and Peter Boghossian to perpetrate the 2018–19 "grievance studies affair," a bad-faith effort intended to satirize and ridicule what they perceived as the shortcomings of social science research.[36] In 2020, Pluckrose and Lindsay published *Cynical Theories*, an attack on the intellectual foundations of the contemporary academy, including postmodernism and critical theory.[37] Pluckrose and Lindsay devote an entire chapter to CRT and intersectionality. This is where, according to Rufo, Lindsay starts proving himself "an encyclopedia of theory connecting all the dots."[38]

So what dots are connected? CRT and intersectionality are addressed in the fifth chapter of *Cynical Theories*. Up to this point, Pluckrose and Lindsay have sought to delegitimize their construction of "postmodern" philosophy and the "applied postmodernism" manifested in (again, their constructions of) various fields of academic critical theory. Because in this telling, all critical theory has origins in Marxism, these theories all intend the revolutionary overthrow of the liberal social order and must be resisted. The analysis is remarkably superficial. Focusing on the "critical" in critical race theory to sum up the academic content of the movement, they suggest that "the word critical here means that its intention and methods are specifically geared toward identifying and exposing problems in order to facilitate revolutionary political change." To address forms of racism subtler than Bull Connor's firehoses, CRT practitioners, according to Lindsay and Pluckrose, "turned to the tools of cultural criticism that were ascendant at the time. This meant adopting critical approaches and, eventually, Theory."[39] By this point in the book, that observation is meant to elicit for readers a dramatic soap opera villain soundtrack. In the same way, CRT's signature critique of liberalism and colorblindness is indicted as "a form of radicalism" indicating its "illiberal nature."

In addition to identifying Patricia Williams and Kimberlé Crenshaw as problematically feminist postmodernists, one of Pluckrose and Lindsay's chief take-aways from their read of CRT is that "one could be easily forgiven . . . for thinking that critical race Theory sounds rather racist itself, in ascribing profound failures of morals and character to white people (as consequences of being white in a white-dominant society)."[40] In other words, they simplistically accuse CRT of the "reverse racism" decried by white Americans since the Supreme Court's *Bakke* decision in 1978.

Their desire? A re-instantiation of colorblind liberalism. In a manner familiar to any race-crit, they suggest that "liberal, egalitarian approaches" embedded in "universal human rights" and "civil rights movements" provide "an achievable goal for the well-meaning liberal individual: treat[ing] people equally regardless of their identity." CRT, on the other hand, "puts social significance back into racial categories and inflames racism" while accepting the "unique voice and . . . counternarrative" of marginalized communities that undoes objective knowledge. The result is "an obsessive focus on race" that "can lead to mob outrage and public shamings" and therefore "is not likely to end well . . . for minority groups [or] for social cohesion more broadly."[41] For Lindsay and Pluckrose, therefore, CRT (along with all forms of scholarship in their broad net of "critical theory") must be understood as a threat to the Western, liberal social order. In this construction, CRT is not merely a competing analytical framework—it is an enemy to be defeated.

By the middle of 2021, school board meetings across the United States were becoming hotbeds of debate over CRT. Equipped with Lindsay's mishmash of pseudo-intellectual misreadings of CRT and a tendency to confuse CRT with any institutional effort to promote diversity, equity, and inclusion, opponents were resourced by right-wing thinktanks while everyone else was left confused.[42] Disinformation crafted by Rufo was at the center of the effort.

In October 2021, CNN covered a school board meeting in Douglas County, Nevada. There, they encountered Bob Russo, who was speaking at his third school board meeting in eight days. "I don't know about you, but I don't want Marxist blood in this country," Russo said to applause from other meeting attendees. Speaking to journalists after the meeting, Russo, a sixty-eight-year-old retiree with no children in local districts, shared why he was speaking out: "I'm concerned about kids being taught theories, ideologies that are going to divide them and set them apart from each other. . . . . I'm concerned about our freedom."[43]

How surprised might Bob Russo be that Derrick Bell, the intellectual godfather of CRT, was a US Air Force veteran, lifelong Christian, and committed family man equally committed to freedom?[44] How surprised might he be to learn that CRT's intellectual foundations are more honestly located in Black and Asian and American Indian liberationist thought than in anything that might have come from Europe? CRT might still spark his concern. But at least that concern would be based on a truth-ful presentation of the movement's histories and commitments rather than the aggressively simple-minded red-baiting of a by-gone American era.

The Obama Factor

CRT and its central founding figure, Derrick Bell, are no strangers to bad-faith arguments in the service of partisan political goals. In 2012, in the midst of President Barack Obama's reelection cam-paign, *Breitbart News* released a video of a 1991 demonstration at Harvard Law School in which a young Barack Obama introduces Bell, encouraging the crowd to "open up your hearts and your minds to the words of Professor Derrick Bell."[45] *Breitbart*, soon joined by Sean Hannity on *Fox News*, sought to discredit Obama through his association with Bell, who had died the year before, in the same way the duo had attempted to harm Obama's first-term candidacy through association with the Rev. Jeremiah Wright.[46] Both Black intellectual leaders—characterized as "radical"—had supposedly taught the impressionable young Obama to "hate America."[47]

The bad-faith argument put forth by white conservative media outlets *Breitbart* and *Fox* was supplemented by the one-man smear campaign long perpetrated by Black conservative economist and political commentator Thomas Sowell. In 1990, in the context of defending Bell's Harvard Law colleague Randall Kennedy against what he perceived to be unfair attacks, Sow-ell had compared Bell to Hitler.[48] In 2012, Sowell was deployed by Hannity to further discredit the recently deceased Bell. Bell himself had long reflected on the fact that his offer to join the Harvard Law faculty in 1969 came in the wake of societal upheav-als following the April 1968 assassination of Martin Luther King Jr. Because of this context, he knew that the offer reflected more than his abilities alone: "For me to go to that position and think that it was simply my talents and not the circumstances would be crazy."[49] When compounded with Bell's sense that "those with substantial litigation experience are looked upon with suspicion," he forthrightly shared that he sometimes struggled with "feelings of inadequacy."[50] For Hannity's audience, Sowell in 2012 disingenuously twisted these words to suggest that Bell knew being appointed "a professor at the Harvard Law School . . . was not something that he merited."[51]

As it turns out, Derrick Bell did (at least initially) influence Barack Obama. In a letter to Bell dated February 28, 1990, a newly elected President Obama—of the *Harvard Law Review*—writes:

> I have not yet had the opportunity to work with you directly (I'm counting on getting into Civil Rights at the Crossroad next year!), but your presence here on campus, your insights at Saturday School, your insistence on speaking truth in a place that does not always place a premium on truth, all of this has been of enormous importance to me during the past year and a half. Indeed, I remember your comments to myself and other insecure [first-years] during our orientation last year; your honesty about the problems at Harvard, but also your belief in our capacity to get something out of the place, told me then and there, on that first day, that I had made a good decision in coming here.
>
> I may be getting my 15 minutes worth of attention, but it is the far more substantial struggle that you have carried on that deserves the accolades. I hope I can keep struggling, wherever I end up, with as much dignity and righteous anger.
> Sincerely,
> Barack Obama
> President[52]

When Obama ascended to the presidency of the United States in 2008, Bell was elated at witnessing this historic triumph.

Shortly after Obama's 2009 inauguration, Bell gave a speech to Yale Law School's Black Law Student Association. There, he shared his joy in having lived to see a day he thought he would never see, though tempered with his signature realism and his

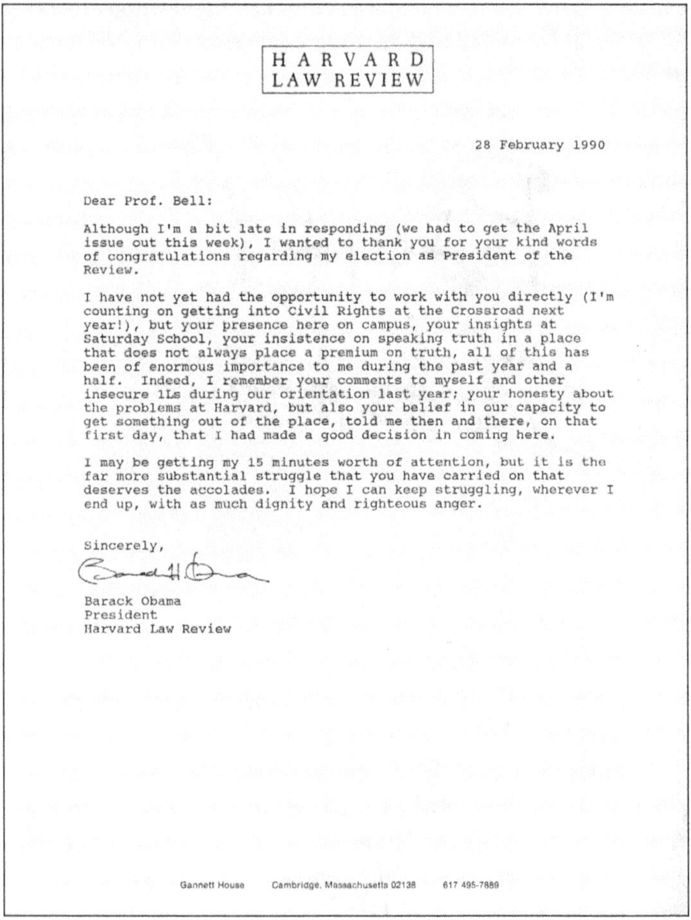

Figure 5.1. Letter from Barack Obama to Derrick Bell, February 28, 1990.
NYU Archive.

awareness of racial interest convergence. "We should not forget
that Obama won only 43 percent of the white vote, even though
he was the much superior candidate . . . competing against a party
(the Republicans) that had left the country in shambles," Bell
wrote. Already in those early months, signs of racial retrenchment

were apparent: "Republicans are trying hard to rebuild the old racial divide-and-conquer strategy. The tactics of division barely masking racism have been successful for hundreds of years."[53]

In the same article, Bell points readers to Ralph Bunche, one of the three Black exemplars he named in his 1954 law school application essay. Bell quotes at length from a 1935 essay from Bunche seeking, in line with W. E. B. Du Bois, to persuade the NAACP to pursue economic development strategies alongside litigation toward full civil liberties. Mark Tushnet summarized this consequential debate in the early years of the NAACP as being between "autonomous legalism" and "economic instrumentalism." Those who preferred the former thought "the expressed norms of fairness embodied in American law could, at least occasionally, be employed with significant effect to remedy racial segregation." The latter group, represented by Du Bois and Bunche, argued that "litigation was likely to be futile unless it was preceded by alteration in the distribution of power and, ultimately, of wealth."[54]

Bunche, in the article Bell cites when seeking to contextualize Obama's presidential victory, is eerily prophetic of key insights of both CLS and CRT when he warns that "instruments of the state are merely the reflections of the political and economic ideology of the dominant group, that the political arm of the state cannot be divorced from its prevailing economic structure, whose servant it must inevitably be." Thus, even while all people of color in the United States might wish to "quaff the full draught of eighteenth-century democratic liberalism," Bunche urged civil rights advocates not to ignore "the quite significant fact that the Constitution is a very flexible instrument and that, in the nature of things, it cannot be anything more than the controlling elements in the American society wish it to be."[55] Litigation is limited, Bunche argues in a way that presages Bell's own tenet of the permanence of race and racism, since "the Supreme Court can effect no revolutionary changes in the economic order" that "fix[es] the Negro in his disadvantaged position."[56] Instead of focusing solely on civil rights lawsuits that, while achieving "a minor and too often illusory victory now and then, are essentially inefficacious in the

long run," Bunche advocated for a non-idealistic, realist strategy focused on "improvement in the condition of the masses of
any American minority group" alongside "the betterment of the
masses of the dominant group. Their basic interests are identical
and so must be their programs and tactics."[57] As Tushnet summarized Bunche's point, "Black progress depended on the betterment of, and alliances with, the white working class."[58] To put it
even more directly, if racism is an elaborate cover for economic
competition, the issue of race will not be dealt with effectively
without tending to economic realities for the whole of society.

Bell understood that in the 1930s, the NAACP chose to eschew
any appearance of connection with Black economic radicals.[59] The
"full draught of eighteenth-century democratic liberalism," which
Bunche saw Blacks in the United States being forced to drink in one
gulp, included unquestioning embrace of free-market capitalism.
In this way, Ralph Bunche himself exemplified the CRT tenet of
challenging dominant ideologies. In this same tradition, President
Obama, despite suspicions to the contrary, never opened the US
economic system to any serious critique. Rather than repudiating
Derrick Bell as he had done with his former pastor, Obama has instead virtually ignored Bell's existence. Although Obama included
excerpts from Bell's *Race, Racism and American Law* casebook—
the basis of the Alternative Course at Harvard Law School—as
part of his "Current Issues in Racism and the Law" course offered
in spring 1994 at the University of Chicago Law School, he makes
no mention of Bell in any of his memoirs or other public writings.
The long reach of "liberal McCarthyism"—the always coercive,
sometimes violent effort to enforce, and sometimes redefine, the
boundaries of thinkable thought—continues its long career.

Keeping Bell in Mind

By fall 1988, Bell offered an elective seminar to Harvard Law
students called "Civil Rights at the Crossroads." Inspired by
Paulo Freire's teaching approaches, Bell co-taught and even
co-published an article about the course with Tracy Higgins

Fordham and Sung-Hee Suh: "Racial Reflections: Dialogues in the Direction of Liberation."[60] This student-centered essay, documenting the details of the course, also features excerpted work of many students enrolled that term. One of these students is now American financier and brief White House director of communications for the Trump administration, Anthony Scaramucci.[61]

Although Scaramucci earned his law degree at Harvard Law School, there are no law libraries with the name Scaramucci on them. He was no "legacy" admit. A self-described "Rockefeller Republican," he first registered for the party on the advice of his father, a proud union man who voted Republican because Joseph M. Margiotta controlled the unions in their Long Island, New York, county. As his dad reasoned, Republicans were helping him with his wages, so he voted with his pocket. It was that simple. Scaramucci worked in his uncle's motorcycle repair shop before attending Tufts University as an undergraduate, and he then earned a spot at Harvard Law in the late 1980s.[62]

"He had an aura about him . . . a pragmatism," Scaramucci said, recalling the lasting impression Derrick Bell left on him. This led Bell to be "honest to a fault," Scaramucci continued.[63] "He was a good man. I loved him."[64] Scaramucci endured countless anti-Italian American stereotypes and insults throughout his life, from his native Long Island to the halls of the White House: "Jersey Shore cast member in the White House, Tony Soprano on the Hudson/Potomac, and mob boss."[65] Scaramucci, young and financially strapped, was impressed when Bell readily affirmed his lived experience of prejudice and discrimination as a white ethnic in the United States.[66] That moment of connection cemented their relationship; Scaramucci went on to work with Bell as his third-year faculty advisor.[67]

Scaramucci is confident that even in 1988, while taking Bell's course and reading Bell's allegorical tales in his newly published book, *And We Are Not Saved*, the students were indeed learning CRT—even if the moniker did not materialize until the following year. "What was interesting about Derrick is he had a scalpel and he cut, making his critiques of the institution and of American society," Scaramucci recalls.[68] A younger Scaramucci had his eyes opened to the realities of structural and institutional racism as an undergraduate student at Tufts, where he studied under Professor James Vance Jr., who in his popular course "Race Awareness in American Society" approached the topic from his military background. Perhaps this sustained background in the academic study of race and racism is why Anthony Scaramucci stands apart from so many other nationally known Republicans—including fellow Harvard Law School educated ones like Senator Ted Cruz—in Scaramucci's refusal to jump onboard the anti-CRT wagon. "It had a direct influence on me," Scaramucci says of his CRT education with Derrick Bell.[69]

Another person influenced by a relationship with Derrick Bell is Randall Kennedy. As a "mentor, friend, and adversary," Kennedy says of Bell, "he was a significant presence in my life."[70] When Bell returned to Harvard Law School in fall 1986, he encountered a young, highly talented Black legal scholar hired to teach civil rights law in the wake of the student protests and boycott of the Greenberg/Chambers mini-course. Bell initially held Kennedy in high esteem as a "gifted young man," seeing him as "a comrade and an eventual successor in . . . racial battles with Harvard."[71] Indeed, early assessments from potential fellow racecrits were positive. "True, Randy Kennedy did go about locking horns with this and that person or idea at CLS—more than once with me and mine—but I didn't find it especially offensive. He's obviously smart," Richard Delgado wrote to Derrick Bell following the January 1987 critical legal studies conference.[72] Bell's response was no less complimentary: "He is constantly involved in protests of this sort and while young and not experienced, I think he has very great potential."[73] That initial collegiality turned to enmity with the 1989 publication of Kennedy's critique of the newly emerging field of CRT, "Racial Critiques of Legal Academia."

By January 1990, controversy surrounding Kennedy's article made it to the *New York Times*. There, Kennedy acknowledged, as he did in the *Harvard Law Review* article itself, that several minority scholars had urged him not to publish the piece, fearing it would be used by white scholars to further discredit minority viewpoints. As Richard Delgado said at the time, "Appointment committees across the land will seize on this article and say, 'See, even Harvard Law School has declared this new critical race theory junk,' and use that as a way of justifying business as usual—that is, minorities won't get hired." Kennedy acknowledged those fears but emphasized the "costs of not speaking frankly about issues."[74]

Writing two days after the *New York Times* story was published, Derrick Bell suggested that the report itself

> shows that the media is ready to accord Kennedy that special celebrity status available to any black willing to speak for whites . . . who are unwilling to criticize blacks for the record. The list of blacks who achieve renown by serving as racial apologists is already too long. I regret that, as I predicted, Kennedy's article is read by so many as an audition to play the role of academic minstrel. A person of Professor Kennedy's talents and potential deserves a reputation built on far more honorable ground.[75]

The tone for much of their future relationship was set. Later that year, when Bell announced that he was protesting Harvard Law School's failure to tenure a Black woman by going on protest leave, Bell told the assembled students, after being introduced by *Law Review* president Barack Obama, that "the goals of diversity will not be served by persons who look black and think white."[76] Kennedy, perhaps with good reason, took that statement personally.[77]

By 1995, Bell described Kennedy as "critical race theory's most politically damaging critic." For Bell, the consequences of Kennedy's choice to speak out were clear: "When a black scholar at a prominent law school tells anyone who will listen that other folks of color are deluded . . . all who rarely listen to scholars of color sit up and take notice. And take notes. And turn those notes into more fuel for the legitimacy debate that has always attended renegade movements."[78] The dividing line could not be clearer.

It would be a mistake, however, for anyone to assume that disciplinary and even ideological disagreement translated for Bell and Kennedy into absolute personal disdain, much less hatred. In fact, their lives were interwoven long before they encountered one another directly.

Although Kennedy was twenty-four years younger than Bell, they shared time in Washington, DC, in the late 1950s. Kennedy was born on September 10, 1954, in Columbia, South Carolina. Kennedy's mother, Rachel, was an elementary school teacher. His father, Henry, drove a truck for the US Postal Service; he carried a gun while on duty. One day, a police officer warned him that Black people couldn't have guns. "A tense standoff ensued, ending in Henry speeding away all the way to Washington, DC. From there, he called Kennedy's mother and told her to pack up: They were moving." As Kennedy recalls, "My parents were afraid for their future in South Carolina. I asked my father once why he moved. His response to me was, 'Because either a white man was going to kill me or I was going to kill a white man.'"[79]

In DC, a young Kennedy competed in tennis matches against Weldon Douglass Rogers, the third child of Jefferson P. and Mary Grace Rogers, who had "absorbed his father's passion for tennis and became a pioneer in what was . . . primarily a whites-only sport."[80] As discussed in chapter 1, the Rogers's DC home provided safety and counsel to leaders like Martin Luther King Jr., other leaders in the SCLC, and to CRT founders Derrick and Jewel Hairston Bell. Their home also welcomed tennis legend and civil rights activist Arthur Ashe Jr., who had known the Rogerses since childhood; in young adulthood he became almost a surrogate son. In 1968, Jefferson Rogers invited Ashe to offer his first public speech on the Black athlete's role in the civil rights movement at the Church of the Redeemer, a community founded, in part, through the efforts of Jewel Hairston Bell. In February 1968, Martin Luther King Jr. wrote to Ashe offering "personal appreciation . . . for your expression of support and solidarity in the fight for justice, freedom and dignity for all people in this country." Ashe had come to King's attention through "Rev.

Jefferson Rogers, a long-time and staunch freedom fighter."[81] Within months of his speech at Redeemer, Ashe would win his first US Open. He would eventually serve on the board of Florida Memorial College (now University), where the Rogerses "worked together to foster educational, economic and social development projects in Miami, partly through a popular Distinguished Lecture Series."[82] Weldon Rogers, through this broad support, had succeeded in integrating the US Lawn Tennis Association at thirteen years old, a feat noted in Raymond Arsenault's biography of Arthur Ashe.[83] Even as Randall Kennedy was working to win matches against Weldon, the broader struggle being led by friends of Derrick Bell, with whom his life would eventually intersect, was ensuring his access to the same courts.

In his chapter, "Derrick Bell and Me," Kennedy shared additional aspects of his personal relationship with Bell that, given their very public disagreements, some could find surprising. Kennedy's wife, Dr. Yvedt Matory, was a surgeon who specialized in breast cancer, the illness that killed Jewel Hairston Bell, Derrick's first wife. "Though she was not Jewel's doctor, Yvedt spent a considerable amount of time monitoring Jewel's care, explaining the treatment that she was receiving, discussing alternatives, and being present to lend support. I sometimes joined Yvedt at Jewel's hospital bedside," Kennedy recalls. "Later, I much appreciated [Derrick's] condolences when Yvedt died and his encouragement in the aftermath of that personal catastrophe."[84] Their personal relationship was renewed in the final months of Bell's life. As Bell's own cancer was "preventing him from attending to his classes as fully as he would have liked," he called Kennedy to ask if he would "be willing to teach a session of his seminar at NYU Law School." Kennedy reports: "I jumped at the chance to participate. I was honored by his invitation and told him so. That was the final time we exchanged words. I taught the seminar a week after he died."[85]

The strength of that personal relationship and mutual esteem has allowed Kennedy to acknowledge Bell's accurate predictions of the current era of US racial politics. In 2017, Kennedy convened

Figure 5.2. Participants in the 1984 *Harvard Law Review* annual banquet. From left to right, Randall "Randy" Kennedy, Judge A. Leon Higginbotham Jr., Stephanie Y. Moore, Charles "Chuck" Jones (one of the Black professors invited to teach in the Alternative Course), and Derrick Bell. Photo courtesy Stephanie Y. Moore.

a panel discussion at Harvard Law School titled "Derrick Bell: The Professor as Protestor," with Patricia J. Williams and Paul Butler. The session was attended by Bell's second wife, Janet Dewart Bell. Speaking extemporaneously after Williams and Butler, Kennedy, after describing his own extensive time in Bell's archive at NYU, said that even "in the grip of that disagreement . . . even at its worst . . . I felt that in an odd sort of way he was on my side and that he wanted the best for me." Although Kennedy never tires of describing himself as an optimist and placing Bell in the pessimist school: "I will say, . . . any student of Derrick Bell's will not be thrown off kilter by what has happened in the United States in the past two years. . . . If you were a close reader of Derrick Bell, he frankly would have prepared you. And for that reason, I got to do a little bit of revision."[86] According to Kennedy, Bell "predicted the backlash, the ferocity of which took many—including me—by surprise. . . . Attentive readers of his writings would not have been surprised by the Trump ascendancy."[87]

To be clear, Bell's prediction of white backlash and retrenchment would hold true no matter the economic failure or success of the Obama administration. Moreover, the rise and endurance of Donald Trump is only symbolic of the current age. Any student of Bell's would not be surprised by the broader racial undercurrents in US political culture. These undercurrents include litigation efforts to outlaw any policies supporting diversity, equity, and inclusion that use the Civil Rights Acts of 1965 and 1966—both of which are intended to assist minority participation in white-dominated society. These litigation efforts also forbid any form of affirmative action, including governmental funding for minority-owned businesses.[88]

Any student of Bell's would not be surprised by the steady drumbeat of police and civilian killings of unarmed or properly licensed Black people—Trayvon Martin, Sandra Bland, Philando Castile, Breonna Taylor, and George Floyd come to mind— killings that gave rise to the Movement for Black Lives.[89] Bell himself, along with any student familiar with the deep roots of the dynamic, ongoing struggle between colorblind liberalism and race-conscious legal theory and policy formation, would not be surprised at the complex processes that forced the resignation of Claudine Gay from her brief, six-month presidency of Harvard University, or Kamala Harris's truncated candidacy for US president, lost to the 2024 re-election of Donald Trump.[90]

In the 2017 panel discussion at Harvard Law School focused on Derrick Bell's legacy as a professor and protester, Paul Butler, now an endowed professor at Georgetown and a legal analyst on MSNBC, said that when he first read Kennedy's "Racial Critiques of Legal Academia," the article "felt a little bit like a blood sport. It felt a little bit Freudian." He acknowledged, however, that "what Professor Kennedy did, which I think a lot of professors would not have done at this time, was to take Derrick Bell seriously. And not Derrick Bell as somebody who was writing about class actions or legal ethics, but Derrick Bell as a critical race theorist. And he took other critical race theorists seriously and critically."[91]

In the context of contemporary bad-faith attacks on CRT, Kennedy's critique stands apart in its effort to at least take the field seriously. Other attempts at critical but serious critique have followed.[92] Once popular discourse on CRT came to be dominated by the likes of media strategists and pundits like Breitbart, Hannity, and Christopher Rufo, however, seriousness could not be expected. When there's at least a good faith attempt to understand and refute an academic position, further conversation is possible. When faced with polemical and sometimes nonsensical attacks on CRT driven more by electoral manipulation techniques than an exchange of ideas, how might proponents of CRT respond?

Conclusion

Story, the Answer from the Beginning

What is CRT? This resounding question is asked by US Senators at Supreme Court Justice confirmation hearings, concerned parents at local school board meetings, and liberal and conservative media pundits alike. Good and bad faith video bloggers and podcasters, presidential debate moderators, lay people and pastors just want to know why this term is constantly in the news and coming out of politicians' mouths. Founders like Kimberlé Crenshaw, Neil Gotanda, Stephanie Phillips, and Teri Miller also grappled with this question as they kicked around terms and concepts in 1989 discussing what exactly unified their nascent group. What *is* CRT?

When Derrick Bell was asked to define CRT, he had a few things to say:

Definition 1: Critical race theory . . . is a new approach to legal theory pioneered by minority scholars. Practitioners, often through the device of either true stories or personal anecdotes or fictional tales, discuss the many ways in which race and law affect each other. There is no unitary perspective. . . . But, as a whole, the perspectives we bring to our work are shaped by having lived our whole lives thinking about and experiencing issues of race—perspectives that, until now, have been ignored by the legal establishment.[1]

Definition 2: My writing was at the forefront of a new school of legal thought now known, and mostly accepted, as critical race theory. Practitioners, often through storytelling and a more subjective, personal voice, examine the ways in which the law has been shaped by and shapes issues of race.[2]

Definition 3: I rather think that this writing is the response to a need for expressing views that cannot be communicated effectively through existing techniques. In my case, I prefer using stories as a means of communicating views to those who hold very different views on the emotionally charged subject of race. People enjoy stories and will often suspend their beliefs, listen to the story, and then compare their views, not with mine, but with those expressed in the story.[3]

Woven throughout Bell's discussions of CRT is his insistence on centering the experiences and unique voices of people of color and communicating these experiences through the method of story. He emphasized story to his fellow race-crits.

In an August 23, 1989, memo to all participants in the July 1989 CRT workshop, Bell updates the group about Richard Delgado's forthcoming essay, "When a Story Is Just a Story: Does Voice Really Matter?," a response to Randall Kennedy's then-recently published "Racial Critiques of Legal Academia."[4] Kennedy's article was clearly a central topic of discussion at this founding CRT moment. Bell's memo encourages all participants to "produce more of the writing that communicates our understanding of law and the society in ways that reflect our experience, insight, and perspective." He continues, "The papers we read and discussed at the Madison Workshop last month are proof that this is not a limited talent."[5]

Bell praises the breadth of Delgado's response, which indicts Kennedy ideologically, disciplinarily, and racially. Delgado first submitted this essay for publication in the summer of 1989 to the *Harvard Law Review*, a journal independent of yet still run by students at Kennedy's place of work. The article didn't find a landing spot until February 1990 with the *Virginia Law Review*. Delgado's critique nods to the clear "interest divergence" Kennedy's article represents; an alignment of a racially minoritized writer "with conservative forces . . . against his own community."[6]

However, Delgado digs deeper and asserts, very much in concert with Bell, that Kennedy's attack on *voice* is the most troubling aspect of the objection. "It urges inattention to difference and a return to sterile canons of conventional excellence," Delgado writes. "Kennedy's fierce individualism may be a useful strategy in economics, where the market is almost always right and the failure of one may lead to a net benefit for all. But it is strikingly inapt in writing and thought, particularly that related to racial justice. Here, inclusion, texture, and diversity of perspective—in short, voice—is everything."[7]

In fall 1988, the Association of Black Faculty and Administrators of Harvard University decided to conduct a survey of the effectiveness of affirmative action across campus. Derrick Bell was cochair of the effort. The first phase of the study involved interviews with all Harvard deans, asking that they provide detailed explanations for the abysmally low numbers of Black faculty at the time: seventeen of 957 tenured, twenty-six of 2,265 on the tenure track.[8] When it came time to do something with all this data, to integrate the interviews and faculty statistics into a report the administrators would actually read instead of "put on a shelf [or] in the wastebasket," Bell devised a plan.[9]

Delivered on October 25, 1988, the association's report began with an opening statement expressing their frustration with Harvard's lip-service approach to diversity and equal opportunity, nodding to the insult of hiring practices that only seriously consider Black candidates if an existing Black faculty member at Harvard dies or resigns. With this "living insult" in mind, the report is not a white paper but instead is a work of "fictional tragedy," which they admit seems unorthodox. The group contends, however, that this is a "well-known African tradition, one that is increasingly used as a medium for scholarly discourse."[10] The report itself explores the hypothetical aftermath of Harvard's hiring priorities after an explosion tragically kills the university's white president and all Black faculty while they meet to discuss affirmative action.

Bell admitted to *Boston Globe* journalist Derrick Z. Jackson that when he first proposed to members of the Association of Black Faculty and Administrators using story for their report, a few "raised questions."

"Would white administrators dismiss the fiction as unprofessional?"

"Isn't it upsetting to pose the killing of the university president?"

Bell's faith in the power of story held him steadfast to the belief that this method of delivery would be "much more powerful than statistics." Referencing some of his literary favorites, Bell told Jackson, "It was Toni Morrison who said we have to sometimes pull back and imagine the unimaginable. Alice Walker said that sometimes you have to choose your soul over convenience. Otherwise, you're just immobilized." Bell continued, "The irony is that our situation right now is not very different than if a bomb had really been dropped."[11]

Bell attached that story, "The Final Report," to his second memo addressed to the July 1989 CRT workshop participants. That protest counterstory was now included in a special issue of the *Michigan Law Review* devoted to the discipline of legal storytelling. The special issue was the result of a joint effort between Richard Delgado and Patricia Williams, who proposed the nontraditional idea to several journals. In a letter of June 1, 1988, Delgado wrote to Kevin Kennedy, editor-in-chief of the *Michigan Law Review*:

> We believe that stories, parables, chronicles, and narratives are potent devices for analyzing mindset and ideology—the bundle of presuppositions, received wisdoms, and shared understandings against a background of which legal discourse takes place. . . . The main cause of Black and brown subordination is not so much poorly crafted or enforced laws or judicial decisions. Rather, it is the prevailing mindset through which members of the majority race justify the world as it is, that is with whites on top and Blacks at the bottom. Ideology makes current social arrangements seem natural and fair.[12]

Kim Lane Scheppele, then professor of sociology at the University of Michigan, in her foreword to the special issue on legal storytelling shared that "along with this dire diagnosis, Delgado proposed a treatment: 'The cure is storytelling,' he announced, 'counterhegemonic' storytelling to 'quicken and engage conscience.'"[13]

After receiving Delgado's letter, Kevin Kennedy met with Lee Bollinger, dean of the University of Michigan Law School; they agreed to move forward with publishing a groundbreaking, interdisciplinary issue on the importance of narrative and legal storytelling. The enthusiastic response to the special issue's call for proposals resulted in an equally interdisciplinary conference held in April 1989. Eric S. Rabkin and Macklin Smith, both English professors at the University of Michigan, provided a writing studies workshop structure for the conference modeled on their joint research.[14] This gathering, directly informed by English studies pedagogical theories and methods, can be considered the founding moment of the key methodology of CRT: counterstory.

Counterstory was fully mobilized, a tool ready to be deployed when the first CRT workshop met in Wisconsin three months later in July 1989. This special issue of the *Michigan Law Review*—containing pieces from Bell, Delgado, Williams, and Mari Matsuda, among others—marks one of the early achievements of CRT. "The issue is worth your perusal," Bell asserted to CRT workshop participants in his September 1989 memo.[15] We agree.

We are living in a momentous time. As the global order slips toward authoritarianism, racial retrenchment is on the rise. Global economic shifts and growing wealth disparities are combining with the climate crisis to create renewed conditions for the exploitation of labor and the unjust distribution of resources. Laws and policies are being altered, modified, and reinterpreted to benefit those classes long invested in building a world that suits their interests. The faces at the bottom of the well, those communities consigned to poverty and degradation, are at ever greater risk of racialized dehumanization and violence.

It is no mistake that CRT—one of the most incisive and forward-thinking tools for critical inquiry and societal interpretation developed in the United States—is now coming under attack. As Derrick Bell observed in 1995, "At a time of crisis, critics serve as reminders that we are being heard, if not always appreciated."[16] The power of CRT is in stories—stories that humanize data, that communicate truths. Although CRT has recently again come under attack, even those of us committed to its tenets and frameworks should not forget that the call is not primarily to defend CRT. Good tools are worth defending because of the good they can do for the sake of the world. When it comes to the storytelling heart of CRT, the point is to effectively humanize data to promote justice, to promote the flourishing of human communities.

Derrick Bell said that the perspectives communicated through CRT "are shaped by having lived our whole lives thinking about and experiencing issues of race—perspectives that, until now, have been ignored by the legal establishment."[17] That establishment is an extension of society as a whole. Storytelling—as a critical method—has the power to make those perspectives heard so dominant classes can no longer avoid the responsibility of listening.

We see the power of storytelling as method in Patricia Williams's longstanding cultivation of her narrative voice while providing critical legal commentary in the *Nation*. We see it in the work of Kimberlé Crenshaw and the African American Policy Forum in her recent book, *#Say Her Name: Black Women's Stories of Police Violence and Public Silence*. We see it in the continued work of Mari Matsuda and Charles Lawrence, producing art exhibits that recover the parallel life stories of women who have fought for Hawaiian sovereignty and reparations. We see it in the ongoing critical writing of Richard Delgado and Jean Stefancic, still chronicling Rodrigo Crenshaw's stories and producing cutting-edge work challenging the boundaries of CRT itself while generously mentoring the next generation of scholar-activists. We see it in the work of Janet Dewart Bell, who since Derrick Bell's death in

Michigan
Law Review

LEGAL STORYTELLING

Foreword   *Kim Lane Scheppele*

Empathy, Legal Storytelling, and the Rule
of Law: New Words, Old Wounds?
         Toni M. Massaro

The Obliging Shell: An Informal Essay on
Formal Equal Opportunity
         Patricia Williams

Difference Made Legal: The Court
and Dr. King
         David Luban

The Cognitive Dimension of the *Agon*
Between Legal Power and Narrative
Meaning
         Steven L. Winter

Stories of Origin and Constitutional
Possibilities
         Milner S. Ball

Public Response to Racist Speech:
Considering the Victim's Story
         Mari J. Matsuda

The Final Report: Harvard's Affirmative
Action Allegory
         Derrick Bell

Storytelling for Oppositionists and Others:
A Plea for Narrative
         Richard Delgado

Persuasion
         Joseph William Singer

A Tale of Two Clients: Thinking About
Law as Language
         Clark D. Cunningham

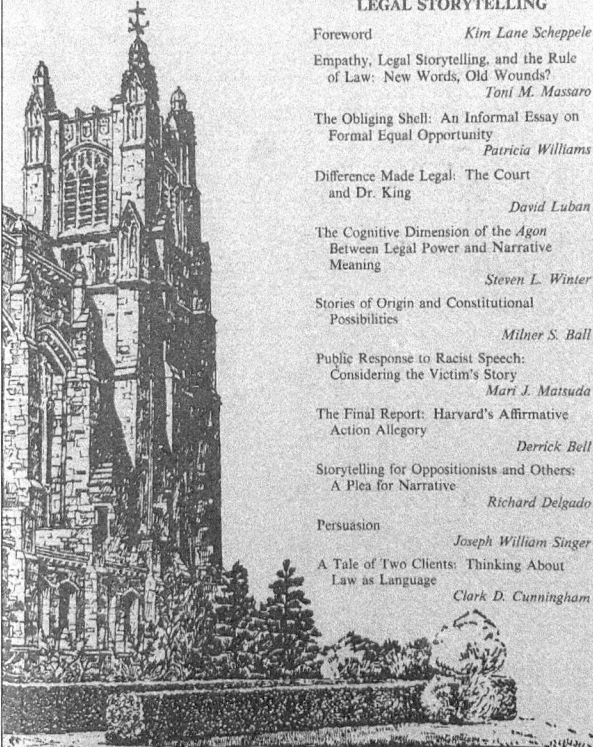

Vol. 87, No. 8   August 1989

Figure 6.1. Cover of the *Michigan Law Review* special issue on legal story-telling. Photo by authors of the issue from the personal archive of Richard Delgado and Jean Stefancic.

HARVARD LAW SCHOOL
CAMBRIDGE · MASSACHUSETTS · 02138

MEMORANDUM

September 30, 1989

TO: Critical Race Theory Workshop Participants and Others

FROM: Derrick Bell

SUBJECT: Legal Storytelling

I am enclosing a reprint of my article, The Final Report: Harvard's Affirmative Action Allegory. Originally, it was an effort to use storytelling as a vehicle of protest (it was the basis of a Harvard black faculty and staff report published last year challenging the University's affirmative action program). Now, it is a contribution in the **Michigan Law Review's** special issue devoted to Legal Storytelling. This is recycling with a vengeance.

The issue is worth your perusal as you may surmise from the table of contents and a portion of the Foreword attached to this memo. As indicated there, Richard Delgado (joined by Pat Williams) wrote several law reviews asking them to consider an issue devoted to storytelling. Michigan accepted and in addition to my piece, the issue contains articles by three other participants in the Workshop, Patricia Williams, Mari Matsuda, and Richard Delgado.

Critical Race Theory Workshop
Participants:

Anita Allen, Georgetown
Taunya Banks, Maryland
Robin Barnes, Wisconsin
Kevin Brown, Indiana
Paulette Caldwell, NYU
John Calmore, Loyola at Los Angeles
Kim Crenshaw, UCLA

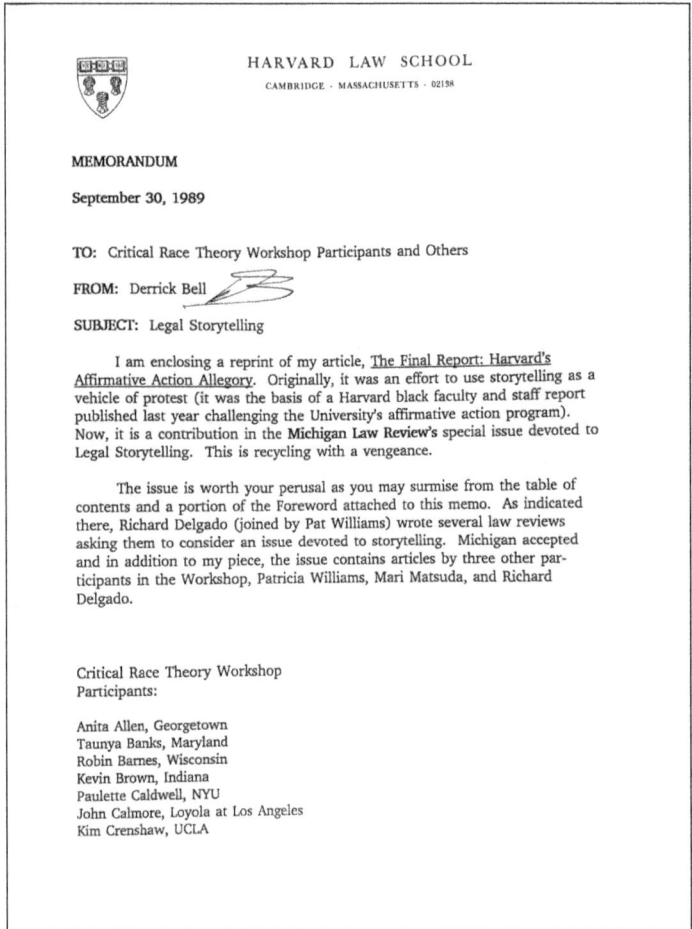

Figure 6.2. Derrick Bell memo to critical race theory workshop participants, September 1989. NYU Archive.

2011 has been the primary torchbearer of his legacy while producing her own projects celebrating the voice and witness of African American women.

In this book, we have shared stories that emphasize and highlight the tenets of CRT. Stories, by their very nature, are more

Harlon Dalton, Yale
Richard Delgado, Wisconsin
Neil Gotanda, Western St. Univ.
Linda Greene, Wisconsin
Trina Grillo, San Francisco
Isabelle Gunning, UCLA
Angela Harris, Berkeley
James Jones, Wisconsin
Mari Matsuda, Hawaii
Teresa Miller, Wisconsin
Philip Nash, CUNY Queens
Elizabeth Patterson, Georgetown
Stephanie Phillips, Buffalo
Benita Ramsey, Wisconsin
Robert Suggs, Arizona State
Kendall Thomas, Columbia
Patricia Williams, Wisconsin

Other Colleagues:

Loretta Argrett, Howard
Regina Austin, Harvard
Deborah Batts, Fordham
Scott Brewer, Harvard
Robert Belton, Vanderbilt
Peggy Davis, NYU
Chris Edley, Harvard
Emma Jordan, Georgetown
Randy Kennedy, Harvard
Charles Lawrence, Stanford
Charles Ogletree, Harvard
J. Clay Smith, Howard
David Wilkens, Harvard

2

accessible than more traditional academic modes of writing. They also more effectively communicate, as Bell said, with "those who hold very different views on the emotionally charged subject of race." We hope this book has offered moments of connection, empathy, and joy along with information and perspective. Stories demonstrate the power of CRT because they illumine the power of human connection and empathetic concern at the heart of CRT.

No explanation of critical race theory is complete without a list of tenets and the names of key people associated with the movement. *The Origins of Critical Race Theory* offers that, along with definitions and key dates. Now we know more about what nurtured and fed the movement; we know more about how we got here. And you are here with us.

We invite you to reflect on how you will respond. What will you do to advance the flourishing of human communities rather than perpetuating the privilege and power of the few over the many? What information will you add to this many-stranded history of CRT? What important people need to be added to the long list of names highlighted here? What truths will you carry forward? What dominant narratives need to be challenged in your own life? What critical race counterstories will you tell?

ACKNOWLEDGMENTS

Just as the story of critical race theory cannot be told without a sprawling cast of characters, a project like this would be impossible without the investment and support of a broad variety of contributors. We are filled with gratitude for the many people who have helped bring this book into existence.

First, we are indebted to Richard Delgado and Jean Stefancic, who have supported the project from its inception. They have served not just as participants who have opened their life stories to us; they have been collaborators and editors throughout the writing process, accompanying us through multiple drafts of this project from the proposal stage, to chapter drafts, to the manuscript in its entirety. It has been an honor and joy to be mentored and encouraged by this dynamic couple. We are no less grateful to Clara Platter at NYU Press for taking a chance on people outside legal studies, and to Brianna Jean, Ainee Jeong, and Richard Feit for their production and editing expertise.

This project would not have been possible without the fleet of librarians and other workers at the NYU Archives. We are especially grateful for the kind support of Janet Bunde and Danielle Nista and know that many other people were involved in delivering boxes and folders.

The Origins of Critical Race Theory's emphasis on humanizing the story of CRT has been aided immensely by the generous participation of people involved with the movement sharing their insights and experiences, either in email communication or interviews. The oral histories generated through these encounters have proven invaluable. In addition to Richard and Jean, we extend our thanks to Stephanie Y. Moore, who, in addition to sharing her oral histories, has provided essential fact checking for historical accuracy while sharing generously from her personal photographic archive. Stephanie has also been a major conduit to other civil rights giants, opening many doors we would have thought impossible before. We are humbled to reprint an image of Jean Fairfax from acclaimed civil rights photographer Rowland Scherman; we share his commitment to documenting the role of women in liberation movements. We are likewise grateful for conversations with the family of Behonor McDonald, including George T. Jackson Sr. and Mrs. McDonald's grandson, Col. G. Torrie Jackson. We are grateful also to the family of Judge Constance Baker Motley, particularly her namesake and niece, Constance Royster.

In addition, we are grateful to Judge U. W. Clemon, Donald Christopher Tyler, Kevin Brown, George Taylor, Stan Stefancic, Mari Matsuda, David Wilkins, David Trubek, Rob Williams, Carol Steiker, Linda Greene, Luz E. Herrera, Anthony Scaramucci, Cristina Cassese, Margaret Montoya, Victor Villanueva, Emma Rodgers, William Miller, Danny Solórzano, and Victor Ray. Our surprise visit to the Zief Law Library at the University of San Francisco, facilitated by Lisa Anderson, brought us into conversation with John Shafer and Mike Muehe.

We are grateful as well for our friends in academia who have been kind enough to comment on the manuscript, offering their encouragement and insight. Jervette Ward, Frankie Condon, Shannon Speed, and Joseph Berra have been wonderful conversation partners. Jaime Armin Mejía offered the most meticulous copyediting support any authors could hope for. And to Burke Gerstenschlager, a masterful editor and conduit of connections (and some of the best Italian food Brooklyn has to offer!).

The University of North Texas provided a supportive environment while the book came together. Research was supported by several College of Liberal Arts and Social Sciences and English and History Department funding sources: the Scholarly Creative Activity Award, Small Grant Award, and Faculty Development Funds. We are grateful to faculty colleagues, particularly Todd Moye. We also acknowledge our excellent UNT students in

ENGL 6810/HIST 6900, ENGL 4230, and ENGL 4150/4230 who have walked with us through this research journey as eager minds and spirits, open to all the stories about CRT that Derrick Bell's archive provides. We are especially grateful to students in the Native American Student Association, for which we are co-advisors, and to our students/collaborators Natali Coronado and Nicholas Durham, who have read drafts and provided insightful feedback.

As always, we have been strengthened through many friendships, especially time spent during NYC research trips, in conversation around our kitchen table, or texting and Zooming from distances near and far: Maria Chaves, Karma Chávez, Ersula Ore, Joanna Sanchez, Marissa Juarez, Erica Cirillo-McCarthy, Elise Verzosa Hurley, Amanda Wray, Tom Do, John Havard, Gavin Johnson, Laura Gonzales, V. Jo Hsu, Vani Kannan, Christina Cedillo, Brittany Ross, Aileen Altuna, Mohammed Mahmoud, Santiago Slabodsky, Nefertiti Takla, Munib Younan, Tarfia Faizullah, Sarah Perry, J. Preston Witt, Anna Hinton, Jo Davis-McElligatt, Priscilla Ybarra, Jessica Enoch, Cheryl Glenn, Keith Miller, and Bob and Teresa Ahern. Family has also been valuable, some even serving as editors and readers! We are thankful for the reading and feedback from Patsy and Ramon Martinez, Cindy Alexander, Caleb Smith, Zion Smith, Olivia Martinez, Esther McGee, the Roark family, and Hailey Fawk (who also was a great NYC host during many Bell-archive research trips!).

Finally, we are grateful for the readers who will encounter this book. We look forward to hearing the stories you will tell!

Recommended Reading

We hope that *The Origins of Critical Race Theory* is a good resource for you. We know, however, that this book is not a comprehensive introduction to CRT. We join a chorus of voices writing on this important topic and encourage you to read further in these sources that we know and trust (full publication for each can be found in the bibliography):

Derrick Bell, *And We Are Not Saved: The Elusive Quest for Racial Justice*

Derrick Bell, *The Derrick Bell Reader*

Derrick Bell, *Faces at the Bottom of the Well: The Permanence of Racism*

Derrick Bell, *Race, Racism and American Law*

Janet Dewart Bell, *Blackbirds Singing: Inspiring Black Women's Speeches from the Civil War to the Twenty-first Century*

Janet Dewart Bell, *Lighting the Fires of Freedom: African American Women in the Civil Rights Movement*

Janet Dewart Bell and Vincent M. Sutherland, eds., *Carving Out a Humanity: Race, Rights, and Redemption*

Eduardo Bonilla-Silva, *Racism without Racists: Color-Blind Racism and the Persistence of Racial Inequality in America*

Paul Butler, *Chokehold: Policing Black Men*

Kimberlé Crenshaw, ed., *#SayHerName: Black Women's Stories of Police Violence and Public Silence*

Kimberlé Crenshaw, Neil Gotanda, Gary Peller, and Kendall Thomas, eds., *Critical Race Theory: The Key Writings That Formed the Movement*

Kimberlé Crenshaw, Luke Charles Harris, Daniel Martinez
    HoSang, and George Lipsitz, eds., *Seeing Race Again: Counter-
    ing Colorblindness across the Disciplines*
Richard Delgado, *The Rodrigo Chronicles: Conversations about
    America and Race*
Richard Delgado and Jean Stefancic, *Critical Race Theory:
    An Introduction*
Richard Delgado and Jean Stefancic, eds., *Critical Race Theory:
    The Cutting Edge*
Adrienne D. Dixson and Celia K. Rousseau, eds., *Critical Race
    Theory in Education: All God's Children Got a Song*
David Theo Goldberg, *The War on Critical Race Theory: Or, The
    Remaking of Racism*
Ian Haney-Lopez, *White by Law: The Legal Construction of Race*
Gloria Ladson-Billings, *Critical Race Theory in Education:
    A Scholar's Journey*
Gloria Ladson-Billings and William Tate, eds., *"Covenant Keeper":
    Derrick Bell's Enduring Education Legacy*
Marvin Lynn and Adrienne D. Dixson, *Handbook of Critical Race
    Theory in Education*
Aja Y. Martinez, *Counterstory: The Rhetoric and Writing of Critical
    Race Theory*
Mari J. Matsuda, Charles R. Lawrence III, and Richard Delgado,
    *Words That Wound: Critical Race Theory, Assaultive Speech,
    and The First Amendment*
Victor Ray, *On Critical Race Theory: Why It Matters & Why You
    Should Care*
Daniel G. Solórzano and Lindsay Pérez Huber, *Racial Microag-
    gressions: Using Critical Race Theory to Respond to Everyday
    Racism*
Francisco Valdes, Angela Harris, and Jerome McCristal Culp, eds.,
    Crossroads, Directions and A New Critical Race Theory
Patricia J. Williams, *The Alchemy of Race and Rights: Diary of a
    Law Professor*
Patricia J. Williams, *Giving a Damn: Racism, Romance, and Gone
    with the Wind*

Robert A. Williams Jr., *Like a Loaded Weapon: The Rehnquist Court, Indian Rights, and the Legal History of Racism in America*

Tara J. Yosso, *Critical Race Counterstories along the Chicana/Chicano Educational Pipeline*

1989 Critical Race Theory Workshop Participants, Madison, WI

Anita Allen, Georgetown
Taunya Banks, Maryland
Robin Barnes, Wisconsin
Derrick Bell, Harvard
Kevin Brown, Indiana
Paulette Caldwell, NYU
John Calmore, Loyola at Los Angeles
Kimberlé Crenshaw, UCLA
Richard Delgado, Wisconsin
Neil Gotanda, Western St. Univ.
Linda Greene, Wisconsin
Trina Grillo, San Francisco
Isabelle Gunning, UCLA
Angela Harris, Berkeley
James Jones, Wisconsin
Mari Matsuda, Hawai'i
Teresa Miller, Wisconsin
Philip Nash, CUNY Queens
Elizabeth Patterson, Georgetown
Stephanie Phillips, Buffalo
Benita Ramsey, Wisconsin
Robert Suggs, Arizona State
Kendall Thomas, Columbia
Patricia Williams, Wisconsin

The Tenets of Critical Race Theory

1. Permanence of race and racism
2. Challenge to dominant ideologies
3. Interest convergence
4. Race as social construct
5. Intersectionality and anti-essentialism
6. Interdisciplinarity
7. Centrality of experiential knowledge and/or unique voices of color
8. Commitment to social justice
9. Accessibility

Permanence of Race and Racism: Racism is endemic and a central, permanent, and "normal" part of US society operating concurrently within multiple forms of social oppression. Derrick Bell describes a racial realism as racism's permanence in addition to its centrality through his assertion that "racism lies at the center, not the periphery; in the permanent, not in the fleeting; in the real lives of . . . [people of color] and white people."[1]

Challenge to Dominant Ideologies: CRT challenges liberal claims of race neutrality, equal opportunity, objectivity, colorblindness, and merit. Concerning education and institutional injustice, CRT's second tenet questions arguments against policies such as affirmative action and interrogates admissions and hiring practices that claim neutrality in their selection of candidates while justifying a passing over of people of color on the "colorblind" basis of merit and "fit."

Interest Convergence: Derrick Bell's theory argues that white elites will tolerate or encourage racial advances for people of color only when such advances also promote white self-interest. This form of "racial progress" (and regression) is cyclical rather than inevitable.

Race as Social Construct: Although biologists, geneticists, anthropologists, and sociologists agree that race is not a biological determinant, humans nonetheless continue to taxonomize human bodies racially. Social constructs of race promote race as fundamental in the structuring and representing of the social world. These racial projects can take many forms and are expressed in everything from legislation that defines the parameters of whiteness to Halloween costumes that caricature an entire race or ethnicity.

Intersectionality and Anti-essentialism: This concept counters the single-axis framework of binaristic racial or gendered analysis. Binary conceptions alone do not accurately account for the intersections of race and gender, thus contributing to the marginalization and exclusion of Black women in feminist theory and in antiracist politics. Twin-skin to intersectionality is anti-essentialism. CRT denounces essentialism, countering culturally racist assumptions that attempt to describe or explain socially constructed racial groups as homogenous in the way they think, act, and believe.

Interdisciplinarity: The premise of interdisciplinarity insists on carving pathways for scholars from disciplines steeped in unyielding commitments to canon. In the spirit of the 1960s activism that resulted in the establishment of ethnic studies, CRT pulls on a variety of scholarly traditions toward centralizing and making sense of experiential knowledge so as to inclusively engage multiple perspectives.

Centrality of Experiential Knowledge and/or Unique Voices of Color: CRT scholars recognize and have developed the methodology of counterstory to relate the racial realities of people of color while also providing methods for minoritized people to challenge dominant ideologies and "common sense" master narratives about race. The CRT narrative recognizes experiential knowledge of people of color as "legitimate, appropriate, and critical to understanding, and analyzing racial subordination."[2]

Commitment to Social Justice: Arguably the most distinguishing characteristic for CRT's narrative method, counterstory is its transparent commitment to a "liberatory and transformative response to racial, gender, and class oppression."[3] CRT and its methodology of counterstory use a narrative method to theorize racialized experience. As a necessary function of counterstory, these narratives serve the purposes of exposing stereotypes, expressing injustice, and offering additional truths through a narration of the researchers' lived experiences, including critical self-reflection on privilege and use of this privilege toward social justice coalition and solidarity.

Accessibility: CRT work has included and always will include a constellation of community, family, laypeople, and non-academics because the work is *for* them, is sometimes *about* them, and is nearly always *inspired by* them. If CRT work is inaccessible to the very people it is for—well, then what's the point? Why do the work if it's inaccessible? The CRT tenet of accessibility is made more practical through the lens of disability studies and the work of DisCrit scholars who work to move accessibility from a conceptual to a material plane, raising awareness of how groups of people are excluded from spaces and practices. Thus, the premise of accessibility envisions a multiplicity of audiences beyond the physically, financially, and conceptually inaccessible ivory tower of academia so as to speak with (rather than for and over) others' communities.

NOTES

INTRODUCTION

Epigraph: Bell, "Foreword: The Civil Rights Chronicles," 71.

1 Martinez, *Counterstory*.

2 Exec. Order 13950, of Sept. 22, 2020, 85 FR 60683, "Combating Race and Sex Stereotyping," https://federalregister.gov.

3 Exec. Order 13950.

4 Christopher Rufo (@realchrisrufo), "We have successfully frozen their brand—'critical race theory'—into the public conversation. . . ." Twitter, March 15, 2021, 2:14 p.m., https://twitter.com/realchrisrufo/status/1371540368714428416?s=20.

5 Harvard Law School, "HLS in the World | Derrick Bell: The Professor as Protestor," November 9, 2017, YouTube, www.youtube.com/watch?v=eEhI-0QGfME&ab_channel=HarvardLawSchool.

6 Alexander, "Foreword," xi.

7 Bell, "Racism," 93.

8 Bell, "Who's Afraid of Critical Race Theory?," 908.

9 As Martinez has noted in *Counterstory* and other previous work, counterstory as methodology is the verb, the process, the CRT-informed justification for the work, whereas counterstory as method is the noun, the genre, the research tool.

10 Ladson-Billings, "Critical Race Theory," 39.

11 See Dixson and Rousseau, *Critical Race Theory in Education*.

12 This was discovered on a letter draft Delgado sent to Bell, ultimately intended for *San Francisco Chronicle* columnist Arthur Hoppe. In this Jonathan Swift–like satire, Delgado argues that what the US needs "is a good Loch Ness monster" since "a love of terror and mystery runs deep in our culture. Why let the Scots have a loch on monsters?" Richard Delgado, "Letter to Arthur Hoppe" (October 18, 1987), MC.138, box 1, folder 15, Derrick A. Bell Jr. Papers, New York University Archive, New York, New York, https://findingaids.library.nyu.edu.

13 Letter from Barack Obama to Derrick Bell, February 28 1990, box 58, folder 14, Derrick A. Bell Jr. Papers.

14 See Bell, Higgins, and Suh, "Racial Reflections: Dialogues in the Direction of Liberation," 1041n17, 1068–69. Anthony Scaramucci, interview by Aja Y. Martinez and Robert O. Smith, November 1, 2023.

15 Harvard Law School, "HLS in the World."

16 Derrick A. Bell Jr., interviewed by Larry Crowe, December 1, 2004, session 1, tape 3, story 3, HistoryMakers Digital Archive. Derrick A. Bell Jr. describes marrying his first wife, Jewel Hairston Bell, https://da.thehistorymakers.org/story/303572. This brief mention of Alain LeRoy Locke illustrates another limit of this book: given constraints of space and scope, we cannot fully develop every intellectual influence on CRT. Locke, for instance, gay and the first Black Rhodes scholar, is widely acknowledged as the "dean" of the Harlem Renaissance, providing an intellectual framework alongside the creative output of writers like Langston Hughes and Zora Neale Hurston. He was a longtime philosophy professor at Howard University, where he mentored the likes of Thurgood Marshall, Ossie Davis, and Martin Luther King Jr. On March 19, 1968, speaking about the Poor People's Campaign in Clarksdale, Mississippi, King said, "We're going to let our young people know that Shakespeare, Euripides, and Aristophanes are not the only poets that have lived in history. We're going to let our children know about Countee Cullen and Langston Hughes. We're going to let our children know that the only philosophers that lived were not Plato and Aristotle, but W. E. B. Du Bois and Alain Locke came through the universe" (quoted in Cone, *Martin & Malcolm & America*, 230).

17 Matsuda, "'Radical Wāhine of Honolulu, 1945' with Mari Matsuda."

18 Fred R. Shapiro, "The Most-Cited Legal Scholars Revisited," *University of Chicago Law Review* 88, no. 7 (November 2021): 1604.

1. DEEPLY ROOTED

1 Derrick Bell, *Still Looking for the Pony*, unfinished manuscript, box 144, folder 17, Derrick A. Bell Jr. Papers. Many parts of this early work provided content in published books, including *Faces at the Bottom of the Well*, *Ethical Ambition*, *Silent Covenants*, and

Confronting Authority. Bell attempted to publish *Still Looking for the Pony* with his *Race, Racism, and American Law* publishers, Little Brown, as a trade follow-up to his highly successful 1974 debut of *Race, Racism, and American Law*. Little, Brown passed on the project.

2 Derrick Bell, "Mississippi Morning" (draft 3), page 9, box 144, folder 17, Derrick A. Bell Jr. Papers.

3 Derrick Bell, Law School Application Essay, box 144, folder 16, Derrick A. Bell Jr. Papers.

4 Bell, *Silent Covenants*, 2.

5 Bell, *Faces at the Bottom of the Well*, 2.

6 Derrick Bell Jr., interviewed by Larry Crowe, December 1, 2004, session 1, tape 3, story 6, HistoryMakers Digital Archive. Derrick A. Bell Jr. describes his experience on US Air Force bases in the South, https://da.thehistorymakers.org.

7 Derrick Bell Jr., interviewed by Larry Crowe, December 1, 2004, session 1, tape 1, story 5, HistoryMakers Digital Archive. Derrick A. Bell Jr. describes his father's family background, https://da.thehistory makers.org.

8 On the Great Migration, see Wilkerson, *The Warmth of Other Suns*.

9 Derrick A. Bell Jr., interviewed by Larry Crowe, December 1, 2004, session 1, tape 3, story 6, HistoryMakers Digital Archive A2004.242. Derrick A. Bell Jr. describes his experience on US Air Force bases in the South, https://da.thehistorymakers.org.

10 We are indebted to William Tate for this insight. See Tate, "The Ethics of Derrick Bell."

11 Derrick Bell, Law School Application Essay, page 3, box 144, folder 16, Derrick A. Bell Jr. Papers.

12 Bell, *Ethical Ambition*, 77.

13 Derrick A. Bell Jr., interviewed by Larry Crowe, December 1, 2004, session 1, tape 2, story 5, HistoryMakers Digital Archive A2004.24. Derrick A. Bell, Jr. describes his experience at Schenley High School, online at https://da.thehistorymakers.org/story/303565.

14 Derrick A. Bell Jr., interviewed by Larry Crowe, December 1, 2004, session 1, tape 2, story 9, HistoryMakers Digital Archive A2004.24. Derrick A. Bell Jr. describes his first wife's career aspirations, online at https://da.thehistorymakers.org/story/303569.

15 "Remembrance of Jewel Bell" (August 1991), box 109, folder 10, Derrick A. Bell Jr. Papers.

16 See interview with Jefferson Rogers by Paul Ortiz (August 14 2012), AAHP 280A, African American History Project, University of Florida Samuel Proctor Oral History Program, transcript online at http://ufdcimages.uflib.ufl.edu.

17 See "Dr. Jefferson P. Rogers Obituary," *Daytona Beach News-Journal* (August 10, 2014). www.legacy.com.

18 Derrick Bell, *Ethical Ambition*, 100–1.

19 Jefferson P. Rogers, in "Remembrance of Jewel Hairston Bell" (August 1991), 14–15, box 109, folder 10, Derrick A. Bell Jr. Papers.

20 Bell, *Ethical Ambition*, 101–2. Both Derrick and Jewel had served in many levels at the camp prior to their time in DC, independently of each other. Derrick cherished the time he spent as program director during law school. See Derrick A. Bell Jr., interviewed by Larry Crowe, December 1, 2004, session 1, tape 2, story 2, HistoryMakers Digital Archive. Derrick A. Bell Jr. describes his experience at Camp James Weldon Johnson, https://da.thehistorymakers.org/story /303562.

21 For an important study comparing Bell and Niebuhr, see Taylor, "Racism as 'The National Crucial Sin.'"

22 Bell's short sermons and prayer compositions for daily prayer in Harvard's Memorial Church and other chapels can be found throughout his archive. See box 11, folder 3; box 19, folder 7; box 21, folder 40; box 23, folder 25; box 24, folder 40; box 40, folder 7, Derrick A. Bell Jr. Papers. Each of these entries represents a different time, primarily in the 1970s, when Bell was a featured speaker at daily prayer. The archive includes many other instances where he spoke in churches, sometimes offering the main sermon on Sunday mornings.

23 Harvard Law School, "HLS in the World | Derrick Bell: The Professor as Protester," YouTube, November 9, 2017, https://youtu.be /eEhI-0QGfME?si=jWWQKUYhnAbtZBXo.

24 Bell, Law School Application Essay, 2.

25 Bell, Law School Application Essay, 4.

26 Bunche, *A World View of Race*, 25.

27 See Bell, *Faces at the Bottom of the Well*; and Bell, "Racial Realism." Bell's understanding of racism's permanence is the crux of contro- versy over whether Bell was in fact a racial pessimist. For

contemporary responses to the concept that shaped CRT, see Delgado, "Derrick Bell's Racial Realism"; and powell, "Racial Realism or Racial Despair?" See also Myrdal, *An American Dilemma*.

28 See Erakat, *Justice for Some*; and Erakat, Li, and Reynolds, "Race, Palestine, and International Law."

29 Bell, *Silent Covenants*, 3.

30 Bell, *Silent Covenants*, 3.

31 Bell, *Confronting Authority*, 18.

32 For more on Hastie's activism within the Roosevelt administration, see McGuire, *He, Too, Spoke for Democracy*; and James, *The Double V*, chapter 11.

33 See the program website, "Hastie Fellowship: Increasing Diversity & Inclusion in the Legal Academy," University of Wisconsin, Madison, Law School, https://law.wisc.edu/hastie/.

34 Trubek, "Foundational Events."

35 Derrick Bell letter to Kimberlé Crenshaw, September 11, 1986, box 18, folder 2, Derrick A. Bell Jr. Papers.

36 Crenshaw, "Race, Reform, and Retrenchment."

37 Crenshaw, "The First Decade," 1359; and Trubek, "Foundational Events," 1506.

38 Bell, Law School Application Essay, 2, 4.

39 Bell, "Black Students in White Law Schools," 545. During the same year he wrote this essay providing insight into Black law student anxieties at predominantly white institutions, he wrote to Judge Hastie, saying, "In any event I am well into my first year and have noted no evidence that my presence has caused the walls of this august institution to crumble" (Bell to William Hastie [February 17 1970], box 2, folder 2, Derrick A. Bell Jr. Papers). This letter is also discussed in Kennedy, *Say It Loud*, 36.

40 Bell, *Confronting Authority*, 18.

41 Derrick Bell, "In Memoriam" (likely 1959), box 144, folder 16, Derrick A. Bell Jr. Papers.

42 Bell, *Confronting Authority*, 20.

43 Motley, *Equal Justice under Law*, 66, 173.

44 Motley, *Equal Justice under Law*, 149.

45 Bell, *Ethical Ambition*, 102; Derrick Bell to Clifford Alexander, June 24 1960, box 1, folder 1, Derrick A. Bell Jr. Papers; C. L. Alexander to Derrick Bell, June 28 1960, box 1, folder 1, Derrick A. Bell Jr. Papers,

confirming the lease arrangement. Riverton Houses was a project built by Met Life Insurance Company.

46 When the lawsuit was first filed in 1961, Charles Dickson Fair served as president of the board of trustees of the State Institutions of Higher Learning for the State of Mississippi.

47 Cited in Brown-Nagin, *Civil Rights Queen*, 195.

48 Motley, *Equal Justice under Law*, 162, 165.

49 Motley, *Equal Justice under Law*, 163.

50 For more on Shores and other Black lawyers in Alabama, see Clemon and Fair, "Making Bricks without Straw."

51 See Krochmal, "An Unmistakably Working-Class Vision," 933.

52 Judge U. W. Clemon, interview by Aja Y. Martinez and Robert O. Smith, February 9, 2024.

53 Clemon interview.

54 Motley, *Equal Justice under Law*, 174.

55 Motley, *Equal Justice under Law*, 164; Bell, *Silent* Covenants, 99; Bell, *Ethical Ambition*, 138. Medgar Evers's spouse, Myrlie, would also shuttle people to and from the airport in her 1957 Chevrolet Nomad station wagon. See Reid, *Medgar & Myrlie*, 114.

56 Bell, *Silent Covenants*, 100.

57 Motley, *Equal Justice under Law*, 151–52.

58 Kynard, *Vernacular Insurrections*, 167.

59 Motley, *Equal Justice under Law*, 183.

60 Motley, *Equal Justice under Law*, 172.

61 Motley, *Equal Justice under Law*, 171.

62 Bell, *Ethical Ambition*, 139.

63 Hudson and Curry, *Mississippi Harmony*, 65.

64 Hudson and Curry, *Mississippi Harmony*, 115.

65 Bell, *Confronting Authority*, 22, citing Rowan, *Dream Maker*, 237.

66 Rowan, *Dream Maker*, 237.

2. RICHARD DELGADO AND JEAN STEFANCIC

Epigraph: Gilbert, "The Abnormal Is Not Courage," 3.

1 This section is drawn from transcripts of US Senate Committee on the Judiciary, "The Nomination of Ketanji Brown Jackson to be an Associate Justice of the Supreme Court of the United States," March 21 2022, www.judiciary.senate.gov.

2 Harris, "Preface," xvi.

3 Ecarma, "Turns out Ted Cruz."

4 See Delgado, "On the Importance of Critical Race Theory."

5 Martinez, *Counterstory*, 18.

6 Pluckrose and Lindsay, *Cynical Theories*, 114.

7 Baucham, *Fault Lines*. On the plagiarism controversy, see Smietana, "Voddie Baucham's Publisher."

8 See US Senate, "The Nomination of Ketanji Brown Jackson."

9 There was quite a bit more going on. See Kerlow, *Poisoned Ivy*.

10 Baum and Miller, "The Hollywood Reporter."

11 Pollard, *Sex and Violence*, 95.

12 Ceplair and Trumbo, *Dalton Trumbo*, chapter 13.

13 Richard Delgado, interview by Aja Y. Martinez and Robert O. Smith, September 2, 2023.

14 Albert Maltz, interview by Joel Gardner (1975, 1976, 1978, 1979). Transcript of a thirty-six-hour interview completed under the auspices of the UCLA Oral History Program. 1.48, tape 21, side 2, December 22, 1978, https://static.library.ucla.edu.

15 Maltz interview, February 13, 1975, tape 1, side 2.

16 Delgado interview.

17 See "Men's U.S. 10,000 Rankings by Athlete," *Track & Field News*, https://trackandfieldnews.com; Delgado interview.

18 Delgado interview.

19 Delgado interview.

20 "Marine Reservist in Trouble," *News Notes of the Central Committee for Conscientious Objectors* 18, no. 4 (July–August 1966), 1, https://content.wisconsinhistory.org; Delgado interview.

21 "Peace Runners Are Searching for Another Car," *Daily Tribune* (Great Bend, Kansas), November 8, 1965, 9, https://access.newspaperarchive.com.

22 Delgado interview.

23 Delgado interview.

24 Delgado, "Metamorphosis," 6–7.

25 Delgado, "Metamorphosis," 6–7.

26 Delgado, "Metamorphosis," 6–7.

27 Delgado, "Metamorphosis," 6–7.

28 Delgado, "Metamorphosis," 6–7.

29 Marchese, "Joyce Carol Oates."

30 Marchese, "Joyce Carol Oates."

31 Jean Stefancic, interview by Aja Y. Martinez and Robert O. Smith, September 2, 2023.

32 Now Case Western Reserve University.

33 For a portion of *Operation Abolition*, see Zinn Education Project, "This Day in History: May 14, 1960: Firehoses Confront Free Speech in S.F. City Hall," Zinn Education Project, www.zinnedproject.org. Resource courtesy Jean Stefancic.

34 Stefancic interview.

35 See "Archibald MacLeish Is Dead: Poet and Playwright was 89," *New York Times*, April 12, 1982, A1.

36 See Delgado and Stefancic, "Panthers and Pinstripes."

37 Stefancic interview.

38 Stefancic interview.

39 Stefancic interview.

40 See "U. W. Clemon: The Equalizer," *Legal Defense Fund News*, July 10, 2014, reposted from *Columbia Law School Magazine*, www .naacpldf.org. These details were confirmed and expanded on in an interview with Judge Clemon by Aja Y. Martinez and Robert O. Smith, February 9, 2024.

41 Stefancic interview.

42 Stefancic interview.

43 King, "Letter from Birmingham City Jail," 95.

44 Stefancic interview.

45 Stefancic interview. john a. powell "spells his name in lowercase in the belief that we should be 'part of the universe, not over it, as capitals signify.'" See https://belonging.berkeley.edu/john-powell.

46 Stefancic interview.

47 Baucham, *Fault Lines*, xvi.

48 Menzie, "'Fault Lines' Author Voddie Baucham."

49 Stefancic interview.

50 Bell, "Foreword."

51 Bell, "Foreword." See Wildman, *Privilege Revealed*.

52 See Grillo, "Anti-Essentialism and Intersectionality"; and Grillo, "The Mediation Alternative." In January 1997, the *University of Minnesota Law Review* devoted an issue to a symposium on Grillo's life and thought. Jean and Richard, along with many other colleagues, contributed pieces.

53 Lawrence, "The Id, the Ego, and Equal Protection."

54 Stefancic interview.

55 Delgado and Stefancic, "Why Do We Tell the Same Stories?"

56 Gilbert, "The Abnormal Is Not Courage," 3.

57 Stefancic interview.
58 Stefancic and Delgado, "Panthers and Pinstripes."
59 See Stefancic and Delgado, *How Lawyers Lose Their Way*.
60 See Stefancic, "Listen to the Voices"; and Stefancic, "The Law Review Symposium Issue."
61 Stefancic interview.
62 John Shafer, interview by Aja Y. Martinez and Robert O. Smith, January 5, 2024, at the Zief Library, University of San Francisco. Special thanks to Lisa Anderson for guiding us on campus. Richard Delgado, for his part, has remarked, "Don't ignore AI or you'll find yourself replaced by a robot at an awkward stage of your career" (*Literary Hub*).
63 Delgado, "Storytelling for Oppositionists and Others."
64 Delgado, "Rodrigo's Chronicle."
65 Richard Delgado, interview by Aja Y. Martinez and Robert O. Smith, September 1, 2023.
66 Richard Delgado, interview by Aja Y. Martinez and Robert O. Smith, June 3, 2023.
67 Email from Richard Delgado to authors, March 11, 2023.
68 Delgado interview, September 1, 2023.
69 Richard Delgado and Jean Stefancic are each contributing single-authored lead articles to *College English*'s September and November 2024 special double-issue on CRT.
70 Delgado interview, September 1, 2023.
71 Delgado interview, September 2, 2023.

3. FINDING GENEVA

 1 Motley, *Equal Justice under Law*, 174.
 2 Motley, *Equal Justice under Law*, 174; On Evers's 1962 Oldsmobile 88, see Ginder, "Biographies: Medgar W. Evers," National Museum of the United States Army, www.thenmusa.org; and Dorman, "Who Killed Medgar Evers?," 52. Mitchell, *Race against Time*, 50. On Medgar Evers's investigatory and organizing roles around the lynching of Emmett Till and the subsequent trial of his killers, see chapter 3 in Reid, *Medgar & Myrlie*.
 3 Motley, *Equal Justice under Law*, 174.
 4 Further information about the offensive mural is drawn from Hudson and Curry, *Mississippi Harmony*. It would be covered by a gray cloth following the passage of the 1964 Civil Rights Act. See

Greene, "Pride and Prejudice." See also the official description of the mural in situ: General Services Administration, "Simka Simkhovitch: Pursuits of Life in Mississippi, 1938," GSA Fine Arts Collection, Public Buildings Service. For a discussion of the mural and its history, see Resnik and Curtis, *Representing Justice*, 113–15.

5 Greene, "Pride and Prejudice."

6 Greene, "Pride and Prejudice."

7 Greene, "Pride and Prejudice"; Motley, *Equal Justice under Law*, 76.

8 Brown-Nagin, *Civil Rights Queen*, 148–49.

9 Greene, "Pride and Prejudice."

10 Greene, "Pride and Prejudice."

11 Greene, "Pride and Prejudice."

12 Greenberg, *Crusaders in the Courts*, 36, 39; Motley, *Equal Justice under Law*, 75.

13 Brown-Nagin, *Civil Rights Queen*, 149.

14 Brown-Nagin, *Civil Rights Queen*, 149.

15 Brown-Nagin, *Civil Rights Queen*, 149.

16 Brown-Nagin, *Civil Rights Queen*, 149.

17 Motley, *Equal Justice under Law*, 77.

18 Greene, "Pride and Prejudice"; Brown-Nagin, *Civil Rights Queen*, 149.

19 Greene, "Pride and Prejudice"; Brown-Nagin, *Civil Rights Queen*, 149.

20 Greene, "A Short Commentary on the Chronicles," 60.

21 Email from Carol Steiker to authors, December 19, 2023.

22 Bell, *And We Are Not Saved*, xii.

23 Bell, "Foreword," 13.

24 Tushnet and Lynch, "The Project of the Harvard Forewords," 470.

25 Bell, "Comments and Introduction," 47.

26 Bell, "Comments and Introduction," 47.

27 Tushnet and Lynch, "The Project of the Harvard Forewords," 470–71.

28 See Bell, "Neither Separate Schools nor Mixed Schools."

29 Bell, "Serving Two Masters," 471.

30 Bell, "*Brown v. Board of Education*," 523, 524.

31 Dudziak, "Desegregation as a Cold War Imperative."

32 Bell, *Shades of Brown*.

33 Bell, "A Holiday for Dr. King," 434n1.

34 Bell, "A Holiday for Dr. King," 435, emphasis in original.

35 Derrick Bell, Handwritten Poems (likely 1950s), box 144, folder 16, Derrick A. Bell Jr. Papers. Also Derrick Bell, "In Memoriam," box 144, folder 16, Derrick A. Bell Jr. Papers.

36 Derrick Bell, "Drafts and Outlines of *Still Looking for the Pony*," box 144, folder 17, Derrick A. Bell Jr. Papers. The drafts contain vivid memoir of Bell's time in Mississippi, especially the story titled "Mississippi Morning."

37 Letter from Timothy C. Robinson to Derrick Bell, box 60, folder 15, Derrick A. Bell Jr. Papers. This letter is from Robinson, vice president and general manager, law division of Little, Brown, expressing regret that Derrick's idea for a trade book "to review progress in education since *Brown* and consider whether or not alternatives to integration as a remedy are educationally and constitutionally acceptable" would not be marketable for the press.

38 Derrick Bell letter to Marcia Ann Gillespie (*Essence*), June 4, 1980, box 23, folder 3, Derrick A. Bell Jr. Papers. Bell eventually had a piece published in *Essence*, the "Electric Slide Protest." See Gordon Chambers to Derrick Bell, April 18, 1996, box 109, folder 19, Derrick A. Bell Jr. Papers.

39 Derrick Bell, "Dependent Status" (likely final revision), pages 9–10, box 23, folder 3, Derrick A. Bell Jr. Papers.

40 Derrick A. Bell Jr., interviewed by Larry Crowe, December 1, 2004, Digital Archive, A2004.242, session 1, tape 6, story 2. Bell describes his characters in "Faces at the Bottom of the Well" and "Gospel Choirs," https://da.thehistorymakers.org/story/303600.

41 Bell "Foreword," 71.

42 Pollak, "Exclusive."

43 Delgado, "Liberal McCarthyism," 1544.

44 Bell, "Foreword," 4.

45 Bell, "Booknotes."

46 Robert A. Williams, interview by Aja Y. Martinez and Robert O. Smith, February 6, 2023.

47 Bell, *And We Are Not Saved*, xi.

48 Bell, "Foreword," 83.

49 Austin, "Resistance Tactics for Tokens," 53.

50 Greene, "A Short Commentary," 61–62.

51 Bell, "Comments and Introduction," 51. Williams, "A Brief Comment," 79–80n1.

52 See, for instance, letter exchange between Derrick Bell and Harold T. Commons, October 24, 1986, box 18, folder 5, and letter exchange between Derrick Bell and Kenneth S. Tollett, November 24, 1986, box 18, folder 5. This same folder contains many other examples of requests for article offprints, which became scarce.

53 Bell, *And We Are Not Saved*, xii.

54 Cobb, "The Man behind Critical Race Theory."

55 Ron Herndon, "Civil Rights Scholar Inspired by Portland Woman," *Portland Observer*, October 19, 2011.

56 Ron Herndon, interview by Aja Y. Martinez and Robert O. Smith, 21 May 2024.

57 On composite characters, see Martinez, *Counterstory*, 23–25.

58 Stephanie Y. Moore, interview by Aja Y. Martinez and Robert O. Smith, October 13, 2023. See also letter to Derrick Bell from Stephanie Y. Moore, January 15, 1987, box 160, folder 6, Derrick A. Bell Jr. Papers. Moore's letter, written while she was clerking for Judge A. Leon Higginbotham Jr., is remarkable for its length, candor, and detailed critique of Bell's draft writing. The letter, as it sits in the archive, contains several marginal notes in Bell's hand, indicating that Moore's comments were incorporated as revisions in subsequent drafts.

59 Derrick A. Bell, Jr. session 1, tape 6, story 2, HistoryMakers Digital Archive A2004.242.

60 Stephanie Y. Moore, interview by Aja Y. Martinez and Robert O. Smith, February 9, 2024.

61 Diehl, "We're Here Because Sonia Sanchez Wants to Reactivate Activism."

62 Bell, "Booknotes" interview.

63 Derrick A. Bell Jr., interviewed by Larry Crowe, December 1, 2004, HistoryMakers Digital Archive A2004.242, session 1, tape 6, story 2. Derrick A. Bell, Jr. describes his characters in "Faces at the Bottom of the Well" and "Gospel Choirs," https://da.thehistorymakers.org /story/303600. By this time, in 2004, Bell was long remarried to Janet Dewart Bell, who certainly is to be included within a pantheon of possible Genevas.

64 See Wing, *Critical Race Feminism*. Bell wrote the foreword to the first edition; Richard Delgado wrote the foreword for the second. *Critical America*, edited by Richard Delgado and Jean Stefancic, is also the home of Delgado and Stefancic, *Critical Race Theory: An*

Introduction. In 1993, Bell received the "Good Brother Award" from the National Political Congress of Black Women. See "Civil Rights and Gender Issues: The National Political Congress of Black Women," C-SPAN, July 31, 1993, www.c-span.org/video/?47287-1 /civil-rights-gender-issues. Janet Dewart Bell was thanked for her role in Bell's prioritizing his presence at the event: "Mrs. Bell thank you for telling him to be here. . . . When his wife learned that we women were going to give him this award, she said 'You change your schedule.'" Finally, see Vastine, "'Our Survival Hope'"; and Vastine's argument that storytelling, informed by intentional engagement with womanist and feminist theory, allows authors of other subject-positions to responsibly participate in conversations with other identities.

65 Bell, "Booknotes" interview.

66 Bell, *Confronting Authority*, 11.

67 Bell, "Booknotes" interview.

68 Box 1, folder 1, Derrick A. Bell Jr. Papers (MC.138), contains letters of recommendation from Jack Greenberg, Robert L. Carter, and Constance Baker Motley.

69 Correspondence from Constance Baker Motley to Martin Levine, January 29, 1968, box 1, folder 9, Derrick A. Bell Jr. Papers.

70 Sara Lawrence Lightfoot, "Remembrance of Jewel Hairston Bell," in *Remembrance: Jewel Hairston Bell*, edited by Derrick Bell (August 1991), page 14, box 109, folder 10, Derrick A. Bell Jr. Papers.

71 Bell, *Ethical Ambition*, 104.

72 Bell, *Ethical Ambition*, 104.

73 Bell, *Ethical Ambition*, 102–3.

74 Derrick A. Bell Jr., interviewed by Larry Crowe, December 1, 2004, session 1, tape 3, story 4, HistoryMakers Digital Archive. Bell describes his marriage to Jewel Hairston Bell, https://da .thehistorymakers.org/story/303573.

75 Bell interview with Larry Crowe.

76 Bell interview with Larry Crowe.

77 Stephanie Y. Moore, interview by Aja Y. Martinez and Robert O. Smith, October 13, 2023.

78 Derrick Bell, "Statement by Derrick Bell at Appreciation Weekend, October 19–20, 1990," in *Remembrance: Jewel Hairston Bell*, edited by Derrick Bell (August 1991), pages 8 and 9, box 109, folder 10, Derrick A. Bell Jr. Papers.

79 Bell, "Statement by Derrick Bell at Appreciation Weekend," page 8.
80 Hudson, *Mississippi Harmony*, 81. Records held by the Wisconsin Historical Society show that among the a thousand or so volunteers who came to Mississippi from the North, three from Carthage, Wisconsin—Dorothy Teel, Hank Werner, and Judy Werner—stayed in the home of Mrs. Behonor McDonald. Other Wisconsin-based volunteers taking part in the Carthage-Harmony Project stayed in the homes of Winson and Dovie Hudson. See Wisconsin Historical Society, "Carthage-Harmony Project volunteers," box 2, folder 4, Hank Werner papers, Z, Accessions, M71–358, https://content .wisconsinhistory.org.
81 Bell, *Silent Covenants*, 102–3.
82 Bell, *Silent Covenants*, 100–1.
83 The American Friends Service Committee (AFSC), an outgrowth of the Quaker movement, was founded in 1917 to provide an alternative for pacifists unwilling to fight in World War I. See the AFSC website, "History," https://afsc.org/history. The Quaker principle of nonviolence, articulated in the seventeenth century, stands in constant tension with the demands of the nation-state. See Hulbert, "Quaker Pacifism in the Context of War."
84 Bell, *Silent Covenants*, 100–1.
85 Egerton, *Speak Now against the Day*, 126. We are indebted to Jean Stefancic for first mentioning this volume to us.
86 Oral history interview with Jean Fairfax, October 15, 1983. Interview F-0013 by Dallas A. Blanchard, Southern Oral History Program Collection (#4007) in the Southern Oral History Program Collection, Southern Historical Collection, Wilson Library, University of North Carolina at Chapel Hill, tape 1, side A, transcript at https://docsouth.unc.edu/sohp/html_use/F-0013.html. Another important oral history interview with Jean Fairfax located in the Southern Regional Council Oral History Collection of the Samuel Proctor Oral History Program recordings in the University of Florida Digital Collections. See Jean Fairfax, "SRC 20 Interviewee: Jean Fairfax," by Brian Ward, February 26, 2003, https://original -ufdc.uflib.ufl.edu.
87 See Niebuhr, "Ten Years That Shook My World."
88 For more on Niebuhr, see Lovin, *Reinhold Niebuhr and Christian Realism*.
89 Egerton, *Speak Now against the Day*, 426–27.

90 Greenberg, *Crusaders in the Courts*, 581n382.

91 Titus, Brown's *Battleground*, 42.

92 Greenberg, *Crusaders in the Courts*, 382–83.

93 Manuel, "Jean Fairfax."

94 Titus, Brown's *Battleground*, 42.

95 See Williams, "Gathering the Ghosts"; and Harrison, "Gathering the Ghosts."

96 Williams, *The Alchemy of Race and Rights*; and Prendergast, *Literacy and Racial Justice*, 53.

97 Williams, "Tribute in Memory of Professor Derrick Bell."

98 Harvard Law School, "HLS in the World | Derrick Bell: The Professor as Protestor," November 9, 2017, YouTube, www.youtube.com/watch?v=eEhI-0QGfME&ab_channel=HarvardLawSchool.

99 Williams, "Tribute in Memory of Professor Derrick Bell."

100 See Derrick Bell, Letter to Patricia Williams, October 9, 1985, box 145, folder 31, Derrick A. Bell Jr. Papers; and Patricia Williams, Memo to Derrick Bell, January 23, 1985, box 145, folder 31, Derrick A. Bell Jr. Papers.

101 Patricia Williams, Memo to Sharon with handwritten note on copy shared with Derrick Bell, undated, box 145, folder 31, Derrick A. Bell Jr. Papers. The allegory is presented at the beginning of her pathbreaking article, "Alchemical Notes," and again in her book, *Alchemy of Race and Rights*. See Williams, "Alchemical Notes."

102 "HLS in the World."

103 Derrick Bell, Letter to Patricia Williams, September 7, 1987, box 27, folder 20, Derrick A. Bell Jr. Papers, enclosing "Bicentennial Celebration: CUNY Law School at Queens College (Flushing, NY)," a script prepared by Bell for public performance with Patricia Williams.

104 Bell, *Ethical Ambition*, 105–6.

105 J Bell, *Lighting the Fires of Freedom*; and Bell, *Blackbirds Singing*.

106 See letter to Derrick Bell from Stephanie Y. Moore, January 15, 1987, page 7, box 160, folder 6, Derrick A. Bell Jr. Papers.

107 Emma Scruggs Rodgers, interview by Aja Y. Martinez and Robert O. Smith, June 29, 2023. Rodgers explained that "sit 'n' runs" happened before there was a clear civil disobedience strategy in place, long before Constance Baker Motley and other NAACP- and LDF-related attorneys developed legal strategies to spring young activists from jail.

108 Harris, "Remembering Dallas' Black Images Book Bazaar."

109 Bell, *Faces at the Bottom of the Well.*

110 Emma Scruggs Rodgers, interview by Aja Y. Martinez and Robert O. Smith, September 27, 2023.

111 Bell, *Race, Racism, and American Law.*

112 Rodgers interview, September 27, 2023.

113 Singley, "Tributes in Memory of Professor Derrick Bell."

114 Kerlow, *Poisoned Ivy*, 87.

115 Letter to Derrick Bell from Carol Steiker, July 3, 1986, box 18, folder 1, Derrick A. Bell Jr. Papers.

116 Bell, *And We Are Not Saved*, xi.

4. CLASH OF THE TITANS

1 Stephanie Y. Moore, interview by Aja Y. Martinez and Robert O. Smith, October 13, 2023.

2 Judge U. W. Clemon, interview by Aja Y. Martinez and Robert O. Smith, February 9, 2024. Judge Clemon continues to be an outspoken advocate of affirmative action. See Clemon, "Time to Expand the Supreme Court."

3 Fair, "U. W. Clemon."

4 Clemon interview, February 9, 2024.

5 Moore interview.

6 See Bell, *The Derrick Bell Reader*, 7.

7 See Derrick Bell, "Memorandum to Dean Bok: Visiting Black Law Professional Program, 1970–1971 School Year," May 22, 1970, box 2, folder 13, Derrick A. Bell Jr. Papers.

8 Crenshaw, "The First Decade," 1347.

9 Tyler and Muldrow, "Letter to the Editor." See also Crenshaw, "The First Decade," 1348.

10 See Horn, "Third World Coalition"; Herrera, "Challenging a Tradition of Exclusion," 61.

11 Crenshaw "The First Decade," 1349; see also Crenshaw, "Twenty Years of Critical Race Theory," 1267.

12 Dorning, "In the Minority"; Crenshaw, "Twenty Years," 1283n102. On COINTEL, see Cunningham, *There's Something Happening Here.* Between 1956 and 1971, FBI covert operations, including direct violence, were used to discredit various civil rights and human rights activists and organizations. For further reading, see the book list provided by the Freedom Archives, www.freedomarchives.org.

13 Crenshaw "The First Decade," 1349; Crenshaw "Twenty Years," 1267.

14 Donald Christopher Tyler, interview by Aja Y. Martinez and Robert O. Smith, February 21, 2024; edits and contributions by Donald Christopher Tyler, March 22, 2024.

15 According to Donald C. Tyler, all BLSA members in attendance at this meeting with Vorenberg, with the exception of Crenshaw, "were members of what some BLSA members derisively called 'Muhammad's Kitchen Cabinet,' also known as 'The Political Action Committee.'" Edits and contributions by Donald Christopher Tyler, March 22, 2024.

16 Crenshaw, "Twenty Years," 1267.

17 Crenshaw, "Twenty Years," 1267.

18 Harvard Black Law Student Association (BLSA) students seized on this statement from Vorenberg, repeating it often in the months that followed. The Third World Coalition letter to the Harvard Law School community, urging boycott of the Greenberg/Chambers course, responded obliquely to this claim, saying, "The lack of Third World professors at Harvard Law School is not due to a vacuum of qualified Third World legal professionals, but rather to the institution's inadequate search methods and the biased criteria it uses to judge prospective Third World faculty candidates" (letter of May 24, 1982, reprinted in Sollors, Titcomb, and Underwood, *Blacks at Harvard*, 457. Student debate regarding the boycott raged in fall 1982 issues of the Law School student newspaper, the *Harvard Law Record*. Given the media firestorm that erupted over the summer, BLSA leaders needed to quote Vorenberg more directly. Donald Tyler, a second-year Law School student appointed to the BLSA executive committee, recalled the group's meeting with Vorenberg to a student newspaper reporter. When the group "specifically requested that [the course] be taught by a black professor," Tyler recalled, "Vorenberg . . . asked if they would not prefer 'an excellent white professor' to 'a mediocre black one.' Tyler said the students objected to Vorenberg's alleged characterization of the choice facing the administration" (Horn, "Third World Coalition," 13). The phrases are quoted again in Tyler and Muldrow, "Goal of a Boycott at Harvard Law." Tyler confirmed his recollection in a 2008 interview with the *Harvard Crimson*; see Phillip, "Race Sparked HLS Tension."

19 Edits and contributions by Donald Christopher Tyler, March 22, 2024.

20 Crenshaw, "Twenty Years," 1267, with edits and contributions by Donald Christopher Tyler, March 22, 2024.

21 Edits and contributions by Donald Christopher Tyler, March 22, 2024.

22 Motley, *Equal Justice under Law*, 150.

23 Motley, *Equal Justice under Law*, 152.

24 Greenberg, *Crusaders in the Courts*, 297.

25 Greenberg, *Crusaders in the Courts*, 294.

26 Motley, *Equal Justice Under Law*, 151; Greenberg *Crusaders in the Courts*, 294.

27 Lomax, *The Negro Revolt*, 186.

28 Greenberg, *Crusaders in the Courts*, 297.

29 Lomax, *The Negro Revolt*, 179–80, 180. Lomax was quoted in Kennedy, "On Cussing Out White Liberals," 171. Lomax's neologism, "go-slowism," from 1962 prefigures Martin Luther King Jr.'s complaint against white moderates: "For years now I have heard the word 'Wait!' It rings in the ear of every Negro with piercing familiarity. This 'Wait' has almost always meant 'Never,'" King wrote in April 1963. "I have been gravely disappointed with the white moderate . . . who constantly advises the Negro to wait for a 'more convenient season.' Shallow understanding from people of good will is more frustrating than absolute misunderstanding from people of ill will" (King , "Letter from Birmingham City Jail," 295).

30 Motley, *Equal Justice under Law*, 151; Greenberg, *Crusaders in the Courts*, 297. For a discussion of Motley's view of the succession controversy, see Brown-Nagin, *Civil Rights Queen*, 127–40.

31 Motley, *Equal Justice under Law*, 150.

32 Motley, *Equal Justice under Law*, 151.

33 Greenberg, *Crusaders in the Courts*, 295.

34 Matsuda, "Looking to the Bottom"; Crenshaw, "Demarginalizing the Intersection of Race and Sex." In her illustration of intersectionality, Crenshaw nods to Sojourner Truth in her 1851 speech "Ain't I a Woman?" and Anna Julia Cooper in her 1892 essay "The Colored Woman's Office," who, like Motley, are Black feminist trailblazers exemplifying the tenet.

35 Motley, *Equal Justice under Law*, 151.

36 Motley, *Equal Justice under Law*, 152–53.

37 For Greenberg's recounting of this conversation, see Greenberg, *Crusaders in the Courts*, 34.

38 Motley, *Equal Justice under Law*, 152.
39 Greenberg, *Crusaders in the Courts*, 502.
40 See Bonilla-Silva, *Racism without Racists*.
41 Jenkins, "Kitchen Bookshelf"; Julia Child, back cover blurb for Jack Greenberg and James Vorenberg, *Dean Cuisine*.
42 Greenberg, "In Memoriam," 5.
43 Greenberg, "In Memoriam," 5–6; See "Elizabeth Vorenberg Obituary," *Boston Globe*, July 21, 2018, ww.legacy.com; "LDF Mourns the Passing of Civil Rights Attorney and Former LDF Litigator Deborah Greenberg," *Legal Defense Fund* , September 21, 2021, www .naacpldf.org.
44 Greenberg, "In Memoriam," 6.
45 Greenberg and Vorenberg, *Dean Cuisine*, 3.
46 "In Memoriam: Jack Greenberg (1924–2016)," Columbia Law School, www.law.columbia.edu.
47 Greenberg, "In Memoriam," 8; Herrera, "Challenging a Tradition of Exclusion," 61, 64.
48 Edits and contributions by Donald Christopher Tyler, March 22, 2024. Vorenberg and Greenberg maintained that Chambers was asked to teach the course first. Stephanie Y. Moore, who worked in the North Carolina law offices of Chambers the summer of 1983 (the summer after the mini-course protest and boycott), objects to this version of events. According to Moore, "As to some of the context provided in this chapter, I would like to just note my very clear recollection before and after arriving at HLS that Dean Vorenberg had only invited Jack to teach the winter term." Email communication with Stephanie Y. Moore, January 15, 2024.
49 Greenberg, *Crusaders in the Courts*, 502.
50 Crenshaw, "Twenty Years," 1267–68.
51 Crenshaw, "Twenty Years," 1268.
52 Greenberg, *Crusaders in the Courts*, 502.
53 Greenberg, *Crusaders in the Courts*, 501; Haberman, "NYC; Soldiering On," B1.
54 Haberman, "Soldiering On," B1.
55 Felber, "'Those Who Say Don't Know and Those Who Know Don't Say,'" 93. The dissertation was edited and published in 2020. The next year, Felber would be summarily fired from his tenure-stream post following a departmental conflict at the University of Mississippi.

56 Derrick Bell, "NAACP News" broadcast transcript, August 16, 1959. General Office File, Black Muslims, 1958–1960, Part 24: Special Subjects, 1956–1965, Series A: Africa-Films, Papers of the NAACP, Library of Congress, cited in Felber, "'Those Who Say Don't Know,'" 79.

57 Miller, "Farewell to Liberals," 238.

58 Derrick Bell Jr. to Loren Miller, November 9, 1962, box 10, folder 5, Loren Miller Papers, cited in Felber, "'Those Who Say Don't Know,'" 254.

59 Greenberg, *Crusaders in the Courts*, 403.

60 Greenberg, *Crusaders in the Courts*, 404.

61 Greenberg, *Crusaders in the Courts*, 406.

62 Greenberg, *Crusaders in the Courts*, 405.

63 Feldman, "Race-Consciousness versus Colorblindness," 159.

64 Bell, "Letters: Legal Defense Fund," 7, 85.

65 Marcus, "Minority Groups Assail Course at Harvard Law." Dave Horn, news editor for the *Harvard Law Record* student newspaper, noted that it was Marcus's own "focusing on the charge that the course was being boycotted because Greenberg was white" which made her report "the catalyst for a media blitz" (see Horn, "Third World Coalition Renews Support for Course Boycott," 13).

66 Crenshaw "The First Decade," 1350n9; and Herrera, "Challenging a Tradition of Exclusion," 61.

67 For the letter exchange, see "The Greenberg-Chambers Incident, Harvard Law School, 1982–1983," in Sollors, Titcomb, and Underwood, *Blacks at Harvard*), 457–74.

68 See Crenshaw, "After Twenty Years," 1276n66. Crenshaw records various efforts by students and some professors, including Bell and Duncan Kennedy, to correct the record.

69 Edits and contributions by Donald Christopher Tyler, March 22, 2024.

70 Bell, "A Question of Credentials," 7, 14. Bell's article was reprinted in *Integrated Education* 20, nos. 3–5 (2006): 99, 100.

71 Christopher Edley Jr., one of two Black professors at Harvard Law School during the controversy, weighed in on the debate through a mainstream news publication. See "The Boycott at Harvard," A23. Randall Kennedy, not yet on a law faculty, published his take as well. See "On Cussing Out White Liberals," 169–72.

72 Greenberg, *Crusaders in the Courts*, 504.

73 Herrera, "Challenging a Tradition," 64. Garcia had not always been in full support of the boycott, wondering if a focus on Greenberg's race would be distracting to broader goals. For Garcia's initial objections, see Horn, "Third World Coalition Renews Support for Course Boycott," 3. For Garcia's communication of the rationale for the change in La Alianza's position, see Garcia, "Letter to the Editor," 11.

74 Crenshaw, "The First Decade," 1348.

75 Tyler and Muldrow, "Goal of a Boycott at Harvard Law."

76 See Herrera, "Challenging a Tradition," 64–65.

77 I Stephanie Y. Moore, interview by Aja Y. Martinez and Robert O. Smith, October 24. 2023.

78 Crenshaw, Gotanda, Peller, and Thomas, *Critical Race Theory*, xxi, xxii.

79 Delgado, "Liberal McCarthyism," 1509.

80 Delgado, "Liberal McCarthyism," 1509.

81 Delgado, "Liberal McCarthyism," 1509.

82 Delgado, "Liberal McCarthyism," 1535; Trubek, "Foundational Events," 1506.

83 Trubek and Trubek "Slaying the Monster."

84 David M. Trubek and Louise G. Trubek, interviewed by Jonathan Simon November 8, 2013, Berkeley Center for the Study of Law and Society, "Conversations in Law and Society: 12. A Conversation with David M. Trubek and Louise G. Trubek," http://www.kaltura.com /tiny/7bcwl.

85 Delgado, "Liberal McCarthyism," 1534.

86 See Crenshaw, "Twenty Years of Critical Race Theory," 1268n44, for Kennedy's comment on *New York Times* coverage of the Greenberg/ Chambers course controversy, expressing his support for student protest and critiquing media bias toward institutional power.

87 Delgado, "Liberal McCarthyism," 1535.

88 See Delgado, "Liberal McCarthyism," 1534; and Kalman, *Yale Law School and the Sixties*, 234, 259–63.

89 Delgado, "Liberal McCarthyism," 1535.

90 See Montoya, "Johns Hopkins University 4.16.20"; and Montoya, "CRT at Harvard, 2020."

91 Cho and Westley, "Historicizing Critical Race Theory's Cutting Edge," 39, 41. For greater context, see Guerrero, *Silence at Boalt Hall*. "Boalt" refers to a now-outmoded informal name for the UC

Berkeley School of Law. See University of California Berkeley School of Law "A Time for Change."

92 Greene, "From Tokenism to Emancipatory Politics," 166. See, "The Ritual of the Minority Law Teachers Conference," 393ff.; and Greene, "Critical Race Theory."

93 Greene, "From Tokenism to Emancipatory Politics," 168, 169. Presentations from the 1985 MLTC were published in a forum by the *University of San Francisco Law Review* 20, no. 3 (Winter 1986).

94 Greene, "From Tokenism to Emancipatory Politics," 171.

95 Greene, "From Tokenism to Emancipatory Politics," 182.

96 Bell was confronted with "a series of lectures by other professors to ensure that my students would gain . . . what it was feared they were missing in my course" (*Confronting Authority*, 115).

97 Richard Delgado and Jean Stefancic, interview by Aja Y. Martinez and Robert O. Smith, April 23, 2023.

98 Bell, *Confronting Authority*, 44–45.

99 Bell, *Confronting Authority*, 47.

100 University of Oregon Division of Equity and Inclusion, "Jewel H. Bell Award."

101 Stanford Black Law Student Association, "Statement of the BLSA at the first 'Enrichment' Session," box 145, folder 27, Derrick A. Bell Jr. Papers.

102 Bell, "The Price and Pain of Racial Perspective," 5. A copy of this column is saved in the box 18, folder 1, Derrick A. Bell Jr. Papers. The article was reprinted in, *The Law and Higher Education*, 1038–41.

103 Gilliam, "An Insult to a Law Professor."

104 All sections were using Brest and Levinson, *Processes of Constitutional Decisionmaking*. See, by way of comparison, Gilliam's incorrectly identifying Bell as Brest's coauthor.

105 Delgado, "An Unanswered Question."

106 See Bell, "Foreword," 5–6; and Bell, "The Real Status of Blacks Today: The Chronicle of the Constitutional Contradiction," in *And We Are Not Saved*, 26–50.

107 Savage, Letter to the Editor, 6.

108 Delgado, "An Unanswered Question."

109 Derrick Bell letter to Gerald (Jerry) Lopez , September 8, 1986, box 18, folder 2, Derrick A. Bell Jr. Papers.

110 Box 18, folder 2, of the Derrick A. Bell Jr. Papers contains several letters from law school deans, friends, and former students who are following the case and its aftermath.

111 Richard Delgado and Jean Stefancic, interview by Aja Y. Martinez and Robert O. Smith, April 11, 2023.

112 Delgado, "An Unanswered Question."

113 Delgado, "Minority Law Professors' Lives," 349–92. The article includes an introduction by Derrick Bell. Gerald Torres assisted in compiling data.

114 For details of that controversy, see Delgado, "Critical Legal Studies and the Realities of Race," 412–13nn30, 31.

115 Delgado, "Storytelling for Oppositionists and Others."

116 See Crenshaw, "Twenty Years," 1282.

117 Delgado, "Imperial Scholar," 577.

118 Quotes drawn from Kennedy, "Racial Critiques of Legal Academia," 1776, 1778.

119 Richard Delgado and Jean Stefancic, interview by Aja Y. Martinez and Robert O. Smith, September 2, 2023.

120 Crenshaw, Gotanda, Peller, and Thomas, *Critical Race Theory*, xxvii–xxviii.

121 See Crenshaw, "Twenty Years," 1290n120.

122 Crenshaw, Gotanda, Peller, and Thomas, *Critical Race Theory*, "Introduction," xxiii.

123 Lawrence, "Foreword," xii, xiii.

124 Edited and expanded versions of their presentations were published in the *Harvard Civil Rights Civil Liberties Law Review* 22, no. 2 (Spring 1987), with a foreword by José A. Bracamonte.

125 Crenshaw, "Twenty Years," 1297.

126 Crenshaw, Gotanda, Peller, and Thomas, *Critical Race Theory*, "Introduction," xxvi.

5. OPEN SEASON

1 See Delgado, "When a Story Is Just a Story," 100, 106, 110. There, he writes "New Race Theorists," when otherwise throughout the essay he refers to the group as "Critical Race Theorists." Delgado—who was also on faculty at Wisconsin Law School during the time this Crenshaw dialogue takes place—composed this essay in July/August 1989 as a response to Randall Kennedy's "Racial Critiques of Legal Academia." With correspondence from Delgado to Derrick Bell in

August 1989, Delgado shares an additional letter sent to Gordon Whitman, a *Harvard Law Review* editor, proposing publication of "When a Story Is Just a Story," in which Delgado describes the "promising new legal movement" as "the emerging new or Critical race theory school of legal scholarship" (Richard Delgado to Derrick Bell, with enclosure, August 3, 1989, box 19, folder 16, Derrick A. Bell, Jr. Papers). While not necessarily reflective of all participants in the July 1989 workshop, Delgado's varied naming of the movement illustrates a dynamic moment in its development.

2 Crenshaw, "The First Decade," 1360.

3 Crenshaw, "The First Decade," 1360.

4 Crenshaw, "The First Decade," 1361.

5 Crenshaw, "The First Decade," 1359; Trubek, "Foundational Events," 1506.

6 Crenshaw, "The First Decade," 1359.

7 Crenshaw, "The First Decade," 1360.

8 Crenshaw, "The First Decade," 1360.

9 Crenshaw, "The First Decade," 1360.

10 Crenshaw, "The First Decade," 1360.

11 Crenshaw, "The First Decade," 1361.

12 Lawrence, "Foreword," xv.

13 Trubek, "Foundational Events," 1506.

14 Bell, *Confronting Authority*, 104–9.

15 See "Harvard Scholar in Sit-In over Tenure Cases," *New York Times*, June 9, 1987, A21.

16 Trubek, "Foundational Events," 1508.

17 Trubek, "Foundational Events," 1511.

18 See, for instance, Lindsay, *Race Marxism*.

19 Trubek, "Foundational Events," 1512.

20 Delgado and Stefancic, "Living History Interview," 225.

21 Ladson-Billings and Tate, "Toward a Critical Race Theory of Education"; Dixson and Rousseau, *Critical Race Theory in Education*, 4–5.

22 Solórzano, Huber, and Huber-Verjan, "Theorizing Racial Microaffirmations," 188.

23 Solórzano, Huber, and Huber-Verjan, "Theorizing Racial Microaffirmations," 188–89. Solórzano is a prolific CRT scholar, counterstoryteller, teacher, and mentor to countless other CRT scholars and counterstorytellers (these authors included). He is

professor of social science and comparative education, and
Chicana/o and Central American studies at the University of
California, Los Angeles, and directs the internationally important
Center for Critical Race Studies in Education at UCLA. Among
many publications and distinguished awards and honors, in 2012,
Solórzano was awarded the Critical Race Studies in Education
Association Derrick A. Bell Legacy Award.

24 Zitser, "Trump Calls on Supporters."
25 Exec. Order 13950, of Sept. 22, 2020, 85 FR 60683, "Combating Race
and Sex Stereotyping," https://federalregister.gov.
26 CRT Forward, UCLA School of Law, Critical Race Studies Program,
https://crtforward.law.ucla.edu.. See also Alexander, Baldwin,
Reinhard, and Zatz, "Tracking the Attack on Critical Race Theory."
27 See Jefferson and Ray, "White Backlash Is a Type of Racial
Reckoning, Too"; and Fortin, "Critical Race Theory."
28 Kruse, "DeSantis' Culture Warrior;" Goldberg, "Meet Christopher
Rufo."
29 Dorman, "Chris Rufo Calls on Trump."
30 Meadows, *The Chief's Chief*, cited in Metzger and Lahut, "Trump
Issued an Executive Order on Critical Race Theory." This sequence
of events is noted as well in Alexander, Clark, Reinhard, and Zatz,
"Tracking the Attack on Critical Race Theory," 10.
31 Christopher Rufo (@realchrisrufo), "We have successfully frozen
their brand—'critical race theory'—into the public conversation. . . ."
Twitter, March 15, 2021, 2:14 p.m., https://twitter.com/realchrisrufo
/status/1371540368714428416?s=20.
32 Christopher Rufo (@realchrisrufo). "The goal is to have the public
read something crazy in the newspaper and immediately think
'critical race theory.'" Twitter, March 15, 2021, 2:17 p.m. https://twitter
.com/realchrisrufo/status/1371541044592996352?s=20.
33 James Lindsay, (@conceptualjames). "Critical Race Theory is falling.
It's end, but not THE end, is coming." Twitter, March 15, 2021, 2:03
p.m., https://twitter.com/ConceptualJames/status
/1371537445599244291?s=20.
34 Jack Murphy, *Jack Murphy Live*, "Panel Show on JML with James
Lindsay and Christopher Rufo," August 3, 2021, YouTube, https://www
.youtube.com/watch?v=fCPvsfR2nsI&ab_channel=JackMurphyLive.
35 On the movement, see Hitchens, Dawkins, Harris, and Dennett, *The
Four Horsemen*.

36 See Mounk, "What an Audacious Hoax Reveals about Academia"; and Pluckrose, Lindsay, and Boghossian, "Understanding the 'Grievance Studies Affair' Papers."

37 Pluckrose and Lindsay, *Cynical Theories.*

38 Jack Murphy, *Jack Murphy Live*, "Panel Show."

39 Lindsey, *Cynical Theories*, 114.

40 Lindsey, *Cynical Theories*, 121.

41 Lindsey, *Cynical Theories*, 133, 134. In their desire to reinstate Enlightenment principles of liberalism, Lindsay and Pluckrose have an aim similar to a previous pair's critiques of CRT. See Farber and Sherry, "Telling Stories out of School." Also see the book-length expansion of the article, Farber and Sherry, *Beyond All Reason.*

42 See, for instance, Kingkade, Zadrozny, and Collins, "Critical Race Theory Battle"; and Hooks, "Critical Race Fury."

43 Lah and Hannah, "Discussions of Critical Race Theory."

44 See Tate, "Afterword."

45 BreitbartTV, "The Vetting: Obama Embraces Racialist Harvard Prof," *Breitbart News*, 2012, www.breitbart.com.

46 In 2008, Obama, while establishing that he was a Christian rather than a Muslim, distanced himself from his former pastor, Jeremiah Wright. See Obama, "On My Faith and My Church."

47 Harris, "The GOP's 'Critical Race Theory' Obsession."

48 Sowell, "Booknotes."

49 Bell, "Booknotes."

50 Bell, *Ethical Ambition*, 103.

51 Sowell, "Derrick Bell and a Revenge Society."

52 "Letter from Barack Obama to Derrick Bell," February 28, 1990, box 58 folder 14, Derrick A. Bell Jr. Papers.

53 Bell, "On Celebrating an Election as Racial Progress." This essay was brought to our attention via Randall Kennedy, *Say It Loud!*, chapter 2.

54 Tushnet, *The NAACP's Legal Strategy*, 11.

55 Bunche, "A Critical Analysis," 315.

56 Bunche, "A Critical Analysis," 316–17.

57 Bunche, "A Critical Analysis," 320.

58 Tushnet, *The NAACP's Legal Strategy*, 12.

59 Bell, "Racial Equality," 511. A critical interest in the relationship between Blacks and Jews in the United States engaged Bell throughout his career.

60 Bell, Higgins, and Suh, "Racial Reflections."

61 Bell, Higgins, and Suh, "Racial Reflections," 1041n17.

62 Anthony Scaramucci, interview by Aja Y. Martinez and Robert O. Smith, November 1, 2023.

63 Anthony Scaramucci, interviews by Aja Y. Martinez and Robert O. Smith, August 4, 2023 and November 1, 2023.

64 Email from Anthony Scarmucci to Aja Y. Martinez and Robert O. Smith, July 18, 2023.

65 Scaramucci interview, November 1, 2023.

66 Scaramucci interviews, August 4, 2023 and November 1, 2023.

67 Scaramucci interviews, August 4, 2023 and November 1, 2023.

68 Scaramucci interview, November 1, 2023.

69 Scaramucci interview, November 1, 2023.

70 Kennedy, *Say It Loud!*, 31.

71 Bell, "The Strange Career of Randall Kennedy," 56. The remainder of this article, a review of Kennedy's book *Race, Crime, and the Law*, provides Bell's most comprehensive assessment of Kennedy's overall project. Bell concludes with a jarring call: "Come home Randy! We advocates of racial justice need you on our side, not in our way" (66). Cf. Bell's 1962 comment on Loren Miller's article, "A Farewell to Liberals," noted above, 119.

72 Letter from Richard Delgado to Derrick Bell, January 30, 1987, box 18, folder 8, Derrick A. Bell Jr. Papers.

73 Letter from Derrick Bell to Richard Delgado, February 12, 1987, box 18, folder 8, Derrick A. Bell Jr. Papers.

74 Rothfeld, "The Law."

75 Bell, "Harvard Law Furor."

76 See Derrick Bell, "Statement," April 24, 1990, page 2, box 55, folder 19, Derrick A. Bell Jr. Papers.

77 See Bell, *Confronting Authority*, 110–11. Here, Bell denies that he intended the statement as a slight against Kennedy, describing it as "off-the-cuff."

78 Bell, "Who's Afraid of Critical Race Theory," 908.

79 Barnett, "Maverick in the Middle."

80 "Obituary: Weldon Douglass Rogers (March 14, 1953–January 29, 2024)," J. Collins Funeral Home, Villa Rica, GA, www.jcollinsfuneral home.com.

81 King, "A Letter to Arthur Ashe."

82 "Dr. Jefferson P. Rogers Obituary," *Daytona Beach News-Journal*, August 10, 2014, www.legacy.com. The Rogers's also established the

Howard Thurman Distinguished Lecture Series, which ran from 1996 to 2011, in partnership with Stetson University. The series featured noted scholars, authors, and civil rights stalwarts, including Derrick Bell (who delivered the inaugural and seven subsequent Thurman lectures), Kwame Ture (formerly Stokely Carmichael), along with US Representative John Lewis, Angela Davis, Rev. Fred Shuttlesworth, Bernestine Singley, and Taylor Branch. The Rogerses also established New Birth Corporation, which eventually acquired, renovated, and continues to preserve the childhood home of Howard Thurman in Daytona Beach, Florida. Qasim Abdul-Tawwab, the Rogers's eldest child, is the current Howard Thurman Home Site Manager for New Birth Corporation.

83 Arsenault, *Arthur Ashe*, esp. 172–73, 206–12.
84 Kennedy, *Say It Loud!*, 67.
85 Kennedy, *Say It Loud!*, 75.
86 Harvard Law School, "HLS in the World | Derrick Bell: The Professor as Protestor," November 9, 2017, YouTube, www.youtube.com/watch?v=eEhI-oQGfME&ab_channel=HarvardLawSchool.
87 Kennedy, *Say It Loud!*, 52.
88 For a legislation-specific example, see D'Innocenzio and Olson, "DEI opponents are using a 1866 Civil Rights Law." For another perspective on the Civil Rights Act of 1866, see Clemon, Karsh, and Mehri, "The Nation's First Civil-Rights Law Needs to Be Fixed."
89 Butler, *Chokehold*, seeks to bring CRT into conversation with the Movement for Black Lives.
90 For the full complement of issues at play, see Harvard Crimson Editorial Board, "Letters to the Editor."
91 Harvard Law School, "HLS in the World | Derrick Bell: The Professor as Protestor."
92 See, for instance, Clark, "A Critique of Professor Derrick A. Bell's Thesis."

CONCLUSION

1 Bell, *Confronting Authority*, 111.
2 Bell, *Confronting Authority*, 171n10.
3 Bell, "Who's Afraid of Critical Race Theory," 894.
4 See Delgado, "When a Story Is Just a Story"; and Kennedy, "Racial Critiques of Legal Academia."

5 Derrick Bell letter to Critical Race Theory Workshop Participants, August 23 1989, box 54, folder 1, Derrick A. Bell Jr. Papers.
6 Delgado, "When a Story Is Just a Story," 109.
7 Delgado, "When a Story Is Just a Story," 110.
8 Jackson, "Shaking Up the Ivy Walls."
9 Bell, "Booknotes."
10 The Association of Black Faculty and Administrators of Harvard University, "Opening Statement," October 25, 1988, page 2, box 28, folder 7, Derrick A. Bell Jr. Papers.
11 Jackson, "Shaking Up the Ivy Walls."
12 Cited in Scheppele, "Foreword," 2075.
13 Scheppele is now Laurance S. Rockefeller Professor of Sociology and International Affairs in the Princeton School of International Affairs and the University Center for Human Values at Princeton University. Scheppele, "Foreword," 2075.
14 Rabkin and Smith, *Teaching Writing That Works*.
15 Derrick Bell, "Legal Storytelling," Memo to Critical Race Theory Workshop Participants and Others, September 30, 1989, box 58, folder 14, Derrick A. Bell Jr. Papers.
16 Bell, "Who's Afraid of Critical Race Theory?," 908.
17 Bell, *Confronting Authority*, 111.

APPENDIX 3
1 Bell, *And We Are Not Saved*, 198.
2 Solórzano and Bernal, "Examining Transformational Resistance."
3 Solórzano and Yosso, "Critical Race Methodology," 26.

BIBLIOGRAPHY

Alexander, Michelle. "Foreword." In *Faces at the Bottom of the Well: The Permanence of Racism*, by Derrick Bell, ix–xix. 25th anniversary ed. New York: Basic Books, 2018.

———. *The New Jim Crow: Mass Incarceration in the Age of Colorblindness*. New York: New Press, 2010.

Alexander, Taifha, LaToya Baldwin, Clark Kyle Reinhard, and Noah Zatz. "Tracking the Attack on Critical Race Theory: A Report from CRT Forward's Tracking Project: An Initiative of the Critical Race Studies Program." *UCLA Law School* (January 12, 2024). https://crtforward.law.ucla.edu.

Arsenault, Raymond. *Arthur Ashe: A Life*. New York: Simon & Schuster, 2018.

Austin, Regina. "Resistance Tactics for Tokens." *Harvard BlackLetter Journal* 3 (1986): 52–53.

Barnett, Lana. "Maverick in the Middle: Randall Kennedy Seeks Nuance in an Age of Absolutism." *Harvard Law Bulletin*, January 31, 2022.

Baucham, Voddie T., Jr. *Fault Lines: The Social Justice Movement and Evangelicalism's Looming Catastrophe*. Washington, DC: Salem Books, 2021.

Baum, Gary, and Daniel Miller. "The Hollywood Reporter, after 65 Years, Addresses Role in Blacklist." *Hollywood Reporter*, November 19, 2012.

Bell, Derrick. *And We Are Not Saved: The Elusive Quest for Racial Justice*. New York: Basic Books, 1987.

———. "Black Students in White Law Schools: The Ordeal and the Opportunity." *University of Toledo Law Review* 2 (1970): 539–58.

———. "Booknotes: Faces at the Bottom of the Well." Interview with Derrick Bell. By Brian Lamb. C-SPAN, September 14, 1992. www.c-span.org.

———. "*Brown v. Board of Education* and the Interest-Convergence Dilemma." *Harvard Law Review* 93, no. 3 (January 1980): 518–33.

———. "Comments and Introduction: The Civil Rights Chronicles Revisited." *Harvard BlackLetter Journal* 3 (1986): 46–51.

———. *Confronting Authority: Reflections of an Ardent Protester*. Boston: Beacon Press, 1994.

———. *The Derrick Bell Reader*. Edited by Richard Delgado and Jean Stefancic. New York: New York University Press, 2005.

———. *Ethical Ambition: Living a Life of Meaning and Worth*. New York: Bloomsbury, 2002.

———. *Faces at the Bottom of the Well: The Permanence of Racism*. New York: Basic Books, 1992.

———. "Foreword: The Civil Rights Chronicles." *Harvard Law Review* 99, no. 4 (1985): 4–83.

———. "Harvard Law Furor (January 7, 1990)." Letter to the editor, *New York Times*, January 26, 1990.

———. "A Holiday for Dr. King: The Significance of Symbols in the Black Freedom Struggle." *UC Davis Law Review* 17, no. 2 (Winter 1984): 433–44.

———. Interviews by Larry Crowe, December 1, 2004. Online at HistoryMakers Digital Archive A2004.242. https://da.thehistorymakers.org.

———. "Letters: Legal Defense Fund." *Civil Rights Review* 3, no. 1 (1976): 7, 85.

———. "On Celebrating an Election as Racial Progress." *Human Rights Magazine*, 2009.

———. Papers. New York University Archive. New York, New York.

———. "The Price and Pain of Racial Perspective." *Stanford Law School Journal* (May 9, 1986).

———. "A Question of Credentials." *Harvard Law Record* 6, no. 14 (September 17, 1982); reprinted in *Integrated Education* 20, nos. 3–5 (2006): 99–100.

———. *Race, Racism, and American Law*. 1st ed. Boston: Little, Brown, 1973.

———. *Race, Racism, and American Law: 1975 Supplement*. Boston: Little, Brown, 1975.

———. "Racial Equality: Progressives' Passion for the Unattainable." Review of *The Lost Promise of Civil Rights*, by Risa L. Goluboff. *Virginia Law Review* 94, no. 2 (April 2008): 495–520.

———. "Racial Realism." *Connecticut Law Review* 24, no. 2 (Winter 1992): 363–80.

———. "Racism: A Prophecy for the Year 2000." *Rutgers Law Review* 42 (1989): 93–108.

———. "Serving Two Masters: Integration Ideals and Client Interests in School Desegregation Litigation." *Yale Law Journal* 85, no. 4 (March 1976): 470–517.

———. ed. *Shades of Brown: New Perspectives on School Desegregation.* New York: Teachers College Press, 1980.

———. *Silent Covenants:* Brown v. Board of Education *and the Unfulfilled Hopes for Racial Reform.* New York: Oxford University Press, 2005.

———. "The Strange Career of Randall Kennedy." Review of *Race, Crime, and the Law* by Randall L. Kennedy. *New Politics* 7, no. 1 (Summer 1998): 55–68.

———. "Who's Afraid of Critical Race Theory?" *University of Illinois Law Review* 4 (1995): 893–910.

Bell, Derrick, Tracy Higgins, and Sung-Hee Suh. "Racial Reflections: Dialogues in the Direction of Liberation." *UCLA Law Review* 37 (1989–1990): 1037–1100.

Bell, Janet Dewart. *Blackbirds Singing: Inspiring Black Women's Speeches from the Civil War to the Twenty-First Century.* New York: New Press, 2024.

———. *Lighting the Fires of Freedom: African American Women in the Civil Rights Movement.* New York: New Press, 2018.

Bonilla-Silva, Eduardo. *Racism without Racists: Color-Blind Racism and the Persistence of Racial Inequality in America.* 6th ed. New York: Rowman & Littlefield, 2021.

Brest, Paul, and Sanford Levinson. *Processes of Constitutional Decision-making: Cases and Materials.* 2nd ed. Boston: Little, Brown, 1983.

Brown-Nagin, Tomiko. *Civil Rights Queen: Constance Baker Motley and the Struggle for Equality.* New York: Vintage, 2023.

Bunche, Ralph J. "A Critical Analysis of the Tactics and Programs of Minority Groups." *Journal of Negro Education* 4, no. 3 (July 1935): 308–20.

———. *A World View of Race.* Bronze Booklet No. 4. Washington, DC: Associates in Negro Folk Education, 1936.

Butler, Paul. *Chokehold: Policing Black Men.* New York: New Press, 2017.

Ceplair, Larry, and Christopher Trumbo. *Dalton Trumbo: Blacklisted Hollywood Radical*. Lexington: University Press of Kentucky, 2015.

Cho, Sumi, and Robert Westley. "Historicizing Critical Race Theory's Cutting Edge: Key Movements that Performed the Theory." In *Crossroads, Directions, and a New Critical Race Theory*, edited by Francisco Valdes, Jerome McCristal Culp, and Angela P. Harris, 32–70. Philadelphia: Temple University Press, 2002.

Clark, Leroy D. "A Critique of Professor Derrick A. Bell's Thesis of the Permanence of Racism and His Strategy of Confrontation." *Denver Law Review* 73, no. 1 (1995): 23–50.

Clemon, U. W. "Time to Expand the Supreme Court." *AL.com*, July 16, 2023. www.al.com.

Clemon, U. W., and Bryan K. Fair. "Making Bricks without Straw: The NAACP Legal Defense Fund and the Development of Civil Rights Law in Alabama 1940–1980." *Alabama Law Review* 52, no. 4 (Summer 2001): 1121–52.

Clemon, U. W., Joshua Karsh, and Cyrus Mehri. "The Nation's First Civil-Rights Law Needs to Be Fixed." *The Atlantic*, August 7, 2020.

Cobb, Jelani. "The Man behind Critical Race Theory." *The New Yorker*, September 13, 2021.

Cone, James H. *Martin & Malcolm & America: A Dream or a Nightmare?* Maryknoll, NY: Orbis, 1991.

Crenshaw, Kimberlé W. "Demarginalizing the Intersection of Race and Sex: A Black Feminist Critique of Antidiscrimination Doctrine, Feminist Theory and Antiracist Policies." *University of Chicago Legal Forum* 1 (1989): 139–67.

———. "The First Decade: Critical Reflections, or 'A Foot in the Closing Door.'" *UCLA Law Review* 49 (2002): 1343–72.

———. "Race, Reform, and Retrenchment: Transformation and Legitimation in Antidiscrimination Law." *Harvard Law Review* 101, no. 7 (May 1988): 1331–87.

———. "Twenty Years of Critical Race Theory: Looking Back to Move Forward." *Connecticut Law Review* 117 (2011): 1253–1352.

Crenshaw, Kimberlé W., Neil Gotanda, Gary Peller, and Kendall Thomas, eds. *Critical Race Theory: The Key Writings that Formed the Movement*. New York: New Press, 1995.

Cunningham, David. *There's Something Happening Here: The New Left, the Klan, and FBI Counterintelligence*. Berkeley: University of California Press, 2004.

Delgado, Richard. "Critical Legal Studies and the Realities of Race—Does the Fundamental Contradiction Have a Corollary?" *Harvard Civil Rights-Civil Liberties Law Review* 23 (1988): 407–13.

———. "Derrick Bell's Racial Realism: A Comment on White Optimism and Black Despair." *Connecticut Law Review* 24, no. 2 (Winter 1992): 527–32.

———. "Imperial Scholar: Reflections on a Review of Civil Rights Literature." *University of Pennsylvania Law Review* 132 (1983): 561–78.

———. "Liberal McCarthyism and the Origins of Critical Race Theory." *Iowa Law Review* 94 (2009): 1506–45.

———. "Metamorphosis: A Minority Professor's Life." *UC Davis Law Review* (2019): 1–32.

———. "Minority Law Professors' Lives: The Bell-Delgado Survey." *Harvard Civil Rights-Civil Liberties Law Review* 24 (1989): 349–92.

———. "Rodrigo's Chronicle." Review of *Illiberal Education: The Politics of Race and Sex on Campus*, by Dinesh D'Souza. *Yale Law Journal* 101, no. 6 (April 1992): 1357–83.

———. "Storytelling for Oppositionists and Others: A Plea for Narrative." *Michigan Law Review* 87 (1989): 2411–41.

———. "When a Story Is Just a Story: Does Voice Really Matter?" *Virginia Law Review* 76 (1990): 95–110.

Delgado, Richard, Aja Y. Martinez, and Victor Ray. "On the Importance of Critical Race Theory—and the Delusional Attacks on It." *Literary Hub*, June 21, 2023. https://lithub.com/.

Delgado, Richard, and Jean Stefancic. *Critical Race Theory: An Introduction*. 4th ed. New York: New York University Press, 2023.

———. "Living History Interview with Richard Delgado and Jean Stefancic." *Transnational Law and Contemporary Problems* 19 (Winter 2010): 221–230.

———. "Panthers and Pinstripes: The Case of Ezra Pound and Archibald MacLeish." *Southern California Law Review* 63 (1990): 907–35.

———. "An Unanswered Question." Tribute to Derrick Bell (October 23, 2011). https://professorderrickbell.com.

———. "Why Do We Tell the Same Stories? Law Reform, Critical Librarianship, and the Triple Helix Dilemma." *Stanford Law Review* 42, no. 1 (November 1989): 207–25.

Diehl, Roberta. "We're Here Because Sonia Sanchez Wants to Reactivate Activism." *Amherst College News* (February 1, 2018).

D'Innocenzio, Anne, and Alexandra Olson. "DEI Opponents Are Using a 1866 Civil Rights Law to Challenge Equity Policies in the Workplace." *Associated Press*, January 14, 2024.

Dixson, Adrienne D., and Celia K. Rousseau, eds. *Critical Race Theory in Education: All God's Children Got a Song*. New York: Routledge, 2006.

Dorman, Michael. "Who Killed Medgar Evers?" *New York Times*, May 17, 1992. www.nytimes.com.

Dorman, Sam. "Chris Rufo Calls on Trump to End Critical Race Theory 'Cult Indoctrination' in Federal Government." *Tucker Carlson Tonight, Fox News,* September 2, 2020.

Dorning, Michael F. P. "In the Minority: Muhammad Kenyatta Fights for Civil Rights." *Harvard Crimson*, November 1, 1982.

Dudziak, Mary L. "Desegregation as a Cold War Imperative." *Stanford Law Review* 41, no. 1 (November 1988): 61–120.

Ecarma, Caleb. "Turns Out Ted Cruz Is Actually Really Good at Driving Up Sales for Anti-racist Literature." *Vanity Fair*, March 25, 2022.

Edley, Christopher, Jr. "The Boycott at Harvard: Should Teaching Be Colorblind?" *Washington Post*, August 18, 1982.

Egerton, John. *Speak Now against the Day: The Generation before the Civil Rights Movement in the South*. Chapel Hill: University of North Carolina Press, 1995.

Erakat, Noura. *Justice for Some: Law and the Question of Palestine*. Stanford, CA: Stanford University Press, 2019.

Erakat, Noura, Darryl Li, and John Reynolds. "Race, Palestine, and International Law." *American Journal of International Law Unbound* 117, no. 2 (2023): 77–81.

Fair, Bryan K. "U. W. Clemon." *Encyclopedia of Alabama*, August 11, 2008. https://encyclopediaofalabama.org.

Fairfax, Jean. "Interview with Jean Fairfax (SRC 20)." Interviewed by Brian Ward, February 26, 2003. Southern Regional Council Oral History Collection of the Samuel Proctor Oral History Program recordings in the University of Florida Digital Collections. https://original-ufdc.uflib.ufl.edu.

———. "Oral History Interview with Jean Fairfax, F-0013 by Dallas A. Blanchard," October 15, 1983. Southern Oral History Program Collection #4007. Southern Historical Collection, Wilson Library, University of North Carolina at Chapel Hill, Tape 1, Side A. https://docsouth.unc.edu/sohp/html_use/F-0013.html.

Farber, Daniel A., and Suzanna Sherry. *Beyond All Reason: The Radical Assault on Truth in American Law*. New York: Oxford University Press, 1997.

———. "Telling Stories out of School: An Essay on Legal Narratives." *Stanford Law Review* 45, no. 4 (April 1993): 807–55.

Felber, Garrett A. "'Those Who Say Don't Know and Those Who Know Don't Say': The Nation of Islam and the Politics of Black Nationalism, 1930–1975." PhD diss., University of Michigan, 2017.

Feldman, Jonathan. "Race-Consciousness versus Colorblindness in the Selection of Civil Rights Leaders: Reflections upon Jack Greenberg's *Crusaders in the Courts*." *California Law Review* 84 (1996): 151–66.

Fortin, Jacey. "Critical Race Theory: A Brief History." *New York Times* (November 8, 2021).

Garcia, Joseph. "Letter to the Editor." *Harvard Law Record*, September 24, 1982.

Gilbert, Jack. "The Abnormal Is Not Courage." In *Monolithos: Poems, 1962 and 1982*. Minneapolis, MN: Graywolf Press, 1984.

Gilliam, Dorothy. "An Insult to a Law Professor." *Washington Post*, August 4, 1986.

Goldberg, David Theo. "Meet Christopher Rufo—Leader of the Incoherent Right-Wing Attack on 'Critical Race Theory.'" *Salon*, August 21, 2021.

Greenberg, Jack. *Crusaders in the Courts: How a Dedicated Band of Lawyers Fought for the Civil Rights Revolution*. New York: Basic Books, 1994.

———. "In Memoriam: James Vorenberg," *Harvard Law Review* 114, no. 1 (November 2000), 5–9.

Greenberg, Jack, and James Vorenberg. *Dean Cuisine: Or, The Liberated Man's Guide to Fine Cooking*. New York: Sheep Meadow, 1990.

Greene, Linda S. "Critical Race Theory: Origins, Permutations, and Current Queries." *Wisconsin Law Review* 2021, no. 2 (November 2021): 259–68.

———. "From Tokenism to Emancipatory Politics: The Conferences and Meetings of Law Professors of Color." *Michigan Journal of Race and Law* 5 (1999): 161–84.

———. "A Short Commentary on the Chronicles." *Harvard BlackLetter Journal* 3 (1986): 60–64.

Greene, Melissa Fay. "Pride and Prejudice: Constance Baker Motley, b. 1921." *New York Times*, December 25, 2005. www.nytimes.com.

Grillo, Trina. "Anti-essentialism and Intersectionality: Tools to Dismantle the Master's House." *Berkeley Women's Law Journal* 16, no. 22 (1995): 16–30.

———. "The Mediation Alternative: Process Dangers for Women." *Yale Law Journal* 100 , no. 6 (April 1991): 1545–1610.

Guerrero, Andrea. *Silence at Boalt Hall: The Dismantling of Affirmative Action.* Berkeley: University of California Press, 2002.

Haberman, Clyde. "NYC; Soldiering on, Half Century after Brown." *New York Times*, April 13, 2004.

Haines, Andrew W. "The Ritual of the Minority Law Teachers Conference: The History and Analysis of the Totemic Gathering of the Shaman to Reconsecrate the Tribal Totem of Law School." *Saint Louis University Public Law Review* 10 (1991).

Harris, Adam. "The GOP's 'Critical Race Theory' Obsession." *The Atlantic*, May 7, 2021.

Harris, Angela P. "Preface." In *Critical Race Theory: An Introduction*, 4th ed., edited by Richard Delgado and Jean Stefancic, xiii–xviii. New York: New York University Press, 2023.

Harris, Laura. "Remembering Dallas' Black Images Book Bazaar with Creator Emma Rodgers." *NBC5-DFW*, February 5, 2021.

Harrison, Pat. "Gathering the Ghosts." *News & Ideas: Harvard Radcliffe Institute*, January 31, 2018. www.radcliffe.harvard.edu.

Harvard Crimson Editorial Board. "Letters to the Editor: On Antisemitism, Plagiarism, and Claudine Gay." *Harvard Crimson*, January 8, 2024.

Herrera, Luz E. "Challenging a Tradition of Exclusion: The History of an Unheard Story at Harvard Law School." *Harvard Latino Law Review* 51, no. 5 (2002): 51–140.

Hitchens, Christopher, Richard Dawkins, Sam Harris, and Daniel Dennett. *The Four Horsemen: The Conversation That Sparked an Atheist Revolution.* New York: Random House, 2019.

Hooks, Christopher. "Critical Race Fury: The School Board Wars Are Getting Nasty in Texas." *Texas Monthly*, November 2021.

Horn, Dave. "Third World Coalition Renews Support for Course Boycott." *Harvard Law Record*, September 17, 1982.

Hudson, Winson, and Constance Curry. *Mississippi Harmony: Memoirs of a Freedom Fighter.* New York: Palgrave Macmillan, 2002.

Hulbert, Emma. "Quaker Pacifism in the Context of War." *Friends Committee on National Legislation*, March 8, 2022. https://www.fcnl.org.

Jackson, Derrick Z. "Shaking Up the Ivy Walls." *Boston Globe*, October 29, 1988.

James, Rawn, Jr.. *The Double V: How Wars, Protest, and Harry Truman Desegregated America's Military*. New York: Bloomsbury, 2013.

Jefferson, Hakeem, and Victor Ray. "White Backlash Is a Type of Racial Reckoning, Too." *FiveThirtyEight*, January 6, 2022. https://fivethirtyeight.com.

Jenkins, Nancy Harmon. "Kitchen Bookshelf; Spring Offerings to Enthrall Armchair Cooks and Travelers." *New York Times*, March 27, 1991.

Kalman, Laura. *Yale Law School and the Sixties: Revolt and Reverberations*, Studies in Legal History. Durham: University of North Carolina Press, 2006.

Kennedy, Randall L. "On Cussing Out White Liberals." *The Nation*, September 4, 1982, 169–72.

———. "Racial Critiques of Legal Academia." *Harvard Law Review* 102 (1989): 1745–1819.

———. *Say It Loud! On Race, Law, History, and Culture*. New York: Pantheon, 2021.

Kerlow, Eleanor. *Poisoned Ivy: How Egos, Ideology, and Power Politics Almost Ruined Harvard Law School*. New York: St. Martin's, 1994.

King, Martin Luther, Jr. "A Letter to Arthur Ashe" (February 7, 1968). International Tennis Hall of Fame. www.tennisfame.com.

———. *A Testament of Hope: The Essential Writings and Speeches of Martin Luther King, Jr.* Edited by James M. Washington. San Francisco: HarperCollins, 1991.

Kingkade, Tyler, Brandy Zadrozny, and Ben Collins. "Critical Race Theory Battle Invades School Boards—With Help from Conservative Groups." *NBC News*, June 15, 2021.

Krochmal, Max. "An Unmistakably Working-Class Vision: Birmingham's Foot Soldiers and Their Civil Rights Movement." *Journal of Southern History* 76, no. 4 (November 2010): 923–60.

Kruse, Michael. "DeSantis' Culture Warrior: 'We Are Now over the Walls.'" *Politico*, March 24, 2023.

Kynard, Carmen. *Vernacular Insurrections: Race, Black Protest, and the New Century in Composition-Literacies Studies*. Albany: State University of New York Press, 2013.

Ladson-Billings, Gloria. "Critical Race Theory—What It Is Not!" In *Handbook of Critical Race Theory in Education*, 2nd ed., edited by

Marvin Lynn and Adrienne D. Dixson, 32–43. New York: Routledge, 2021.

Ladson-Billings, Gloria, and William F. Tate, eds. *"Covenant Keeper": Derrick Bell's Enduring Education Legacy*. New York: Peter Lang, 2016.

———. "Toward a Critical Race Theory of Education." *Teachers College Record*, 97 (1995): 47–68.

Lah, Kyung, and Jack Hannah. "Discussions of Critical Race Theory, Covid-19 Rules Whip Up School Board Meetings to the Dismay of Students." CNN, October 31, 2021.

Lawrence, Charles R., III. "The Id, the Ego, and Equal Protection: Reckoning with Unconscious Racism." *Stanford Law Review* 39, no. 2 (January 1987): 317–88.

———. "Foreword: Who Are We? And Why Are We Here? Doing Critical Race Theory in Hard Times." In *Crossroads, Directions, and a New Critical Race Theory*, edited by Francisco Valdes, Jerome McCristal Culp, and Angela P. Harris, xi–xxiv. Philadelphia: Temple University Press, 2002.

Lindsay, James . *Race Marxism: The Truth about Critical Race Theory and Praxis*. Orlando: New Discourses, 2022.

Lomax, Louis E. *The Negro Revolt*. New York: Harper & Row, 1962.

Lovin, Robin W. *Reinhold Niebuhr and Christian Realism*. Cambridge, UK: Cambridge University Press, 1995.

Maltz, Albert. Transcripts of Interviews by Joel Gardner (1978). UCLA Oral History Program. Los Angeles, California. https://static.library .ucla.edu.

Manuel, Diane Casselberry. "Jean Fairfax: Still Devoted to Proving Justice Is Possible." *Christian Science Monitor*, February 2, 1984.

Marchese, David. "Joyce Carol Oates Figured Out the Secret to Immortality." *New York Times Magazine*, July 16, 2023.

Marcus, Ruth. "Minority Groups Assail Course at Harvard Law." *Washington Post*, July 26, 1982.

Martinez, Aja Y. *Counterstory: The Rhetoric and Writing of Critical Race Theory*. Champaign, IL: National Council of Teachers of English, 2020.

Matsuda, Mari J. "Looking to the Bottom: Critical Legal Studies and Reparations." *Harvard Civil Rights-Civil Liberties Law Review* 22 (1987): 323–99.

———. "'Radical Wāhine of Honolulu, 1945' with Mari Matsuda." Center for Biographical Research. YouTube video, 1:01:18. www.youtube.com /watch?v=4cFohp_Q48s.

McGuire, Phillip. *He, Too, Spoke for Democracy: Judge Hastie, World War II, and the Black Soldier*. New York: Bloomsbury, 1988.

Meadows, Mark. *The Chief's Chief*. St. Petersburg, FL: All Seasons Press, 2021.

Menzie, Nicola A. "'*Fault Lines*' Author Voddie Baucham Confused or Making Things Up, Richard Delgado Says in Response to Misquote on 'Righteous Actions' of Whites." *Faithfully Magazine*, August 3, 2021. https://faithfullymagazine.com.

Metzger, Bryan, and Jake Lahut. "Trump Issued an Executive Order on Critical Race Theory after Seeing a Segment about it on Tucker Carlson's Show: Book." *Business Insider*, December 7, 2021.

Miller, Loren. "Farewell to Liberals: A Negro View." *Nation*, October 20, 1962.

Mitchell, Jerry. *Race against Time: A Reporter Reopens the Unsolved Murder Cases of the Civil Rights Era*. New York: Simon & Schuster, 2021.

Montoya, Margaret. "CRT at Harvard, 2020." Prezi presentation. https: //prezi.com.

———. "Johns Hopkins University 4.16.20." Prezi presentation. https: //prezi.com.

Motley, Constance Baker. *Equal Justice under Law: An Autobiography*. New York: Farrar, Straus Giroux, 1999.

Mounk, Yascha. "What an Audacious Hoax Reveals about Academia." *The Atlantic*, October 5, 2018.

Myrdal, Gunnar. An American Dilemma: The Negro Problem and Modern Democracy. New York: Harper and Row, 1944.

National Political Congress of Black Women. "Civil Rights and Gender Issues: The National Political Congress of Black Women." C-SPAN, July 31, 1993. www.c-span.org.

Niebuhr, Reinhold. "Ten Years that Shook My World." *Christian Century* 56, no. 17 (April 26, 1939): 542–45.

Obama, Barack. "On My Faith and My Church." *Huffington Post*, March 14, 2008.

Olivas, Michael A. *The Law and Higher Education: Cases and Materials on Colleges in Court*. Durham, NC: Carolina Academic Press, 1989.

Phillip, Abby D. "Race Sparked HLS Tension: Lack of Faculty Diversity Sparked Boycotts at HLS." *Harvard Crimson*, June, 1 2008.

Pluckrose, Helen, and James Lindsay. *Cynical Theories: How Activist Scholarship Made Everything about Race, Gender, and Identity—And Why This Harms Everybody*. Durham, NC: Pitchstone, 2020.

Pluckrose, Helen, James Lindsay, and Peter Boghossian. "Understanding the 'Grievance Studies Affair' Papers and Why They Should Be Reinstated: A Response to Geoff Cole." *Sociological Methods & Research* 50, no. 4 (November 2021): 1487–1945.

Pollak, Joel B. "Exclusive: Kagan's Handwritten Notes to Bell on Critical Race Theory." *Breitbart News*, April 25, 2012. www.breitbart.com.

Pollard, Tom. *Sex and Violence: The Hollywood Censorship Wars*. New York: Routledge, 2015.

powell, john a. "Racial Realism or Racial Despair?" *Connecticut Law Review* 24, no. 2 (Winter 1992): 533–51.

Prendergast, Catherine. *Literacy and Racial Justice: The Politics of Learning after* Brown v. Board of Education. Carbondale: Southern Illinois University Press, 2003.

Reid, Joy-Ann. *Medgar & Myrlie: Medgar Evers and the Love Story that Awakened America*. New York: Mariner, 2024.

Resnik, Judith, and Dennis Edward Curtis. *Representing Justice: Invention, Controversy, and Rights in City-States and Democratic Courtrooms*. New Haven, CT: Yale University Press, 2011.

Rogers, Jefferson P. Interview with Jefferson P. Rogers by Paul Ortiz, August 14, 2012. African American History Project, University of Florida Samuel Proctor Oral History Program, AAHP 280A, Gainesville, Florida.

Rothfeld, Charles. "The Law: Minority Critic Stirs Debate on Minority Writing." *New York Times*, January 5, 1990.

Rowan, Carl. *Dream Makers, Dream Breakers: The World of Justice Thurgood Marshall*. New York: CTR, 1993.

Savage, Mark. "Letter to the Editor." *Stanford Law School Journal*, May 9, 1986.

Scheppele, Kim Lane. "Foreword: Telling Stories." *Michigan Law Review* 87, no. 8 (August 1989): 2073–98.

Shapiro, Fred R. "The Most-Cited Legal Scholars Revisited." The University of Chicago Law Review 88:7 (November 2021): 1595–1604.

Singley, Bernestine. "Tributes in Memory of Professor Derrick Bell: Bernestine Singley." *Derrick Bell Official Site*, October 16, 2011. https://professorderrickbell.com.

Smietana, Bob. "Voddie Baucham's Publisher Defends *Fault Lines* against Plagiarism Claims." *Religion New Service*, August 3, 2021.

Sollors, Werner, Caldwell Titcomb, and Thomas A. Underwood, eds. *Blacks at Harvard: A Documentary History of African-American Experience at Harvard and Radcliffe*. New York: New York University Press, 1993.

Solórzano, Daniel G., and Dolores Delgado Bernal. "Examining Transformational Resistance through a Critical Race and Latcrit Theory Framework: Chicana and Chicano Students in an Urban Context." *Urban Education* 36, no. 3 (May 2001): 308–342.

Solórzano, Daniel G., Lindsay Pérez Huber, and Layla Huber-Verjan. "Theorizing Racial Microaffirmations as a Response to Racial Microaggressions: Counterstories across Three Generations of Critical Race Scholars." *Seattle Journal for Social Justice* 18 (2020): 185–215.

Solórzano, Daniel G., and Tara J. Yosso. "Critical Race Methodology: Counter-Storytelling as an Analytical Framework for Education Research." *Qualitative Inquiry* 8, no. 1 (February 2002): 23–44.

Sowell, Thomas. "Booknotes: Preferential Policies." Interview with Thomas Sowell. By Brian Lamb. C-SPAN, May 24, 1990. www.c-span.org.

———. "Derrick Bell and a Revenge Society." Interview with Thomas Sowell. By Sean Hannity. *Fox News*, March 13, 2012. YouTube video, 8:22. https://www.youtube.com/watch?v=wxYu9omxvho&ab.

Stefancic, Jean. "The Law Review Symposium Issue: Community of Meaning or Reinscription of Hierarchy?" *University of Colorado Law Review* 63, no. 3 (1992).

———. "Listen to the Voices: An Essay on Legal Scholarship, Women, and Minorities." *Legal Reference Services Quarterly* 11, nos. 3–4 (1992): 141–49.

Stefancic, Jean, and Richard Delgado. *How Lawyers Lose Their Way: A Profession Fails Its Creative Minds*. Durham, NC: Duke University Press, 2005.

Tate, William F. "The Ethics of Derrick Bell: Oh How He Loved Us." In *"Covenant Keeper": Derrick Bell's Enduring Education Legacy*, edited by Gloria Ladson-Billings and William F. Tate, 181–89. New York: Peter Lang, 2016.

Taylor, George H. "Racism as 'The National Crucial Sin': Theology and Derrick Bell." *Michigan Journal of Race & Law* 9 (2004): 269–322.

Titus, Jill Ogline. *Brown's Battleground: Students, Segregationists, and the Struggle for Justice in Prince Edward County, Virginia*. Chapel Hill: University of North Carolina Press, 2011.

Trubek, David M. "Foundational Events, Foundational Myths, and the Creation of Critical Race Theory, or How to Get along with a Little Help from Your Friends." *Connecticut Law Review* 43 (2011): 1505–12.

Trubek, David M., and Louise Grossman Trubek. "Conversations in Law and Society 12. A Conversation with David M. Trubek and Louise G. Trubek." Interview by Jonathan Simon, November 8, 2013. Berkeley Center for the Study of Law and Society. www.kaltura.com.

———. "Slaying the Monster: Defending Academic Freedom against McCarthyism at the University of Wisconsin in the 1950s." Unpublished manuscript on file with authors, 2024.

Tushnet, Mark V. *The NAACP's Legal Strategy against Segregated Education, 1925–1950*. Durham: University of North Carolina Press, 1987.

Tushnet, Mark, and Timothy Lynch. "The Project of the Harvard Forewords: A Social and Intellectual Inquiry." *Constitutional Commentary* 11, no. 3 (Winter 1994/95): 463–500.

Tyler, Donald Christopher, and Cynthia Muldrow. "Letter to the Editor: Goal of a Boycott at Harvard Law." *New York Times*, August 17, 1982.

University of California Berkeley School of Law. "A Time for Change: Contextualizing the Removal of 'Boalt Hall' from the Law School's Identity." https://www.law.berkeley.edu.

University of Oregon Division of Equity and Inclusion. "Jewel H. Bell Award: Honoring Jewel Hairston Bell." https://inclusion.uoregon.edu.

US Senate Committee on the Judiciary. "The Nomination of Ketanji Brown Jackson to Be an Associate Justice of the Supreme Court of the United States: Transcript." March 21, 2022.

Vastine, Stephanie. "'Our Survival Hope': Geneva Crenshaw as Derrick Bell's Womanist Muse." *Feminist Formations* 32, no. 2 (Summer 2020): 235–57.

Wildman, Stephanie M. *Privilege Revealed: How Invisible Preference Undermines America*. 2nd ed. New York: New York University Press, 2021.

Wilkerson, Isabel. *The Warmth of Other Suns: The Epic Story of America's Great Migration*. New York: Random House, 2010.

Williams, Patricia J. "Alchemical Notes: Reconstructing Ideals from Deconstructed Rights." *Harvard Civil Rights Civil Liberties Law Review* 22, no. 2 (Spring 1987): 401–34.

———. *The Alchemy of Race and Rights: Diary of a Law Professor*. Cambridge, MA: Harvard University Press, 1991.

———. "A Brief Comment, with Footnotes, on the Civil Rights Chronicles." *Harvard Blackletter Journal* 3 (1986): 79–82.

———. "Gathering the Ghosts" *The A-Line: A Journal of Progressive Thought* 1:3–4 (August 2018).

———. "Tribute in Memory of Professor Derrick Bell." Derrick Bell Official Site, October 11, 2011, https://professorderrickbell.com/.

Wing, Adrien Katherine. *Critical Race Feminism: A Reader*. 2nd ed. New York: New York University Press, 2003.

Zitser, Joshua. "Trump Calls on Supporters to 'Lay down Their Very Lives' to Defend US against Critical Race Theory." *Business Insider*, March 13, 2022.

INDEX

Page numbers in *italics* indicate figures.

240 | INDEX

48, 147; promotion of classical liberalism, 149, 212n41. *See* Rufo, Christopher

Loch Ness monster, 7, 187n12

Lomax, Louis, 113, 118–19, 204n29

Lopez, Gerald "Jerry", 134

Lorde, Audre, 87

Lumbee (Tribe of North Carolina), 83

Lynch, Timothy, 78

MSNBC, 161

Madison, Wisconsin, 30, 127, 129, 140, 143, 164; Lake Mendota, 30, 140

MacLeish, Archibald, 58, 63, 65

Maltz, Albert, 51–52

Manhattan Institute, 146

Marcus, Ruth, 122, 206n65

Margaret Morrison Carnegie College, 22. *See* Carnegie Mellon University

Margiotta, Joseph M., 155

Marshall, Thurgood (Justice), 18, 28, 105, 107–8, 110, 112, 114, 118–19, 136, 143; admiration of local civil rights workers, 42; and Alain LeRoy Locke, 188n16; assignment of *Meredith v. Fair* to Constance Baker Motley, 35; aversion to civil disobedience, 34–35, 38; as mentor to young lawyers, 108; pragmatism of, 113–14; sexism of, 35, 112, 114; as Supreme Court Justice, 105, 136

Martin, Trayvon, 161

Martinez, Aja Y., 1, 5–6, 8; *Counterstory: The Rhetoric and Writing of Critical Race Theory* (book), 1, 5

Marxism, 21, 49, 143, 147–49; vulgar, 143. *See* critical theory (European)

Maryville College, 57–58

Matory, Yvedt, 159

Matsuda, Mari, 5, 10, 114, 126, 130, 138, 145, 167–68; "looking to the bottom" (concept), 114. *See* prosopography

Mays, Benjamin, 23

McCarthy, Joseph (Senator), 50, 127; McCarthyism, 51

McCulloch v. Maryland, 134

McDonald, Behonor, 16, *17*, 41–42, 92–94, 101, 200n80; source of Derrick Bell's motto, 16, 94, 101

McGee, Henry "Hank", 84

McMillan, Terry, 103

Meadows, Mark, 146

Meredith, James H., 18, 34–38, 40–41, 70–71, 90, 107, 113

Meredith v. Fair, 37–41, 70, 72, 112; and Constance Baker Motley, 34–38, 40–41, 113

Michigan Law Review (special issue on legal storytelling, 1989), 166–167, *169*. *See* counterstory

Miles College, 107

Miller, Loren, 119, 121

Miller, Teresa "Teri", 140, 163

Mills, Billy, 53

Mize, Sidney (Judge), 70, 72, 74–75

Monaghan, Peter, 145

Monti, Daniel J., 84

Montoya, Margaret, 5, 129

Moore, Stephanie Y., 76, 86–*87*, 91, 101, 106, 108, 126, 198n58, 205n48; an editor of Bell's "Civil Rights Chronicles", 76, 86, 101, 198n58;

ABOUT THE AUTHORS

AJA Y. MARTINEZ is author of the multi-award-winning book *Counterstory: The Rhetoric and Writing of Critical Race Theory*. She is the 2023 recipient of the National Council of Teachers of English National Intellectual Freedom Award.

ROBERT O. SMITH (Chickasaw) is author of *More Desired Than Our Own Salvation: The Roots of Christian Zionism*.

www.ingramcontent.com/pod-product-compliance
Lightning Source LLC
Chambersburg PA
CBHW030150310326
41914CB00099B/1784/J